Strategic Supply Chai

MW00680895

The supply chain is at the heart of every successful business organization's decision-making process. This textbook explains how to create a winning supply chain management strategy by spotlighting how senior executives in European and US companies have turned their supply chains into strategic weapons designed to convert threats, risks and outside pressures into competitive advantages.

Strategic Supply Chain Management contains 20 real-world cases, all of which have been field researched by a top author team and tested out in the classroom. Each case adopts an executive leadership perspective to illuminate the real dilemmas faced by managers. The authors draw on their extensive classroom and industry experience to ensure that the writing style is geared towards an executive education readership.

This elite case package will provide a complete teaching resource and authentic learning experience for MBA and executive education classes in supply chain management throughout the world.

Carlos Cordón is LEGO Professor of Process Management at IMD, Switzerland. He is an expert on business models, value chains and process management and is the co-author of *The Power of Two: How Smart Companies Create Win–Win Customer–Supplier Partnerships that Outperform the Competition* (Palgrave Macmillan, 2008).

Kim Sundtoft Hald is Associate Professor in Supply Chain Management and Performance Management at Copenhagen Business School, Denmark. He has published in leading international academic journals, including *Industrial Marketing Management*, *Management Accounting Research* and *Global Journal of Flexible Systems Management*, and has contributed to several books, such as *Leading in the Top Team: The CXO Challenge* and *Managing the Global Supply Chain*.

Ralf W. Seifert is Professor of Operations Management at IMD and Professor of Technology and Operations Management at the College of Management of Technology at Ecole Polytechnique Fédérale de Lausanne (EPFL). He is director of the Mastering Technology Enterprise (MTE) programme and has designed and directed numerous company-specific general management programmes. Based on his work with companies, Professor Seifert has co-authored more than 30 case studies, winning five case awards. He continues to actively research issues of supply chain strategy, supply chain finance and technology management and has more than 50 articles and international conference presentations to his credit.

Strategic Supply Chain Management

Carlos Cordón, Kim Sundtoft Hald and Ralf W. Seifert

Routledge
Taylor & Francis Group

NEW YORK AND LONDON

First published 2012
by Routledge
2 Park Square, Milton Park, Abingdon, Oxon OX14 4RN

Simultaneously published in the USA and Canada
by Routledge
711 Third Avenue, New York, NY 10017
Routledge is an imprint of the Taylor & Francis Group, an informa business

British Library Cataloguing in Publication Data
A catalogue record for this book is available from the British Library

Library of Congress Cataloging in Publication Data
Cordon, Carlos.
Strategic Supply Chain Management / Carlos Cordón, Kim Sundtoft Hald and Ralf W. Seifert.
p. cm.
Includes bibliographical references and index.
1. Business logistics—Management. 2. Strategic planning.
I. Hald, Kim Sundtoft. II. Seifert, Ralf W. III. Title.
HD38.5.C67 2012
658.7—dc23
2011038416

ISBN: 978–0–415–59175–1 (hbk)
ISBN: 978–0–415–59176–8 (pbk)
ISBN: 978–0–203–12445–1 (ebk)

Typeset in Times New Roman
by Bookcraft Ltd, Stroud

Printed and bound in Great Britain by
TJ International Ltd, Padstow, Cornwall

In memory of Thomas E. Vollmann, our superb mentor, colleague and friend

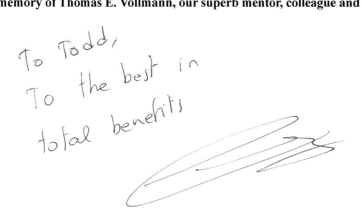

To Todd,
To the best in
total benefits

Contents

Illustrations

List of figures

List of tables

Introduction

This book positions supply chain management at the center of firms' strategic decision making and execution processes. By means of case studies of real companies, it illustrates how European and US executives have turned their supply chains into strategic weapons designed to convert threats, risk and outside pressures into core competitive advantages.

Executives will find the book useful because of its focus on executive decision making and strategy in the extended enterprise-crossing boundaries between firms and regions. The book provides a solid foundation for understanding the challenges, strategies, dilemmas and opportunities involved in both process and relationship design within and across companies in global supply chains.

No other book currently on the market positions supply chain management at the center of firms' strategic decision making and execution processes, or demonstrates how executives across functions in the firm can help turn supply chain threats and dilemmas into strategic opportunities and value.

This book is intended for a broad cross-section of executives. More specifically, its purpose is to inspire executives at all levels and across all functions within a firm, in terms of how they can help turn the firm's transformation processes into core strategic weapons. With its examples of best practices and the associated dilemmas, this book is a good reference for supply chain management executives.

How the book is organized

Unlike most books about supply chain management – textbooks and casebooks alike – this one is not organized around the different disciplines within the field. Instead it deals with the executive decision and management process and focuses on the key questions and dilemmas a broad cross-section of executives may face when supply chain challenges arise. The book is organized around three themes/chapters, with an introductory and a concluding chapter.

Chapter 1 provides a general introduction to the challenge of thinking strategically about supply chain management. It includes a discussion of the extended supply chain, incorporating the traditional flow of goods, information and finances. It then extends these and points to the importance of three additional flows of strategic importance to the supply chain: the exchange of risks, the exchange of ideas and innovations, and the flow of personal relations and perceptions. It also outlines in more detail the purpose and structure of the book.

In Chapter 2, the *why* and *where* questions pertaining to strategic supply chain management are discussed and illustrated using examples. Why do companies/ executives face these problems? Where should they go next? Via four case studies, this chapter provides the executive reader with hands-on ideas and tools for identifying and leveraging strategic opportunities in existing transformation and supply chain systems.

Chapter 3 focuses on the *what* questions. Faced with a dilemma, what should the executive do next? A range of actual decision-making problems, all related to supply chain practices, are illustrated in the six cases included. This section helps supply chain and non-supply chain executives to identify and respond to supply chain dilemmas.

Chapter 4 turns to the *how* question. How exactly can the strategy and any decisions taken be implemented? How can executives avoid execution failure and long, costly implementation processes? The collective learning from five US and European firms illustrating how they approached the supply chain execution and implementation challenge is presented and synthesized, and key takeaways for executives are shared.

Chapter 5 leverages the knowledge from the first four chapters, and discusses how executives working in the field of supply chain management or a related area can assess their existing supply chain and realign it with a new strategic direction. A process framework is presented.

The philosophy: Learning with cases

Case studies are indispensable for modern education as they permit interactive learning based on rich, complex and authentic situations. From the authors' experience, the use of cases has a lasting impact as the students actively participate in the analysis and resolution of practical problems. The exchanges with both teachers and class participants can leverage group knowledge and create a highly dynamic learning environment that students greatly appreciate.

The majority of the cases included in the book have already been successfully used in executive education programs at IMD and other business schools, although there is some new case material. The book is also relevant as a best practice guide for executives working in supply chain management.

1 Thinking strategically about supply chain management

In this book supply chain management is understood to be the design and operation of the entire chain from the raw material to delivery of the final product to the customer. The expression 'From the farm to the plate', coined by food industry executives, encapsulates this idea. There is no generally accepted definition of supply chain because the task of managing this entire end-to-end process has changed over the last 20 years from a fragmented tactical view to a strategic integrated view.

In line with this way of understanding the supply chain, the most advanced companies have an executive vice president of global supply chain who works directly with the CEO to manage the entire process. Typically, this person is responsible for customer service, logistics and distribution, manufacturing, sourcing and planning, and often also quality, IT and sustainability.

It could be said, then, that the supply chain provides the infrastructure for a corporation's business model and thus determines its profitability and future. Furthermore, the trend over the last 20 years to outsource many activities has tremendously increased the role of the supply chain as the backbone of the company.

There is even an emerging view, with the current emphasis on business models, that the key to a business model's profit formula is the supply chain or value chain. For example, in 2010 many companies stated that most of their profit increase was a direct result of supply chain improvements. The supply chain should thus be considered as a value adder rather than a source of costs. When it functions well, it plays a major role in improving revenue and implementing the firm's value proposition for the end-consumer, as well as its vision and strategy.

The second defining feature that distinguishes strategic supply chain management from conceptual flow coordination is the involvement of a senior executive as the supply chain manager. This ensures that supply chain management is no longer confined within the boundaries of a single function, but instead entails the strategic involvement of several functions reporting to the same senior supply chain executive.

The objective of this book is to provide a collection of best practices and highlight the main challenges that companies face in managing the supply chain. Within the case studies we also use the terms 'demand chain management' and 'value chain' because the executives from the individual companies use them. While this might be considered just a semantic issue, many companies have spent considerable time discussing who is responsible for what and exactly what is included in the supply chain.

The extended supply chain

Over the last few decades many value chains have become much more fragmented as a consequence of the drive towards outsourcing. Thus, while decades ago much of the added value of a product or service was created within one company, today most of it is created externally. For many companies suppliers represent more than 50% of the supply chain costs, so the greatest potential for improvement involves working with suppliers.

Similarly, for many companies innovation mainly originates outside the organization. In recognition of this, Procter & Gamble (P&G), for example, has created a 'Connect and Develop' portal where customers, suppliers and other third parties can buy and sell ideas. As an innovative company, P&G is thus able to cultivate creativity. Figure 1.1 illustrates these flows with a model of this extended supply chain.

Traditionally, the supply chain has been described as consisting of three main flows: (1) the flow of goods from the supplier to the manufacturer, to the distributor, and finally to the retailer in order to reach the consumer, as well as reverse flows related to repairs and material recovery; (2) the flow of information, ranging from order placement and forecast sharing to updating supply chain partners on available capacity and expected delivery dates; and (3) the financial flows including trade credit arrangements.

Three other flows that circulate in both directions are equally important: (1) the exchange of risks between customers and suppliers; (2) the exchange of ideas and innovation; and (3) the personal relations and perceptions of different parties regarding the others in the supply chain.

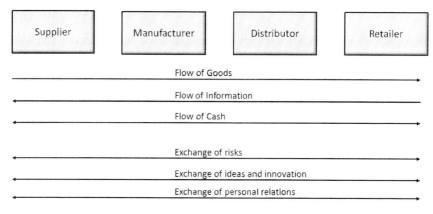

Figure 1.1 Fundamental supply chain flows

The exchange of risks is of a special nature; many risks cannot be totally transferred. A company might believe that it has transferred the risk to a supplier because it is specified in the contract, but experience shows that it is frequently not transferred. The BP Gulf of Mexico platform disaster in 2010 illustrates this point. BP might have believed that the risk had been transferred to its supplier, Transocean, which owned the platform. Yet, while Transocean's top managers received a bonus in 2011 for good safety performance in 2010, BP came in for a lot of criticism for its safety record and its CEO was forced to resign following the disaster, not the supplier's CEO. Clearly, the disparity between BP's actual risks and those perceived by the supplier is considerable.

With the exchange of ideas and innovation that happens through the supply chain, companies can react fast by bringing out new products in response to consumers' wishes while also taking into consideration suppliers' innovative ideas. Companies like Victoria's Secret created 'councils of suppliers' to foster the development of ideas from suppliers to its stores (see Chapter 2, Case 2.2). The Numico (A) case (see Chapter 3, Case 3.1) is an excellent example of how these exchanges of ideas and innovation create a comparative advantage for both the customer and the supplier.

Finally, personal relations are extremely important because they allow companies to evaluate if the customer or supplier is a reliable business partner. If the relationship works well, it can foster extraordinary performance in the other flows. We will see in Chapter 4 how these personal relations must be managed proactively to achieve this. In particular, the Freqon case (see Chapter 4, Case 4.5) explicitly shows the role relationships play in the success of partnerships between customer and suppliers. In the same chapter we provide several useful models for developing successful win–win relationships.

From a function to a vital company process

Comparing definitions of the supply chain across different firms we often find considerable diversity in scope and meaning. Some organizations include only logistics and warehousing in their supply chain while others include the upstream aspect of sourcing and managing suppliers. One shared feature, however, is that today most companies regard their supply chain as the principal process.

An important challenge for many companies is setting up a supply chain organization with sufficient decision-making power to manage it. In some firms, an executive VP works directly with the CEO and is in charge of the whole chain. In others, a supply chain executive is in charge of coordinating the process without having direct line responsibility over the parts of the process. Finally, in some other cases, if the corporation is divided into business units, each unit has its own supply chain organization.

As with all organizational structures, centralization of the supply chain organization has its dilemmas. On the one hand centralization, and the resulting integration, provides opportunities for increasing speed to market, reducing supply risks, reducing supply costs and improving supply quality. These potential benefits have led to a clear trend towards supply chain integration and centralization over the last two decades. On the other hand it can also result in more fragile supply systems, where risks may spread more easily. These and other dilemmas will be discussed in the other chapters, particularly Chapter 3.

We are also seeing for the first time a drive towards insourcing and nearshoring, which facilitates coordination along the supply chain. It is fair to say that the outsourcing trend of the 1990s and 2000s was made easier because companies had learned how to create and develop close relations with suppliers. However, the possibility of transferring and managing risk properly was generally overestimated, as the BP case mentioned earlier, shows.

The impact of the supply chain on the environment is also tremendous. For example, Unilever has openly stated on its website that the impact on water consumption of its products is mainly through customers and suppliers. It estimates that 50% of the water used in relation to its detergents can be attributed to the consumer and another 50% to the raw materials it sources (the supply chain). The water it adds to the product represents less than 0.1%, as depicted in Figure 1.2. Thus, the only way for Unilever to reduce its water footprint is to work through the supply chain and the consumer rather than focusing on internal use.

We conclude from these developments and their impact on the bottom line that the supply chain has become by far the most important process in a majority of companies. We see industries totally transformed by companies using the supply chain as the main lever for competitive advantage, like Zara in the fashion business, Dell in the computer business, Luxottica in the eyewear industry, and many others.

From operations to finance, leadership, innovation and risk management

In many companies the supply chain has a fundamental impact on finance, leadership, innovation and risk management. This is mainly because a process that spans the whole company substantially influences many functions.

The supply chain's impact on a company's finances and the world financial system is extraordinary. Some economists have estimated that the amount of money passing through the accounts receivable and accounts payable books – referred to as the trade working capital – of companies worldwide is almost twice the monetary mass of the world financial system. At the company level, the impact

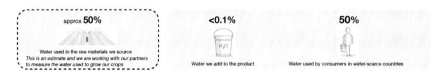

Figure 1.2 Unilever 2008 baseline study across seven countries

Source: Company website

is so strong that we often find CEOs asking their supply chain executives for marketing funds instead of approaching the financial market. Also, practices like supply chain finance and creating negative working capital through the supply chain have become commonplace in that they allow firms to benefit from their customers' sound financial conditions. The Numico King Project case (see Chapter 3, Case 3.3) is a perfect example of this type of approach.

From a leadership point of view, managing the supply chain is a challenge in that it requires influencing and obtaining the trust of different organizations and their respective functions and people. It is well known that managing change in a single company or organization is a difficult enough task. Doing it across several firms or organizational structures functioning together in a chain or network is a tremendous challenge.

Similarly, converting a top management team into a high performance team is a characteristic of great leadership. Leading two teams from different companies towards a high performance partnership requires at least two great leaders who trust each other. The relationship between LEGO and DHL (see Chapter 4, Case 4.4) is a prime example of this kind of situation, where the joint commitment of the leaders of both companies was expressed in the meeting of what they called 'the four musketeers'.

We believe that, for many companies, the amount of innovation emanating from suppliers is equal to or greater than that generated internally, as illustrated in Chapter 3 with the Numico example. The company stated that in 2005 its research budget was around €50 million and its purchases from suppliers amounted to €800 million. Numico estimated that its suppliers allocate around 6% of their sales to research, representing €48 million (based on sales to Numico). While the latter fully controlled the €50 million it spent on research internally, it did not have much influence over the €48 million spent by its suppliers whose investment could in effect subsidize Numico's competitors if they benefited from the innovation or if Numico was not willing to listen to its suppliers' ideas.

Finally, the most important risks for companies are those related to suppliers in terms of lack of supply, quality issues and potential bankruptcy. For example, in August 2010[1] the *Wall Street Journal* reported that companies like Ericsson, GE and others in the electronics industry were experiencing supply shortages. Ericsson said that this had cost the company between US$400 and $550 million. Similarly, Toyota's famous recall of millions of vehicles because of an accelerator pedal problem derived from issues at both Toyota and the pedal supplier.

The supply chain: An integrative view of a company's business model

Because the supply chain process spans the whole company, it probably provides the best integrative view of the company and its value chain. CEOs have only recently begun to grasp how crucial the supply chain is in defining the company's business model. Indeed, the 2008/09 financial crisis led many of them to conclude that their current business models are not sustainable and that the supply chain is fundamental to the profit generation capability of their organizations. They are thus trying to understand more about how the supply chain functions. They are also now asking supply chain and purchasing executives to take part in discussions on what the company's next business model should be. This is relatively new to some of these executives so they, in turn, are now trying to understand how business models work and how the supply chain defines the profit engine of a business model.

An excellent illustration of the supply chain being the backbone of the company is the case of Luxottica, the world leader in eyewear manufacturing, distribution and retailing (see Chapter 2, Case 2.1). The story of the company's evolution, from a one-man molding workshop, to the industry leader, alongside brands such as Ray-Ban and Chanel, describes how the company was built on the strengths of the supply chain.

In the following chapters, you will find cases that describe the challenges involved in transforming supply chain management from a series of straightforward material and information flow coordination tasks into a highly strategic enterprise. A set of models and considerations to help understand the challenges of developing a state-of-the-art supply chain are discussed.

Chapter 2 looks at how firms can link their supply chains to their business model. We argue that two basic components of a company business model are driven by supply chain considerations: the level of vertical and horizontal integration and the level of risk and how it is managed. The case studies are:

Case 2.1 Luxottica: Sustaining growth in challenging times

Case 2.2 MAS Holdings: Providing design to delivery solutions to the global apparel industry

Case 2.3 Nestlé: Quality on the boardroom agenda (A)

Case 2.4 Nestlé: Quality on the boardroom agenda (B)

Chapter 3 considers the multiple dilemmas that supply chain executives face and that have no optimal solution, including flexibility vs. efficiency, the best global footprint, capital allocation, process organization, and how to accelerate improvements. The case studies are:

Case 3.1 Numico: Delivering innovation through the supply chain (A)

Case 3.2 Numico: Transforming the supply chain to support new realities (B)

Case 3.3 Numico: King Project

Case 3.4 ABB transformers

Case 3.5 Hewlett-Packard: Creating a virtual supply chain (A)

Case 3.6 Hewlett-Packard: Creating a virtual supply chain (B)

Chapter 4 continues with the leadership perspective, but focuses on how to make the supply chain work. Here we discuss and present cases on managing relations with external partners as well as on the challenges of risk and reward sharing in the supply chain. The case studies are:

Case 4.1 Novo Nordisk Engineering: Running for fast-track project execution

Case 4.2 Building partnerships: Reinventing Oracle's go-to-market strategy

Case 4.3 LEGO: Consolidating distribution (A)

Case 4.4 LEGO: Consolidating distribution (B)

Case 4.5 Freqon: Buyer–supplier evolution?

Case 4.6 Unaxis: Going Asia (A)

Case 4.7 Unaxis: Going Asia (B)

Chapter 5 concludes with the important discussion on supply chain alignment and how firms can ensure that their current supply chain set-up and design correspond to their current market requirements. The case studies are:

Case 5.1 The 'mi adidas' mass customization initiative

Case 5.2 Hilti: Gearing the supply chain for the future (A)

Case 5.3 Hilti: Reflections and outlook (B)

Note

1   'Suppliers Strain to Pick up Pace.' *Wall Street Journal*, 6 August 2010.

2 The supply chain: Key driver of your business model

In the last few years many companies have moved from a market-driven strategy to a more supply-driven business model. We have seen profit warnings in companies that could not meet demand due to lack of components, CEOs resigning because suppliers took excessively high risks, as well as considerable instability in prices because of the uncertainty of supply. Irrespective of whether companies follow an innovation or a cost leadership strategy, the supply side of the business has become much more relevant than before.

While some executives are discovering that the supply chain is an important part of the business model of their companies, other organizations have succeeded by making the supply chain the very backbone of their business model. Nurturing a distinct supply chain capability and competing in the marketplace in this way can be very powerful. Today supply chain and sourcing executives are members of the top management team and CEOs are rushing to learn much more about supply chain.

It is easy to see how important the supply chain is in the business model by making a simple comparison. A typical business today might have a profit and loss account as shown in Table 2.1. Supply chain costs, which include operations and what is paid to suppliers, typically represent around 70% of the value of sales in a manufacturing company.

On the one side, in the example described in Table 2.1, we can see in column two that a 10% increase in sales leads to a 30% increase in profits; on the other side, a 10% reduction in supply chain costs increases profitability by 70%.[1] Thus, the supply chain is a fundamental aspect of the company's business model.

Two basic components of a company's business model are driven by supply

Table 2.1 Effect on profitability of sales increase vs. supply chain improvement

	Base	*10% sales increase*	*10% supply chain improvement*
Sales ($)	100	110	100
Supply chain costs ($)	70	77	63
SG&A ($)	20	20	20
Profit ($)	10	13	17

chain considerations: (1) the level of vertical and horizontal integration; and (2) the level of risk and how it is managed.

Vertically and horizontally integrated supply chains

The level of vertical integration is the degree of integration up and down a supply chain. For example, if a retailer starts manufacturing the products it sells, it is increasing its level of vertical integration. Vertical integration may be upstream or downstream. The interesting question is, how many consecutive steps in the supply chain should the company control and own? Two extremes are the Ford Motor Company in the 1920s and Lacoste today. Ford was known in the early 20th century for owning all of the supply chain tasks, from managing the plantations that produced rubber for the tires, to tire making, car assembly and delivery. By contrast, Lacoste is an almost fully outsourced company: manufacturing and distribution are entirely outsourced, while marketing and design are largely outsourced.

The level of horizontal integration is the breadth of activities at the same point in the supply chain. A typical method of increasing the level of horizontal integration is to acquire other companies or brands in the same business. For example, supermarkets that are moving toward selling a larger variety of non-food items are increasing their level of horizontal integration. Another example is Volkswagen's efforts to merge with Porsche: by merging with another brand in the same field, Volkswagen was able to consolidate its activities and thereby achieve economies of scale.

Although in the last century we have seen many companies pursue a much lower level of vertical integration, this evolution does not mean that companies must strive for vertical disintegration. If anything, today there are extremely successful corporations like Inditex (the owner of the Zara fashion chain) and Luxottica (the world leader in eyewear) that have a high level of vertical integration, but there are also thriving companies like Hewlett-Packard that have a very low level of vertical integration. Thus, it cannot be said that a high or low level of vertical integration on its own is the key to success. The main advantages and drivers of vertical integration of supply chain flows are:

Flow of goods: Fast response to market needs, lower inventories, access to markets, access to materials and, sometimes, consistent quality.

Flow of information: Fast information from the markets, reduced coordination and transaction costs and elimination of price distortions that reduce potential profitability.

Flow of cash: Faster cash-to-cash cycles, reduced receivables, increased availability of cash.

Flow of risks: Allows holistic allocation and management of risk for the chain, reduces uncertainty about supply and demand, prevents opportunistic actions from third parties and captures all of the value in the chain.

Flow of ideas: Faster flow of ideas and innovation.

Flow of personal relations: Creates trust fast because 'We are working for the same company.'

Even companies that have a high level of vertical integration compared to competitors do not integrate everything. For example, Luxottica has a high level of vertical integration but the company does not make lenses for eyewear. This is because there are also important disadvantages to vertical integration:

Flow of goods: Possible exclusion from access to markets or to materials. Customers and suppliers might perceive the company as a competitor. Vertical integration may also lead to difficulty in balancing supply and demand.

Flow of risks: Inefficiencies due to lack of supplier competition, lack of flexibility due to investments upstream or downstream, inability to invest in new competencies as a result of being anchored in nurturing existing ones.

Over the last century we have seen a move toward more horizontal integration and less vertical integration. The main advantage of horizontal integration is the possibility of achieving economies of scale. In particular, companies look for the following aspects of scale advantages:

- Manufacturing and operations like logistics.
- Purchasing power.
- Advertising scale.
- Selling power against customers.

The elimination of barriers between countries (e.g. the European Union, the NAFTA – North American Free Trade Association) has created larger markets, allowing even more important economies of scale.

However, practice has shown that there are also disadvantages to horizontal integration, usually due to added complexity and diseconomies of scale. Typical examples are:

- Excessively big factories might be a challenge to manage.
- Exceedingly large companies might face antitrust scrutiny.
- Oversized brands might represent too high a risk: one small instance can damage the whole brand.

Finally, some executives maintain that economies of scale is a concept of the past that no longer exists. They argue that small operations can be as effective as big ones if properly managed.

There is no optimal vertical or horizontal level of integration per se. It depends on the company's circumstances, the competition, the configuration of the value chain and the evolution of the technology and industry. A particularly useful framework to help understand that evolution, is the clockspeed concept developed by Charles Fine at MIT.[2]

The clockspeed concept

Fine's concept is based on his research on supply chains in different industries. He states that companies and supply chains evolve at different speeds in different industries. For example, the consumer electronics industry evolves extremely fast with product life spans of several months, compared to the aerospace industry in which airplanes last for decades.

There are three distinct clockspeeds at which different parts of the organization change: (1) the organization clockspeed; (2) the process clockspeed; and (3) the product clockspeed. The product change clockspeed is the fastest, while the organization one is the slowest.

A result of this research was the double helix of industries about vertical integration. The process is described in Figure 2.1. This double helix synthesizes the evolution of industries with respect to vertical integration. Two main forces are at play in this development: (1) the complexity of managing a vertically integrated industry; and (2) the pressure to appropriate profits from an invention in the value chain.

An interesting example is the evolution of the bicycle industry in the US. In 1899 more than 300 assemblers of components bought from big suppliers in order to make bicycles. By 1905 only 12 bicycle companies were still making standard products. This consolidation was driven by economies of scale. The Schwinn Company gained a technological edge with several components and, in order to appropriate most of the profits from this innovation, it integrated vertically. By 1930 Schwinn dominated the industry in the US. The mountain bike, a huge innovation in the 1970s, required very different capabilities and the industry was disintegrated, with hundreds of companies making different kinds of mountain bikes. Subsequently, a Japanese company, Shimano, developed innovations in mountain bike components and started to dominate and integrate the industry again.

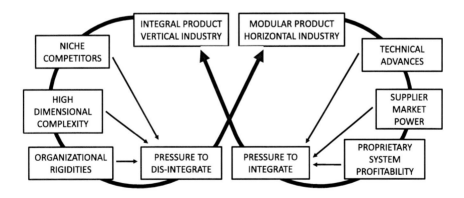

Figure 2.1 Charles Fine's double helix

Source: Adapted from Fine, C.H. *Clockspeed: Winning Industry Control in the Age of Temporary Advantage.* New York: Perseus Books, 1998.

This example illustrates how technological innovation, economies of scale and the pressure to appropriate profits from innovation drive vertical integration and disintegration.

Finally, we must add that the appropriate level of vertical integration depends on the history of the company. A well-established company with a set of existing capabilities might find it appropriate to retain those capabilities, whereas a newly created company might find it more useful to buy the required competencies from suppliers.

Identifying and managing supply chain risks

The need to identify and manage risks in the supply chain is nothing new for companies. What is relatively new, however, is the high level of scrutiny that companies face from customers and the public in general about the consequences of not properly managing risks. In particular, well-known companies are expected to manage risks more effectively than ever before. For example, it is estimated that 5,000 people die in the US each year from food poisoning. Very few of these instances, if any, are due to products from large manufacturing companies, yet such cases tend to be overly reported by the media while food poisoning originating in the home kitchen barely rates a mention.

In order to manage the supply chain it may be useful to ask yourself a few questions, such as: What are the sources of risk in the supply chain? Have they been mapped out? How can you avoid them?

Several trends in society and in the way companies are managed today add to the long list of risks that might emerge from the supply chain (see Table 2.2).

Table 2.2 Types and drivers of risk in a supply chain

Type of risk	Source (risk driver)
Supply risks	Disruption of supply, inventory, schedules and technology access; price escalation; quality issues; technological uncertainty; product complexity; frequency of material design changes.
Operational risks	Breakdown of operations; inadequate manufacturing or processing capability; high levels of process variations; changes in technology; changes in operating exposure.
Demand risks	New product introductions; variations in demand (fads, seasonality and new product introductions by competitors): chaos in the system (the bullwhip effect on demand distortion and amplification).
Security risks	Information systems security; infrastructure security; freight breaches from terrorism, vandalism, crime and sabotage.
Macro risks	Economic shifts in wage rates, interest rates, exchange rates and prices.
Policy risks	Actions of national governments like quota restrictions or sanctions.
Competitive risks	Lack of history about competitor activities and moves.
Resource risks	Unanticipated resource requirements.

Source: Adapted from Manuj, I. and J.T. Mentzer. 'Global Supply Chain Risk Management.' *Journal of Business Logistics*, Vol. 29, No. 1, 2008: 133–155.

Logically, companies should protect operations from all potential risk occurrences and balance the reward–risk ratio (see Figure 2.2). However, it is challenging to mitigate supply chain risk without eroding profits. An interesting analogy posed by Chopra and Sodhi[3] in their work on supply chain risk management is this: How can the manager adopt a stock portfolio manager's way of operating? In managing supply risk, the company should ask: How can we achieve the highest possible profits for varying levels of risk and do so efficiently? Two options are available: (1) move to a greater level of efficiency by reducing risk for the same or higher rewards; or (2) remain at the current level of efficiency and accept reduced risk and lower rewards.

Some risks are essentially unacceptable today and it is not possible to totally pass the risk on to another player in the supply chain, otherwise the whole chain will suffer when a problem occurs. The key is to develop knowledge to minimize risk and the cost of protecting against it.

Companies that are best at identifying and avoiding supply chain risks have often previously been damaged by major supply chain disruptions. Thus, it seems that companies tend to take out supply chain disruption risk insurance only after part of their house has burned down. For example, telecommunications manufacturer Sony Ericsson (at that time L.M. Ericsson) was nearly broken in 2000 (see textbox overleaf). To avoid similar instances, shortly thereafter top management implemented a thorough risk management system to mitigate the effects of any future supply disruptions. The system includes: (1) a risk management organization; (2) supply chain risk identification and assessment systems; (3) mitigation plans; and (4) procedures for responding to severe risks if and when they occur.[4]

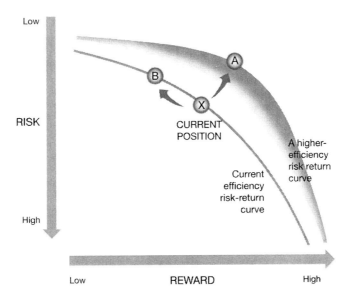

Figure 2.2 Risk–reward-tradeoffs

Source: Chopra, S. and M.S. Sodhi. 'Managing Risk to Avoid Supply-chain Breakdown.' *Sloan Management Review*, Fall 2004: 53–61.

'On March 17, 2000, lightning hit a power line in Albuquerque, New Mexico. The strike caused a massive surge in the surrounding electrical grid, which in turn started a fire at a local plant owned by Royal Philips Electronics, N.V., damaging millions of microchips. Scandinavian mobile phone manufacturer, Nokia Corporation, a major customer of the plant, almost immediately began switching its chip orders to other Philips plants, as well as to other Japanese and American suppliers. Thanks to its multiple-supplier strategy and responsiveness, Nokia's production suffered little during the crisis. In contrast, Telefon AB L.M. Ericsson, another mobile phone customer of the Philips plant, employed a single sourcing policy. As a result, when the Philips plant shut down after the fire, Ericsson had no other source of microchips which disrupted production for months. Ultimately, Ericsson lost $400 million in sales. Ericsson has since implemented new processes and tools for preventing such scenarios. These two dramatically different outcomes from one event demonstrate the importance of proactively managing supply chain risk.'

Designing supply chain response strategies

Have you prepared your supply chain based on a worst case scenario? What if a quality problem that is perceived as compromising the safety of thousands of your customers suddenly erupts and spreads like wildfire in the media? Do you know how to respond? The best companies reduce the consequences of potential events by reacting fast and in an aligned and coordinated manner; every member involved in the compromised supply chain has a specific role and knows exactly what to do, what not to do, what to say and how to respond internally and externally.

Another issue here is the notion that what is important is the customers' perceptions, not whether they are right or wrong. If customers or the media think that your products are dangerous or even potentially deadly, you should respond as if they are!

Managing a crisis is a top management issue. The first key point is to have a clearly defined way to decide when something is indeed a crisis. Then, the company must have a process in place to manage the crisis. This is both an operational and a public relations issue: The company needs to act and it needs to inform. One (no matter how good) without the other is a disaster. If the crisis hits, the issue is a CEO issue and should be dealt with accordingly. In other words, the response has to be measured, fast and coordinated. Evidence indicates that not facing up to the problems early on, or trying to minimize the cost of responding, often results in much greater costs. Based on our experience studying responses to supply chain crisis situations, we have developed a list of dos and don'ts.

The dos and don'ts of supply chain crisis management

- Do inform top management immediately.
- Do be accessible to the media.
- Do be as open and as frank as possible when dealing with the media.
- Do appoint a single spokesperson for the entire company to avoid presenting conflicting versions of the incident.
- Do secure the backing of the regulatory authorities in order to reassure the public.
- Do begin with the assumption that consumers are right when they complain that a product is defective.
- Do remember to keep clients, suppliers and personnel well informed.
- Don't wait for a crisis to happen to develop a strategy for handling crises.
- Don't answer 'no comment' – it invariably implies that the company has something to hide.
- Don't keep your employees in the dark – they are greatly concerned with the image of their company and also want to see that their management team can deal with a crisis.

Bringing strategic flexibility into supply chains

Strategic flexibility pertains to a firm's ability to adjust to changes in global consumer requirements for its products. These changes sometimes appear overnight or emerge over only a few months. Take for example the 2008/09 financial crisis that completely changed consumer buying behaviour across a broad section of industries within an extremely short period of time.

The key question is whether your supply chain – and the position of your firm within it – is robust enough to tackle such pressures. Can your firm adjust its objectives with the support of its superior knowledge, capabilities and supply chain positioning?

Flexibility in a supply chain can take multiple forms depending on whether it relates to the firm (or strategic) level or to the way the firm is embedded in the wider supply network[5] (see Table 2.3). Some companies use such a classification tool to assess their current robustness and ability to adapt to changing patterns of demand.

An important mechanism for improving flexibility is to constantly rebalance supply chain integration levels in order to keep up with an ever-changing environment. In addition, offering modular products and targeting diverse customer segments (e.g. hedging product offerings) have proven to be winning strategies for companies in times of crisis and facing fluctuating customer demand.

Table 2.3 Measuring the level of flexibility in a supply chain

	Flexibility dimension	Description
Strategic flexibilities (firm level)	New design	Speed (and cost effectiveness) at which the firm can design and introduce new products into the system.
	Expansion	Ease with which the firm can add long-term capacity to the system.
	Market	In-house ability to adapt to changes in the market environment.
Supply chain flexibilities (network level)	Robustness	Range of market change with which the existing supply chain configuration is able to cope.
	Reconfiguration	Potential to realign or reinvent the supply chain in response to (or in anticipation of) market change.
	Relationship	Ability to build collaborative relationships both up- and downstream, including for new product development.
	Logistics	Potential to rapidly send and receive products cost-effectively as customers and sources of supply change.
	Organizational	Ability to align (or redistribute) skills to meet the current needs of the whole supply chain.
	Inter-organizational information systems	Ability to align information systems with existing supply chain entities to meet changing information needs.

Source: Adapted from Stevenson, M. and M. Spring. 'Flexibility from a Supply Chain Perspective: Definition and Review.' *International Journal of Operations & Production Management*, Vol. 27, Iss. 7, 2007: 685–713.

Cases in this chapter

2.1 Luxottica: Sustaining growth in challenging times

What are the strategic implications of extending the level of vertical and horizontal integration? This is one of the central questions raised in the Luxottica case. The company is the world leader in eyewear manufacturing, distribution and retailing, with leading brands like Ray-Ban and Sunglass Hut. The case demonstrates how Luxottica, unlike its competitors, pursued a vertical integration strategy and acquired wholesalers and, later on, several retail outlets as a strategic move in order to avoid coming under pressure from big customers. The case also illustrates how the supply chain management was more effective in an integrated chain and how Luxottica escaped the disadvantages of vertical integration described earlier in this chapter.

First, Luxottica integrated forward from mold making to manufacturing, assembly, wholesale, retail and internal production in response to the founder's desire to capture more value from the whole chain. The move allowed the company to gain a better understanding of customer needs and a 20% reduction in unit manufacturing costs compared to those of its main competitors.

Second, by integrating all manufacturing activities and producing internally, Luxottica achieved greater flexibility and an ability to respond more rapidly to changing market trends. The firm did not have to coordinate with supply chain partners. Moreover it had a direct link to end customers coming into its retail stores, allowing it to get a much stronger feel for changing end-customer preferences compared to its competitors, which did not have this direct link. In fact, having developed this knowledge and competency, Luxottica was able to offer its services in managing the collections of other retail customers.

Third, the Luxottica example illustrates how a high level of vertical integration can also provide the opportunity to implement a strong IT infrastructure, leading to increased information transparency throughout the supply chain. As a result of its computerized link between selling, production and distribution elements of the chain, Luxottica was able to monitor worldwide inventory and sales trends on a daily basis and respond to them quickly. Likewise, it was able to deliver products in 24 hours, whereas some of its competitors took a week because of their more complicated three-tier distribution systems.

The 2008/09 crisis created a challenge for Luxottica. A company that has been used to growing for so many years needs to continue growing to maintain the momentum and the existing culture. However, its high level of vertical integration did not allow for a lot of growth. Potentially, Luxottica could continue its horizontal integration by acquiring more brands and more retailers. Such a strategy might lead Luxottica to diseconomies of scale. The company could also risk becoming too dominant. Furthermore, some independent retailers might feel too dependent on a single competitor. Thus, Luxottica might face the disadvantages of vertical and horizontal integration.

2.2 MAS Holdings: Providing design to delivery solutions to the global apparel industry

This multinational based in Sri Lanka is the major supplier of Victoria's Secret, the leading lingerie retail chain in the US. Since its foundation as a joint venture between a Sri Lankan entrepreneur and a Victoria's Secret sourcing arm, the company has grown into a multinational with operations in Sri Lanka, Madagascar, China and Mexico.

The case illustrates the challenges of managing a global supply chain with manufacturing bases in low cost countries as well as issues related to links between manufacturing operations in Sri Lanka and the strategies of US and European customers.

Many of these dilemmas arise from the fact that the company is based in Sri Lanka. Though the labor supply is abundant here, the company is encountering several managerial challenges. The lack of technically skilled manpower, cultural issues pertaining to dealing with customers located across the globe as well as the inability to have constant and direct (physical) communications with the customer at all times are bound to take their toll as MAS continues to grow rapidly.

The immediate issues in the case revolve around how best to organize MAS Holding's various business lines to fulfil customer demand and decide what level of vertical integration the company should pursue in order to circumvent these challenges. It is particularly interesting that the company created many joint ventures with different partners to obtain vertical and horizontal integration, without requiring too many resources and too much time to acquire the competencies needed.

The challenge that the company is facing relates to the elimination of textile quotas, which will expose all companies to a new competitive landscape. The company needs to work out how to leverage the coordination of the value chain and whether forward integration to retail in the Indian subcontinent might be a logical next step.

2.3 and 2.4 Nestlé: *Quality on the boardroom agenda (A and B)*

These two cases are set in the context of Nestlé and its quality management process. They reflect the high level of scrutiny that companies face from customers and the public in general and the consequences of not managing risks properly. The (A) case concentrates on the issues related to the impact of poor quality management and what might happen if quality is not a top priority. It illustrates some major quality fiascos which prove that – even for companies with good quality management practices – it is still possible to end up in serious trouble. The case also demonstrates how quality issues in a company need much more than the attention and awareness of internal operations and managers. They need the best internal controls, the ability to control quality throughout the supply chain, and a highly responsive mechanism to deal with any crisis that might occur.

The (B) case examines these ideas in the context of Nestlé and its different units. The case describes some operating units of the Nestlé organization, which have different potential exposure to quality problems – and therefore different approaches to quality management. The importance of supply chain management and its role in quality management is highlighted, along with the potentially vulnerable aspects of several specific chains.

The case illustrates the fragility of managing quality in an extended supply chain. This fragility is a direct result of the growing tendency for companies to adopt longer supply chains and the resultant challenges in terms of traceability and designing products, processes and logistics system solutions for improved quality. Nestlé is not at all poorly managed in terms of quality, quite the contrary. But it is constantly investigating how to perform even better – being at the absolute forefront of quality management is not just some vague public relations promise.

Case 2.1
Luxottica: Sustaining growth in challenging times

Manuel Burneo, Carlos Cordon and Dominique Turpin

In June 2009, Andrea Guerra, CEO of Luxottica, met with his management team
to review the company's growth strategy for the next five years. He commented:

> After years of sustained growth, global markets are now experiencing not so
> much a crisis as a structural reset of the world. Now we must be as responsive
> as possible and as flexible as ever in adapting to the new scenario.

Luxottica, headquartered in Milan, Italy, was the largest eyewear company in
the world with sales surpassing €5 billion in 2008. Although its name was not
widely recognized outside its home country, some of its eyewear brands, Ray-Ban,
Oakley, Chanel and Prada, for example, and retail brands, such as Sunglass Hut
and LensCrafters, were world renowned.

Luxottica was one of the most vertically and horizontally integrated companies
in the world, with over 6,150 retail stores and a brand portfolio that included 12
house brands and 18 license brands (*refer to* **Exhibit 1**).

During the 2008/09 economic downturn, Luxottica had continued to reinforce
its global leadership, and its singular business model proved resilient. In turn, its
closest competitor, Safilo, manufacturer of Carrera, Armani and Gucci, was being
rescued from imminent bankruptcy by Dutch retail investment group HAL Holding.

Guerra insisted that 'Growth is in the DNA of Luxottica,' recognizing the many
challenges, opportunities and dilemmas that he had to face 'in this new world':

a)   Is it time to modify or dramatically change our business model?
b)   Should we continue with retail and brand acquisitions?
c)   How should we manage our large portfolio of brands?
d)   Where should our geographical focus be?

History of Luxottica

The founder and chairman of Luxottica, Leonardo Del Vecchio, began his career in
Milan as an apprentice in a factory making molds for automobile logos and eyeglass
frames. In 1958, at the age of 23, he opened his own molding shop making tools
for the manufacture of eyeglass frames. In 1961 Del Vecchio moved to Agordo, in
northeast Italy and founded Luxottica, a contract manufacturer of eyewear parts.
Soon he was producing his own frames and competing with his original customers.

In 1967 Del Vecchio decided to focus on the production and sale of finished eyeglass (spectacle) frames and created the Luxottica brand. The company integrated all the manufacturing processes, from design to frame production. Del Vecchio explained:

> By mastering all the technologies, we became very competitive on price without having to compromise our quality.

Vertical integration of the manufacturing process

Del Vecchio continued to systematically integrate his eyeglass business, focusing on technological advances throughout the 1970s. Observing that it was not materials that drove cost increases but retooling to accommodate fashion changes, Del Vecchio began to tackle that side of his business. He began to devise automated molding and milling equipment.

Perhaps most importantly, Del Vecchio guided Luxottica's implementation of computerization. By the end of the 1970s, the company had integrated all facets of its process, from design to manufacturing and inventory control. This early application of computer technology not only gave Luxottica a significant cost advantage over its competitors but also allowed small production runs. This factor would become increasingly important as the influence of ever-changing fashion trends impacted the eyewear industry.

Expansion in wholesale distribution

In 1974 Luxottica acquired the distributor of its product line in Italy, and during the early 1980s continued to pursue vertical integration by acquiring independent optical distributors and forming wholesale subsidiaries in Europe and North America. Over the course of the decade, Luxottica acquired 9 of its 12 international distributors and took significant equity positions in the remainder. The company expanded its computerized ordering, inventory services and just-in-time delivery.

Horizontal integration: Merging eyewear and fashion

In the late 1980s, in parallel to the vertical integration development, Luxottica increased its product lines to include the design, manufacture and distribution of designer frames through license agreements with major fashion houses. Del Vecchio reasoned that people who might not be able to afford a Giorgio Armani suit might opt instead for the designer's eyewear.

In the early 1990s the company continued to extend its distribution network by opening new commercial subsidiaries and expanded its product lines to the fast-growing sunglasses segment by acquiring Vogue in 1990 and Persol in 1995.

Furthermore, Luxottica shifted from its traditional trade-only promotions to consumer advertising with large-scale image-oriented campaigns.

Expanding the vertical and horizontal integration

In 1995 Luxottica took its most significant step toward vertical integration with the hostile US$1.4 billion takeover of United States Shoe Corporation, owner of LensCrafters, North America's biggest retail optical chain with 870 stores. Luxottica thus became the world's first eyewear manufacturer to enter the retail market.

Before entering the retail market, Luxottica sold to individual opticians (90% of US sales) and optical chains throughout its wholesale business. Del Vecchio believed the acquisition of LensCrafters was the only way to prevent the company from being squeezed between shrinking insurance allowances for optical frames and discount chains like Wal-Mart. He remarked, 'I would have risked a lot more by sitting back.'

After a year of conflicts with its wholesale customers, Luxottica's revenues evolved strongly, jumping from €419 million in 1994 to almost €1.25 billion in 1996 and €1.9 billion in 1999.

The company made a further important move in 1999 by acquiring the famous Ray-Ban brand.

Global eyewear leader in the 21st century

Between 2000 and 2005, Luxottica consolidated its leadership in the industry by acquiring retail chains all round the world, including Sunglass Hut in 2002, the world's biggest distributor of premium sunglasses; OPSM Group in 2003, the number one optical player in the Asia-Pacific region; and Cole National in 2004, owner of North America's number two optical retail chain, Pearle Vision.

It was also in 2004 that Andrea Guerra (then 38) became the first CEO to 'come from outside' the company.

In 2007, Luxottica acquired California-based Oakley, the world's leading sports optical company and according to Guerra the only significant eyewear brand not yet included in Luxottica's brand portfolio. Not only was Oakley a world-renowned brand but also the deal included a retail network of over 300 stores.

(*Refer to* **Exhibit 2** *for a summary of financial highlights and* **Exhibit 3** *for a diagram of the business model.*)

The eyewear industry

Overview

The estimated size of the worldwide retail eyewear industry was more than €50 billion in 2007. This market included sales of prescription frames (39%), lenses (34%), sunglasses (15%), contact lenses (10%) and non-prescription reading glasses (2%). The market share of the main product categories was expected to remain unchanged.

By region, the North American market was worth more than €20 billion at retail prices, followed by €15 billion in Europe and €8 billion in Japan.

Industry observers segmented the eyewear market into three broad price categories: high-end (luxury) prescription frames and sunglasses, which generally sold at prices of over €100; mid-range (fashion) with prices ranging from €30 to

€100; and the lower end of the market with prices of under €30. Luxottica operated in the medium and high price market and was totally absent from the low price segment which was very large in terms of units, but where the added value was minimal and the competition very tough.

Italian manufacturers enjoyed worldwide leadership in the production of eyewear frames, both for spectacles and sunglasses. They had a share of nearly 25% of world production, mainly concentrated in medium and high price products (where the Italian producers' market share was estimated to be 50%).

A mature industry

The marketing manager explained:

> In contrast to the double-digit growth rates recorded in the past, the eyewear market in developed countries is now a maturing industry with prescription frames growing at roughly 2% to 3%. The sunglasses market is more volatile and had been growing until the 2008 world economic downturn at more than twice the rate of the rest of the market due to an increased awareness of both the useful benefits (i.e., eye protection) and trendy appeal.

The retail president observed:

> The sunglasses business was relatively underdeveloped, especially in North America where one-third of the population did not wear sunglasses, and the market for units above $30 represented roughly 10% of the total (40% of value). Indeed, 20% of sunglasses sold in North America were by Wal-Mart. By contrast, in Europe, people purchased a lower number of sunglasses but of better quality and the average price per unit was €80 ($112).

Guerra considered that major growth opportunities were expected through the development of new markets. Industry observers envisioned China becoming one of the world's largest eyewear markets over the following five to ten years. However, main players in the mid and high end of the market were struggling to recover their investments in China. Indeed, at the end of 2009 Safilo sold its loss-making retail businesses in China.

Optical and sunglasses retail

The retail eyewear business included independent opticians and optometrists, optical retail chains, specialty sunglasses retailers and duty-free shops. In recent years, the emergence of optical departments in mass retailers resulted in significant competition. For instance, Wal-Mart was the market leader in North America in terms of units sold.

Optical stores sold eyeglasses and contact lenses based on prescriptions written by optometrists or ophthalmologists and operated much like other retail stores.

Some large chains bundled a retail store with an optometrist and an optical laboratory for the fastest service. It was estimated that 75% of sales were influenced or even decided by the opticians.

A typical store held an inventory of 500 frames in 100 different styles. The product mix between optical frames and sunglasses varied considerably across regions, for example in Europe, sunglasses represented around 50% of the mix and in North America, roughly 20% on average.

Economies of scale were driving the consolidation of both producers and distributors of eyewear. For example, in 2008 large retail chains held 60% of the market, up from 40% five years earlier.

Competition

The prescription frames and sunglasses industry was highly competitive and fragmented. Luxottica was the industry leader and the only significant player operating in the two segments: (1) manufacturing and wholesale distribution; and (2) retail distribution.

Luxottica's closest competitors were the large manufacturers and distributors of prescription frames and sunglasses: Safilo, Marchon, De Rigo, Marcolin, Charmant Group, Silhouette International, Menrad, Viva International (Highmark) and Stylemark (*refer to Exhibit 4*). The competition focused on fashion and brands. Luxottica was the only company designing, producing and distributing almost 100% of its frames and sunglasses.

In the retail segment, competitors included a large number of small independents and several chains of optical stores. Even though Luxottica was the only global retail player, in recent years, retail chains and optical departments in discount retailers had been winning market share, especially in North America where the main competitors were Wal-Mart, Eye Care Centers of America (Highmark), National Vision and US Vision.

In Europe, individual country regulations made the creation of a truly pan-European retail chain complex. The main players included Pearle Europe and Grandvision (part of HAL Investments), Fielmann, D&A, and General Optica (*refer to Exhibit 5*).

The optical lenses manufacturing segment was more concentrated with four companies accounting for more than 50% of the global market: Essilor (Luxottica's largest supplier and closest business partner), Carl Zeiss Vision, Hoya and Rodenstock (*refer to Exhibit 6*).

Business model: A vertically and horizontally integrated company

Leonardo Del Vecchio, who had developed Luxottica's structure, had seen great potential in a 'vertical' strategy ever since he had decided to make entire frames rather than just components. Vertical integration of manufacturing was gradually accompanied by the expansion of direct distribution, first wholesale and, from 1995, retail. Eliminating the middleman allowed Luxottica to capture value in every point of the value chain.

The vertically integrated business model was the common platform for a portfolio of 30 brands internally managed by independent teams with a differentiated mission, value proposition and marketing mix. Each team worked with the marketing and design departments to develop collections of 20 to 40 models for every brand, generating more than 3,000 different styles every year. Each license brand was managed by a key account manager who acted as a link between Luxottica and the licensors.

The coexistence of wholesale and retail distribution in North America

In North America, the retail division accounted for 85% of sales and the wholesale division for the remaining 15%. Luxottica was the market leader with a share of roughly 20%. This number was estimated to double in the mid- and high-price eyewear market.

In 1994, in the early years of Luxottica's presence in the retail business, the company had faced channel conflict with its wholesale clients who were reluctant to be sourced by a 'competitor'; sales of the segment fell 25% in North America. This conflict declined over time as Luxottica had maintained equitable pricing across the channel. The retail president commented:

> We all have the same products and sell at the same price; furthermore, if our competitors in retail do promotions or offer discounted eye exams, we prefer not to react even if we are able to.

Luxottica's main strategy had been shifting the industry toward more fashionable and profitable items. Improvements in its assortment and customer service, coupled with a faster reaction to market trends constituted an important defense from what the management team considered the 'real threat,' the mass retailers like Wal-Mart, which offered eyewear at very low prices.

The European distribution dilemma: Retail brands vs. product brands

Luxottica did not operate optical retail stores in continental Europe. Guerra commented, 'The European retail market is too fragmented and our wholesale business is huge, so we prefer not to take the risk of competing with our clients.'

The European wholesale business represented 25% of total sales and almost 40% of the operating profits. Moreover, Luxottica had an average 40% share of the main European markets in terms of value. (*Refer to* **Exhibit 7** *for a description of Luxottica structure and key operational metrics.*)

A member of the management team commented:

> Most of the best-selling eyewear brands in the world are from European designers. This makes it relatively more relevant to own retail stores in the rest of the world since customers in Europe know the product brands well and tend to spend more money on fashion and luxury. (*Refer to* **Exhibit 8**.)

An analyst argued:

> If Luxottica affirms its key to success is its vertically integrated business model, why does it have very different levels of integration in North America (fully integrated), Europe (no retail) and the rest of the world (something in the middle)?

Innovating in wholesale: The STARS initiative

As an alternative to direct participation in the retail business in certain regions, Luxottica launched a singular solution, the STARS Program. Using its know-how in retail and infrastructure, Luxottica provided its most important wholesale clients with:

- A comprehensive assortment
- Inventory management – automatic replenishment
- Promotion management – merchandising – pricing
- New product introductions
- IT services and store design among other services.

Operations: Manufacturing and logistics

The entire production was made in Luxottica's manufacturing facilities and distributed through a single logistics platform which in turn served the wholesale distribution network and Luxottica's own retail stores.

The company's main production sites were located in northeast Italy. It had two plants in China, which concentrated on the more labor-intensive lines of production, and the Oakley facility in the US. In 2008, production reached 40 million frames and sunglasses.

Distribution networks: Wholesale and retail

The wholesale network comprised 43 wholly or majority-owned subsidiaries operating in principal markets, over 2,000 sales representatives and approximately 100 independent distributors. Wholesale customers included retailers of mid- and premium-priced eyewear such as independent opticians, optical and sunglasses chains, optical superstores, sunglasses specialty stores, sporting goods and specialty sports stores and duty-free shops. Europe represented almost 60% of the wholesale revenues.

Luxottica's retail division operated the largest group of optical stores in the US and Canada based on both sales and store count. It also owned the largest specialty retailer of sunglasses in the world based on revenues and was the leading player in the Australian prescription segment. The retail business consisted of 5,695 corporate-owned store locations and 560 franchised locations (*refer to* **Exhibit 9**).

In 2006 Luxottica expanded its retail presence in China by acquiring three premium retail chains to become a leading operator of premium optical stores in the three top optical markets. Luxottica stores around the globe sold a wide range of frames, lenses and other ophthalmic products and services. In 2008, Luxottica's house and licensed brands represented approximately 72% of the total sales of frames based on units sold by the retail division.

Marketing

Marketing and advertising activities were designed primarily to enhance Luxottica's image and its brand portfolio and to drive traffic into its retail locations. In 2008, advertising expenses amounted to approximately 7% of net sales (roughly €365 million).

Vertical integration and scale gave Luxottica complete control of the end-customer shopping experience and the means to develop product brands.

Brand portfolio

Luxottica's brand portfolio integrated house brands, which accounted for over 65% of all units sold, with license brands, including some of the best known names in the global fashion and luxury industries. None of the license agreements represented more than 6% of total sales in 2008.[1]

Manufacturing and design know-how, extensive direct distribution capability and direct retail operations enabled Luxottica to differentiate each brand offering in terms of style, geographical distribution, display and communication. (*Refer to Appendix I.*)

Ray-Ban, Luxottica's stellar brand, had gone through a breathtaking turnaround since it was acquired in 1999. With a constant double-digit growth, it was the top-selling brand worldwide in 2008 and represented roughly 40% of all units sold by Luxottica. (*Refer to Appendix II for more details.*)

Safilo and Luxottica

Although Luxottica and Safilo had shown similar strategies and results in the past, they had had very different track records over recent years (*refer to Exhibit 10*). Moreover, the loss-making Safilo had been rescued *in extremis* at the end of 2009, while Luxottica was generating record cash flows.

Until the late 1980s the two companies had had comparable sales and business models with a strong focus on manufacturing and wholesale. Almost 50% of their sales were derived from license brands and in both cases the North American market represented around 50% of sales.

In the early 1990s, Luxottica had decided to integrate all its manufacturing activities and to produce internally, while Safilo outsourced 20%. The result was a unit manufacturing cost that was 20% lower for Luxottica.[2] It also gave Luxottica more flexibility and a more rapid response to market trends.

Luxottica also led the race toward control of the wholesale channel by acquiring its distributors worldwide. In addition, online monitoring of sales, production and distribution processes enabled the daily supervision of worldwide inventory and sales trends. Luxottica was able to deliver products within 24 hours while Safilo took a week because of its three-tier distribution system.

Safilo made a higher proportion of its sales to a few big optical chains that had high bargaining power, whereas Luxottica sold to many small clients. As a result, Luxottica's average unit price was almost 30% higher,[3] and its inventory turnover was three compared with two for Safilo. Luxottica also benefited from all the intangible advantages such as faster reaction to fashion trends, better service, commercial edge, and so on.

In the five years prior to its entry into the retail business, Luxottica had recorded operating margins of 22%, vastly superior to Safilo's 10%. The strong cash generated by Luxottica fuelled its external growth while Safilo concentrated on organic growth and license agreements.

In contrast with Safilo, Luxottica placed great importance on its portfolio of house brands and retail activities. In 2008, house brand sales represented more than half of total sales and its retail business accounted for 60% of net sales. Safilo, for its part, derived 80% of sales from 28 license brands and less than 10% from its retail segment.

Moreover, in 2009 Safilo announced that it would focus on its core business and sell its loss-making retail activities acquired in previous years in an attempt to follow Luxottica's business model.

The growth challenge

Guerra was confident that the worst-ever economic conditions Luxottica had had to face were over and anticipated that things would soon be back to normal.

Vertical and horizontal integration had provided the company with a broad range of growth options. With limited financial resources due to previous acquisitions and the economic downturn (*refer to **Exhibit 11***), the company's main challenge now was to identify the soundest initiatives.

As he opened the meeting, Guerra stressed:

> We have been very successful so far, but tomorrow's success is never guaranteed. Even if historical annual growth rates of more than 15% appear impossible under current conditions, don't forget that growth is the DNA of the company.

Manufacturing and Wholesale		Retail	
House Brands	**License Brands**	**House Brands**	**License Brands**
• Arnette • Eye Safety Systems • K&L • Luxottica • Mosley Tribes • Oakley • Oliver Peoples • Persol • Ray-Ban • Revo • Sferoflex • Vogue	• Anne Klein • Brooks Brothers • Bulgari • Burberry • Chanel • Chaps • Club Monaco • Dolce & Gabbana • DKNY • Donna Karan eyewear • Miu Miu • Polo Ralph Lauren • Prada • Salvatore Ferragamo • Tiffany & Co • Tory Burch • Versace • Versus	• BrightEyes • Budget Eyewear • David Clulow • Ilori • Laubman & Pank • LensCrafters • Oakley • OPSM • PearleVision • Sunglass Hut	• Sears Optical • Target Optical

Exhibit 1 Brand portfolio

Source: Company website

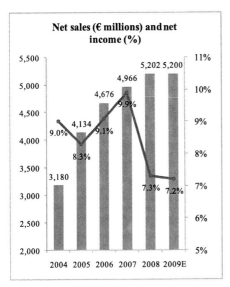

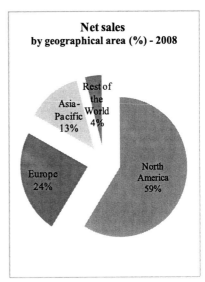

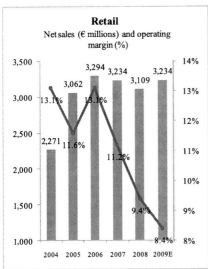

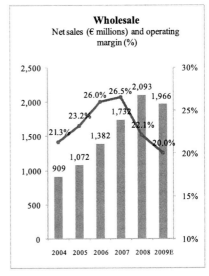

Exhibit 2 Financial highlights

Source: Annual reports – Presentations

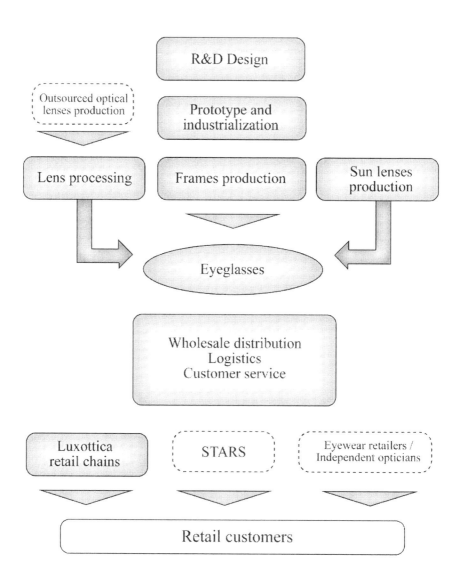

[ ] Luxottica presence in the eyeware value chain

Exhibit 3 Vertically integrated business model

Source: www.luxottica.com – IMD elaboration

	Sales (2008) (€ million)	Country	Main group brands	Main license brands	Main markets
Luxottica	5,202		Ray-Ban, Oakley	Prada, Dolce & Gabbana, Chanel, Polo Ralph Lauren	Global
Safilo	1,148		Carrera, Safilo	Armani, Gucci, Dior, Yves Saint Laurent	Global
Marchon (VSP)	NA	US	Marchon, Flexon	CK, Nike, Karl Lagerfeld	US
De Rigo	582		Police	Givenchy, Guess	
Charmant	200		Charmant	Lacoste, Sprit	Global
Silhouette	NA		Silhouette	Adidas, Daniel Swarovski	
Menrad	NA		Menrad	Joop, Davidoff	
Viva Int.	NA	US	Viva	Tommy Hilfiger	US
Marcolin	187		Marcolin	Roberto Cavalli, Timberland, Tods	Global
Stylemark	NA	US	Polaroid Eyewear	Perry Ellis, Dockers, Disney	US

Exhibit 4 Manufacturing and wholesale competitors

Source: Companies' websites – IMD elaboration

	Sales (2008) (€ million)	Main market	Number of stores (2008)
Luxottica retail	2,600	US	4,826
Wal-Mart	1,300	US	4,100
ECCA (Highmark)	384	US	430
Vision	NA	US	690
National Vision	NA	US	500
Pearle Europe (HAL Holding)	1,102		2,587
GrandVision (HAL Holding)	930		1,235
Fielmann	903		600
D & A (De Rigo)	NA		376
General Optica (De Rigo)	NA		205
Sunglass Hut (Luxottica)	NA	Global	81
David Clulow (Luxottica)	NA		64

Exhibit 5 Retail competitors

Source: Companies' websites – IMD elaboration

	Sales (2008) (€ million)	Country
Essilor	3,074	
Carl Zeiss Vision	892	
Hoya	865	
Rodenstock	481	

Exhibit 6 Eyeglass lenses manufacturers

Source: Companies' websites

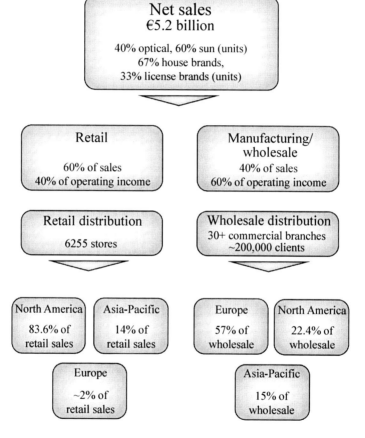

Exhibit 7 Luxottica structure and key operational metrics (2008)

Source: Company reports – SEC Form 20-F – IMD elaboration

Rank	Brand	Country of origin	Eyeware license
1	Louis Vuitton	France	-
2	Gucci	Italy	Safilo
3	Chanel	France	Luxottica
4	Rolex	Switzerland	-
5	Hermès	France	-
6	Cartier	France	-
7	Tiffany & Co	US	Luxottica
8	Prada	Italy	Luxottica
9	Ferrari	Italy	Marcolin
10	Giorgio Armani	Italy	Safilo
11	Bulgari	Italy	Luxottica
12	Burberry	UK	Luxottica
13	Dior	France	Safilo
14	Polo Ralph Lauren	US	Luxottica
15	Zegna	Italy	De Rigo
16	Ferragamo	Italy	Luxottica

Exhibit 8 The leading luxury brands 2008

Source: Interbrand, 2008 Leading Luxury Brands

	North America	Asia-Pacific	China/Hong Kong	Europe	Africa and ME	South Africa	Central and South America	Total
LensCrafters	966		170					**1,136**
Sunglass Hut and ILORI	1,708	208	6	82		68		**2,072**
Pearle Vision	425							**425**
Sears Optical	878							**878**
Target Optical	331							**331**
Oakley retail locations	127	15		10		2	2	**156**
OPSM group		521						**521**
David Clulow (UK)				59				**59**
Bright Eyes		49	68					**117**
Franchised locations	391	114		10	39		6	**560**
Total	**4,826**	**907**	**244**	**161**	**39**	**70**	**8**	**6,255**

Exhibit 9 Luxottica retail segment by region (as of December 2008)

Source: Luxottica SEC Form 20-F

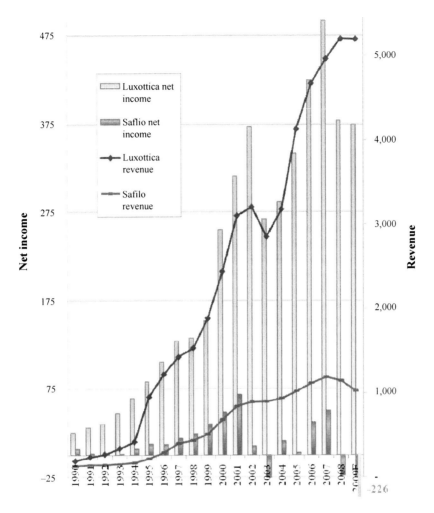

Exhibit 10 Luxottica vs. Safilo: Revenue and net income 1990–2008 (€ million)

Source: Annual reports and SEC Forms 20-F

During the economic downturn, demand for eyewear plunged and Luxottica also experienced a consumer shift toward lower entry price products that favor rivals like Wal-Mart.

After several years of strong growth, in 2009 the CEO's guideline was solidity of the balance sheet and cash flow generation. This implied CAPEX reduction, cost cuts in many areas and deleveraging (Net debt/EBITDA = 2.7x).

When Guerra joined Luxottica in July 2004 as the first CEO from outside the company, he took over the command of a €3 billion company with considerable prospects for growth and cash. In only five years, Guerra oversaw the integration of Pearle Vision in North America; expanded the brand portfolio with significant license agreements (notably Dolce & Gabbana, Ralph Lauren, Burberry and Tiffany & Co.); started the retail business in China; and acquired Oakley, the last significant eyewear brand left in the industry.

In 2008, revenues peaked at €5.2 billion and the same figure was expected for the end of 2009. Guerra faced a much more challenging situation. On the one hand, a mature industry with lower 'psychological' prices for fashion and luxury eyewear than two years previously; on the other hand, a portfolio of 30 brands, considered to be the maximum number of manageable brands. Additionally, as a result of its debt level, Luxottica had limited cash for investments or acquisitions even if its main competitors were in a worse financial position.

Some of the key growth initiatives included the STARS program and geographical expansion in emerging markets, especially China where growth rates in recent years had been significant and the wholesale and retail businesses were developing together. However, this region still represented less than 10% of total sales.

Exhibit 11 Luxottica during the 2008/2009 economic downturn

Appendix 1 Brand portfolio

House brands

LUXOTTICA☆	Created in 1967, this was the first line to be manufactured by Luxottica. The brand is characterized by its classic style, clean-cut design and high-quality frames.
Sferoflex	Sferoflex takes its name from the patented flexible hinge enabling the temples to conform to the shape and size of the face. Sferoflex prescription frames target people demanding a classic, reliable and comfortable product.
VOGUE eyewear	Vogue styles, mainly designed for women, stand out for their innovative design, for the wide variety of colors and frames and for the fashionable details on the temples.
MOSLEY TRIBES *Persol*	Created in 1917 and acquired by Luxottica in 1995, Persol is a living legend of "Made in Italy" eyewear. The brand is characterized by high-quality lenses and comfortable fit with a heritage of history and tradition.
Ray-Ban GENUINE SINCE 1937	Style, tradition and freedom of expression are the key values behind Ray-Ban, the best-selling sunglasses and optical frames in the world. Ray-Ban is characterized by high-quality lenses and materials as well as clean-cut design, traditionally favored by celebrities. Its "authenticity" has been enhanced with a modern approach and extensive marketing campaigns.
REVO	Revo is characterized by an innovative lens based on a technology developed by NASA, offering maximum protection against ultraviolet and infrared light. Revo targets people needing perfect vision for outdoor sports or specific protection of the eyes.
arnette	Created in California according to the principle that doing things your own way is not only the *right* way, it's the *only* way, Arnette targets the 3S generation – surf, skateboard and snowboard. Arnette has a highly appealing design and provides good comfort and functionality for those who enjoy dynamic and extreme sports.
K&L EYEWEAR	K&L addresses the needs of emerging markets maintaining global distribution. K&L is a fresh brand for a dynamic young public who are careful about their look.
OAKLEY	Established in 1975 and acquired by Luxottica in 2007, Oakley is one of the leading sports performance brands in the world. Oakley, holder of over 600 patents, is unique in its blend of technology, design and art across its products making it one of the most iconic and inimitable brands on the market.

License brands

Brooks Brothers (logo)	Brooks Brothers collections are characterized by affordable style, functionality, lightness and slender lines that reflect the unique features of the style of this American brand.
BVLGARI (logo)	Bvlgari eyewear is distinguished by the high quality of its materials, attention to detail and elegant design. This product line addresses a clientele who seek a distinctive and exclusive product.
Salvatore Ferragamo EYEWEAR (logo)	The Salvatore Ferragamo collections are characterized by painstaking attention to detail and trimming as well as an original use of materials and choice of colors. The eyewear collection is inspired by the tradition of craftsmanship of this fashion house, reinterpreted in a contemporary mode.
CHANEL	The Chanel product line, targeting sophisticated, trendy, sleek and refined people, reflects the essential characteristics of the brand: style, elegance and class.
ANNE KLEIN NEW YORK	This product line targets successful professional women who place an emphasis on image and comfort.
PRADA	Prada collections have a forward-thinking approach and style, enabling the brand to anticipate and often inspire trends across all sectors. Sophisticated, elegant and refined, Prada products are identified by their strong character and unique style.
MIU MIU	The Miu Miu brand addresses a sophisticated, free-and-easy clientele particularly attentive to new trends and expresses Miuccia Prada's vision of an alternative style. The Miu Miu brand is urban, young, sophisticated and sensual, a "new classic."
VERSACE	Versace is a fashion and lifestyle brand for contemporary men and women who love glamorous luxury and distinctive personal style. Versace eyewear's refined and innovative design is a celebration of timeless exclusivity and fashion forward elegance.
VERSUS	The Versus brand was designed by Versace to target the younger generations who are more price conscious.
DONNA KARAN EYEWEAR	This product line reflects the design sensibility and spirit of the Donna Karan collection, offering men and women sophisticated styling in modern and lightweight materials.

License brands continued

DKNY DONNA KARAN NEW YORK	DKNY is easy-to-wear fashion with an urban mindset, the New York City street-smart look. DKNY eyewear caters to modern, urban, fashion-conscious women and men with multifaceted lifestyles: international, eclectic, fun and real.
DOLCE & GABBANA	Dolce & Gabbana eyewear collections are an expression of ultimate luxury. They are characterized by modern, fashionable shapes, prestige materials and sumptuous detailing, such as logos in Swarovski crystals or elegant metal circles.
D&G DOLCE & GABBANA	The D&G eyewear collection has a youthful, provocative and cosmopolitan spirit at more affordable prices.
BURBERRY ESTABLISHED 1856	Leading British luxury and fashion brand, Burberry influences its eyewear collections with the brand's core values of form and function and the essence of classic style re-interpreted always with a relaxed and distinctly British attitude.
POLO RALPH LAUREN	The Polo collection focuses on refined designs, inspired by the heritage of Polo Ralph Lauren apparel. Polo is the ideal collection for men who appreciate quality and tradition and are seeking classic styles with a fresh design.
RALPH LAUREN	In a range of designs from vintage silhouettes to glamorous oversized shapes, the Ralph Lauren eyewear collection gives the modern woman striking ways to make her own style statement.
CHAPS EST. 1978	Chaps features easy to wear designs in the classic tradition of Polo Ralph Lauren. The line offers a designer name to the young consumer at competitive prices.
CLUB MONACO	Club Monaco offers quality eyewear of uncompromising style and affordable luxury. The styling targets men and women between 20 and 40 who are urban professionals, style enthusiasts who appreciate design at mid-level prices.
TIFFANY & CO.	For 169 years, Tiffany & Co. has designed and produced standard-setting jewelry and accessories. The first collection of Tiffany & Co. eyewear, launched exclusively by Luxottica early in 2008, remains true to the brand's highest standards.
TORY BURCH	Tory Burch is a sophisticated American brand at an accessible price point for women of all ages. The first eyewear collection was launched in 2009.

Main retail brands

sunglass hut	Acquired by Luxottica in 2001, Sunglass Hut is recognized as a leader in specialty sun retailing with almost 2,000 Sunglass Hut locations around the world (1,600 in North America).
	Luxottica products represent 80% of Sunglass Hut sales.
LENSCRAFTERS	LensCrafters operates a retail network of 1,136 stores, of which 966 are in North America and 170 in China. LensCrafters is the largest optical retail chain in North America in terms of sales.
	LensCrafters stores offer a wide selection of prescription frames and sunglasses, mostly made by Luxottica. It is known for providing convenient access to eye exams by Independent Doctors of Optometry at or next to LensCrafters, a wide choice of frames and lenses and one-hour service.
PEARLE VISION	Pearle Vision is the second-largest optical chain in North America after LensCrafters. Although both brands address the mid- to high-end customer bracket, their positioning is complementary. Pearle Vision focuses on eye care and the vision insurance segment (less fashion content) and addresses more price conscious customers. Its stores are mostly located in strip malls instead of the conventional malls where most LensCrafters and Sunglass Hut stores are located. In addition, Luxottica has franchised Pearle Vision locations located throughout North America.
	Pearle Vision operates 450 store locations and has 390 franchise locations throughout North America.

Source: Annual reports – www.luxottica.com

Appendix II The Ray-Ban turnaround

When Luxottica acquired Ray-Ban in 1999, the brand had been declining for some years. During the 1990s, Ray-Ban had product and quality issues, pricing conflicts, uncontrolled distribution and little advertising investment. Ray-Bans were sold in camera shops, tobacconists, discount stores, mass retailers – just about anywhere.

A former brand manager explained:

> The first step in Ray-Ban's turnaround was comprehensive market research to identify the 'DNA' of the brand. Luxottica shut down the manufacturing facilities and halted sales of the world's most popular sunglasses brand for six months. Distribution was re-opened in a selective way, elevating the status of the brand. Manufacturing was transferred to Italy and prices were standardized across the world and went up from a minimum of $29 to a minimum of $89.

Through multimillion marketing campaigns, Ray-Ban was repositioned from 'my parents' sunglasses to something cool.' The new approach was very fashion-oriented with three or four collections every year and adapted quickly to trends by sending prototypes to the market before production. Luxottica has invested roughly $15 million a year ever since in consumer marketing and trade marketing in North America alone.

The brand manager observed:

> The acquisition of Sunglass Hut in 2001 allowed Luxottica to pack, sell and distribute Ray-Ban in the exact way it was planned. At the same time, control of the 'last mile' provided Luxottica with quick and direct feed-back from consumers.

Ray-Ban, which also added prescription frames to its product line, has generated annual sales growth of roughly 20% since 2003 and is the world's top-selling brand in both sun and prescription eyewear.

Case 2.2
MAS Holdings: Providing design to delivery solutions to the global apparel industry

Atul Pahwa, Carlos Cordon and Donald A. Marchand

December 2004. Colombo, Sri Lanka. Mahesh Amalean, Chairman of MAS Holdings (MAS), looked back on the stellar performance of the group companies. Gap, Marks & Spencer, Nike and Victoria's Secret, some of the apparel company's more prestigious customers had just conferred manufacturing and supplier excellence awards on it, a testimony to the firm's customer-centric ethos.

But the winds of change were gathering force. By mandate of the World Trade Organization (WTO), from January 2005, a quota-free international textile trade regime was to replace country-specific textile quotas for goods entering WTO member states including the EU and USA. Small apparel manufacturers were not expected to survive the anticipated wave of consolidation and it was widely accepted that Chinese firms could corner as much as 50% of the worldwide market.

Amalean faced several operational issues. The company had just embarked on an internal reorganization to focus its 16 loosely held joint ventures around three key product lines. In recent years, it had also taken several steps to change its focus from being a contract manufacturer to positioning itself as a full service provider for its customers.

Some of the questions that lay ahead of Amalean were:

- How should MAS be organized to best meet customer demands in a rapidly changing, fashion-driven industry where both speed and flexibility in operations were critical to success?
- How vertically integrated should MAS become? Should it invest in building a retail brand? Or should it go downstream and bring raw material suppliers in-house? Or instead focus on configuring its supply chain to optimize its existing business processes?
- How should MAS manage and deploy its IT systems to improve knowledge sharing and information management capabilities across the organization, and perhaps strive for a competitive edge?

The global textile and apparel industry

The apparel and textile industry comprised $375 billion of trade between WTO member states. Under the auspices of the General Agreement on Tariffs and Trade (GATT), various countries imposed import restrictions in the 1950s and 1960s to protect their domestic markets and this led to the Multifiber Agreement (MFA) of 1974. By 1994, a plan to phase out the MFA was reached. The WTO, which replaced GATT in 1995, instituted the Agreement on Textiles and Clothing (ATC) to oversee the abolition of quotas by January 1, 2005. (*Refer to **Exhibit 1** for the evolution of the textile and apparel industry agreements through 2005.*)

Sri Lanka's textile and apparel industry

While the textile industry in Sri Lanka was encouraged by the government as an import substitution mechanism in the 1960s and 1970s, the apparel segment gained ground in the 1980s as a vibrant export industry. Spurred by the liberalization of the Sri Lankan economy in 1977, foreign investment and interest in Sri Lanka continued to rise.

There were over 1,000 apparel companies from 55 different countries operating in Sri Lanka employing 450,000 people. Low labor costs ($50–$100 per person per month), a high literacy rate (92%) and financial incentives were key drivers in the continual growth of the industry. Sri Lanka had also invested significantly in modern ports and in power and telecommunications infrastructure. In addition, Sri Lanka was known to consistently follow stringent labor standards and practices. The apparel industry accounted for $2.5 billion and 53% of the country's total exports. (*Refer to **Exhibit 2** for further data.*)

There were, however, some weaknesses in the environment. The ethnic conflict that had engulfed the island nation for over 20 years continued, and Sri Lanka lacked a developed raw materials base (it had to import 150,000 tons of fabric annually).

The origins of MAS Holdings

In 1981 Mahesh Amalean, armed with a chemical engineering degree, joined the 60-year-old family textile business temporarily, while awaiting his diploma. Amalean happened upon an opportunity to supply the European retailer C&A with a small order of 12,000 garment pieces and soon convinced the family elders to pursue an export-oriented strategy to grow the business. The initial order was well received and soon larger orders followed. In the coming years, Amalean also secured contracts from Izod, Calvin Klein and Jordache.

In 1985, eager to branch out on his own, Amalean sold his shares in the family business and invested his entire savings in a unit with 40 sewing machines, managing the business himself.[4] In 1986, he attracted the attention of Martin Trust, CEO of MAST Industries. MAST was a leading supplier (and, since 1978, a subsidiary) of The Limited Inc., a retailer based in Columbus, Ohio.[5]

Trust saw skilled manufacturing abilities and a charismatic entrepreneur who had gradually built up an impressive client base. He immediately offered Amalean a 50–50 joint venture opportunity to build a manufacturing unit to supply MAST with women's synthetic dresses, which at the time were not under the quota regime. Both sides shook hands, each invested about $45,000 (it was all Amalean could afford) and began to build the infrastructure for the joint venture.

Women's dresses came under quota before production could begin, and Amalean decided to take on women's lingerie, a product category that was still quota-free.

Unfazed by the complexity of the product category, he convinced Trust to set up a visit to one of MAST's suppliers in China, for he had the technical know-how but not the product knowledge to manufacture lingerie. Trust agreed and, at Amalean's behest, also set up a meeting with the president of Victoria's Secret.

At this meeting, Amalean and Trust convinced Victoria's Secret's president to give Amalean a small order. Realizing that he was competing against the current sourcing arms of Victoria's Secret in the Philippines, China and the US, Amalean worked diligently to deliver the goods on spec, on time and at the agreed price.

Victoria's Secret soon came back to Amalean to let him know that his products were flying off the shelf. The combination of price and product quality was second to none. And they immediately offered to book 100% of his capacity for the next three years. Elated, yet cautious about putting all his eggs in one basket, Amalean instead offered 60% of his capacity. Although confident that his low cost, high quality operation in Sri Lanka could meet the needs of the lingerie marketplace, Amalean recognized two shortcomings of the current operation.

First, to scale his operations[6] he would require seasoned professional managers, able to interact with the customer at all levels of the organization. Amalean considered himself more of an entrepreneur and realized that as the operations grew in size, his role would grow to one of nurturing talent, not single-handedly controlling the business. Second, while the company's manufacturing quality and capabilities had passed a vital test with the customer, Amalean was also aware that the company's success was due to the relationship with MAST – their joint venture combined the access to markets that MAST provided with the manufacturing excellence of the Sri Lankan operation.

Expanding the MAS portfolio

The joint venture philosophy

Over the next three years, as MAS slowly built up its lingerie product portfolio with Victoria's Secret, there was a shift in the market from a functional to a more fitted, fashion-oriented product. Eager to tap into this lucrative arena, and aware of the highly technical nature of the manufacturing process, MAS and MAST together approached Triumph[7] to suggest a joint venture collaboration.

The first meeting took place in April 1990, at Triumph's Hong Kong production facility. Triumph executives carefully scrutinized MAS, its experience, technology and capabilities before agreeing to visit Sri Lanka. At the same time they offered Amalean the opportunity to walk through the Triumph operations – seven floors of 25,000 sq ft each, with a total of 2,000 workers, was a sizable operation. Amalean marveled at the size and complexity of the operations, while realizing that Triumph's minimum requirements for the size of a potential Sri Lankan venture would be four times the size of the largest facility that MAS currently operated back in Sri Lanka.[8]

In August 1990, Triumph's president, satisfied with a visit to MAS in Sri Lanka, committed to one of the first joint ventures in the company's history. It brought together German technology and world-class manufacturing techniques, with retail access to the best market for intimate apparel (the US) and the low cost Sri

Lankan base. The three sides, MAS, Triumph and MAST, quickly agreed that each would hold an equal share in this new company, Bodyline.

By this association with Triumph, MAS learned how to manage large businesses. MAS decided not to influence the running of the plant but instead accepted the systems, processes and procedures/practices instituted by Triumph. In MAS, Triumph saw a level of immaturity in business processes, yet considerable future potential and even guided Bodyline to the detail of reviewing and approving every official communiqué with outside partners. Also, Triumph saw the joint venture as a vehicle to get into specialty stores at a slightly higher price point.

Victoria's Secret, through MAST, was able to utilize the formula of Triumph technology and the MAS manufacturing base to tap into the evolving lingerie market and offer increasingly relevant products to an industry turning away from functional products toward rapidly changing fashion trends.

This joint venture symbolized the cornerstone of the MAS philosophy of building partnerships on a formula of trust, openness, fair play and mutual understanding. MAS made sure that its relationship management with its partners was very strong, with emphasis on close dialogue, a personal relationship and trust, not purely on numbers.

Over the years, MAS built up several other joint ventures with leading industry players like Noyon Dentelle (lace), Pacific Textiles, Prym Newey (permanent safe fastenings), Sara Lee Courtaulds Textiles, Speedo International[9] (swimwear) and Stretchline (elastics). Wherever possible, the venture was set up as an equal partnership. This way, no partner had an edge over the other.

Every joint venture at MAS was developed along the same principles. As Amalean explained:

> It's not a magic formula. Both partners are equal – and make an equal commitment to the project. Both partners bring to the table the same value in terms of the business. We agree upfront on the role of each partner. The fact that we are in [Sri Lanka], we take on the responsibility of managing the business – once orders are taken, we manage the process from there onward. And we outline this very clearly in the joint venture agreement. We also identify the responsibility of the other partner(s). With Triumph, it was their responsibility to provide the product development and technical [solution] that we would thereafter use to manufacture the product. MAST Industries, with their association with Victoria's Secret, took the responsibility of bringing business into this project. So the specific roles were identified early.

> Was this easy? It was challenging! We had Americans and the American culture, Germans with their culture, and Sri Lankans with their culture. It was important to understand the culture the partners had in their business. I believe the magic, if anything, is to understand how each of the partners works, what is important to them, what their expectations are, and then to build your structure to support that – your organization and people, getting them to understand your partner and their way of working.

Understanding the roles was vital to the success of such a project. An issue related to manufacturing meant that Triumph's or MAS Holdings' opinion on the matter would count more than the opinion of another partner. Similarly, if it were a marketing-related issue, then a partner such as MAST would have considerably more say.

Backward vertical integration

In the early years, it was a challenging task to get elastic from the UK and China and expect the color to match the fabric coming from Korea. Because of such difficulties, MAS pressed ahead with procuring a local base of raw material and thereby better coordinating the production process to obtain consistency and quality in the finished product.

There was another thought behind starting backward integration projects – MAS knew that if it were to be competitive and sustain its business in the region, it would need to source its primary components from within the region (south and southeast Asia), if not from Sri Lanka.[10] Once WTO quota restrictions were lifted and manufacturing units consolidated to gain economies of scale, there was a strong possibility that there would be less movement of raw material between different regions. Sri Lanka had almost no raw material or technical resources to compete with regional manufacturing in places like China, and thus began MAS's efforts to backward integrate into manufacturing processes (*refer to **Exhibit 3***).

A loosely held coalition of companies

At the heart of the joint venture philosophy was the tenet that the companies under the MAS Holdings umbrella would work with each other in an 'arm's-length' supplier–customer relationship. This ensured a considerable amount of operational freedom for each business unit manager, the development of an entre-preneurial spirit, and even a competitive environment, where the business units even battled each other for business, something that happened frequently.

For example, Slimline and Linea Clothing both manufactured ladies' underwear and routinely competed with each other for Victoria's Secret business. Similarly, Unichela and Shadowline competed for business from Gap. (*Refer to **Exhibit 4** on details of operations of MAS Holdings in December 2004.*)

Utilizing technology and information to manage growth

In 1997, MAS became only the fourth apparel manufacturer worldwide (and the first in Asia) to implement an SAP enterprise resource planning (ERP) solution for the apparel industry.[11] It was an ambitious project for the $140 million company, which aimed to link seven of the group companies on a single system that would track details from the time the purchase order was entered to the time the money was collected from the customer. By linking the purchase order module to the sourcing and production functions, the company wanted to evaluate profitability at a sales order level. There was no senior manager equivalent to the CIO or CTO directing these efforts, and all coordination was done at the business unit level. Amalean commented:

> There is no one de facto owner of the IT group and its strategy. There is a team that handles the networking. There is a MASSAI – MAS Strategic Action Initiatives – team that handles strategic initiatives including technology. These teams, which are led by a member of the MAS corporate board, include operational people and managers, act as hunters for new ideas and set priorities.

> To date, MAS has had a very decentralized structure. That is the reason we have not had a corporate-driven emphasis on IT. We have provided autonomy to the business units to make decisions. Where economies of scale can be created, we get together in MASSAI and look to see how best to implement a solution that can be used across the group.

MAS began a pilot with Slimline in 1998, using external consultants, and 18 months and $2 million later completed the task. During this time, MAS developed a shadow team to track the implementation, and subsequently this internal team completed the rest of the implementation in the other six companies by 2001 and with an additional spend of $2 million. IT expenditures totalied just under 0.5% of annual revenues.

Spinning off IT services

In 2002, MAS spun off its internal SAP team into a separate company, Rapier Consulting. With both a functional and a technical understanding of deploying solutions in the apparel industry, Rapier aimed to operate as a profit center by providing services to MAS group companies as well as external clients. Amalean noted:

> We looked at the potential opportunities for the resources we had built. We spoke to SAP and realized that this part of the world did not have such expertise. We deliberated within MAS on this diversification into an IT-focused business and nevertheless focused on the business opportunity that lay in front of us.

MAS group companies were free to implement the specific SAP modules they deemed most important for their respective businesses. However, Rapier had also created a customized product offering – by developing a pre-configured solution of SAP at one-sixth of the price of a standard implementation, it was now able to commit to a fast implementation (two months), which included training and data migration services, and also guaranteed a 99% solution fit for a typical contract manufacturer.[12]

Over the following two years, Rapier's revenue split was 60% MAS and 40% external and it was widely expected that as much as 70% of its revenues would come from external clients in 2005. As Vajira DeSilva, CEO of Rapier noted:

> Rapier is probably the only consultancy company to stem from the apparel and textile industry. We have built a knowledge-based organization around the SAP Apparel and Footwear solution, which we are able to offer to external clients. I believe, these attributes will give Rapier an edge over our competition.

In addition, there was a second wholly owned subsidiary, Sabre Technologies, which had internally developed a real-time production system. External solutions would have cost three times what it cost MAS to develop its in-house system, and besides, this allowed MAS to get quick turnaround and support from the internal team as well as to customize the solution to its specific requirements.

Valuing information and IT usage at MAS

Although the initial emphasis was on the deployment of IT systems across the organization, there came a realization that the appropriate usage of these systems would enhance their value. There was no performance measurement for usage by people across the organization; instead there was only emphasis on SAP training, based on job profile. One of the IT managers said:

> We monitor how many people use the intranet on a monthly basis. We try to get the users to be more IT savvy. Though people don't necessarily use it correctly, and problems crop up. The success of the application depends on the functional manager's use of the system.

The IT group was responsible for making sure that people knew what was available, that data entry personnel were trained in the necessary systems (to ensure that there was a high level of accuracy in the data input), and that there was an intranet forum to facilitate discussion on necessary IT-related activities. The systems had been deployed as a matter of competitive necessity and allowed for some productivity gains along the way, a trend uniform across the industry.

> The first couple of years we struggled to get people disciplined to work on the integrated system and to understand the implications [of doing so]. We put a lot of effort into building awareness. Today, I still don't think we are using the systems to the optimal levels. At an operational level, I would say, yes.[13] It has become a day-to-day practice to make decisions [using SAP]. On a tactical level, we are half way. On a strategic level, I still cannot see that the people have matured enough to make the decisions based on the system.

There were some good, though scattered, attempts at linking up with some key customers to exchange transactional data. In late 2004, MAS had piloted a web-based application whereby customers could check the status of an order in real time. It expected to fully develop and roll out the application in 2005.

But there was still much work to be done to gain the true value from using such systems. Moving beyond competitive necessity, MAS truly desired a transparent model where information flowed through the value chain, from its customers down to its various suppliers.

Developing information systems for 2005 and beyond

There was no information or knowledge transfer between MAS and its key suppliers of raw materials via ERP systems. Written purchase orders and telephone calls complemented other manual forms of exchange in a process that was flexible and manageable for small volumes but quickly got unwieldy as the number of transactions increased.

Similarly, knowledge and information transfer within the MAS group companies was limited. Although the ERP system was in place across multiple group companies, because the individual businesses had customized their SAP installations, they had created virtual islands of information that were difficult to collate, analyse and use at the group level.

There were visible cracks in this information exchange mechanism. As MAS grew business with its customers, there were multiple points of contact with them. A customer who was serviced by more than one of the group companies would receive a call from one of them for some specifications and then a while later receive a similar call from yet another company. And customers were becoming increasingly irate about the duplicated efforts required to reach out to the highly decentralized operations within MAS. (*Refer to* **Exhibit 5** *for process and information flow linking various activities within MAS.*)

Organizational culture at MAS

Amalean's humble beginnings and focused vision in the lingerie industry, his never-ending quest for perfection, and his warm and affable nature soon attracted a nucleus of like-minded people into the organization. The company was full of passionate, hardworking and inquisitive minds that did not hesitate before challenging norms, but did so within defined limits. By December 2004, MAS employed 30,000 people in eight countries.

A sporting mindset

MAS encouraged people to push the limits. Walking down the corridors of MAS offices, one could see images of sporting heroes all around. The logic behind this, according to Dian Gomes, Managing Director of Unichela:

> Athletes inspire people. One of our HR people ran the 400 meters in the Olympic Games, and now she is training for the World Championships. It takes a lot for them to train, then come here and do a decent job. But it inspires the other people in the organization. In a way, this competitive spirit is in our DNA. And this gives us humbleness and courage.

This was not a unique example. The company team won the Sri Lankan Women's Cricket Championship six years in a row, its women's rugby team won the national championships in 2002, and there were a number of champion boxers on the staff (Gomes was a boxing champion in his youth!).

Staff achievements went beyond professional sports. One of the people instrumental in writing an award-winning help-desk software package (MAS was the only non-IT company in Sri Lanka to win such an award) went on to win the World Mathematics Olympiad and then an MIT scholarship.

A young and dynamic organization

MAS was a young organization. The average age of senior management was well under 50. The youngest CEO in the group companies was 28. With an emphasis on championing employees and creating an egalitarian culture, MAS developed a competency development program across all ranks of the organization. The goal was to create a place of learning that would lead to personal development and finally increased contributions to the daily work.

The company believed that it had not only the right processes but also the right people. Therefore, 60 outstanding managers had been put on a fast-track development involving a 'cross-pollination' of personnel from various functional areas across the group companies. These fast-trackers, as they were called, were heralded as the future leaders of the organization.

A culture of performance

Some of the performance culture was directly attributable to MAS's ability to create an environment where failures were seen as opportunities to learn, not just things to frown upon. There was a clear understanding of expectations from the line level managers, which emphasized focusing on corrective actions quickly if necessary. Creating a culture of behavior correction was a challenge, but it was proactively tackled at MAS, according to Gomes:

> As a [business unit manager], I spend a lot of my time training and talking to people. Most of my managers are young and there will be mistakes. But these are the future CEOs. There have been a few times I have delegated and that almost cost me my job – I allowed them to take the decision and ultimately I am responsible for that. I saved [the situation] but I call that living on the edge.

> But I have the courage to do that. I'd rather do that and fail than be a control freak. When [the management team] is young, on behavioural aspects they make wrong calls – on the selection of people, I think I could make a better judgment. On the processes, they are fine. It's when they get into subjective areas that they tend to make mistakes.

The costs of failures were monitored but not dwelled on. If a shipment should have gone by sea but, due to management or operational issues, had to go via air freight, if production needed to go into overtime, if excess raw material was ordered – as Gomes said, 'It isn't brain surgery – correct it, get on with it.'

> You have to create a culture where people admit when they make a mistake, even if it's [going to cost] a million dollars. We can remedy it. Lots of people tend to admit it when it gets bigger. They try and manage it themselves in the meanwhile. I think this is a unique approach, since we are a mix of a family business and a multinational. A multinational would enforce things more rigidly – decisions would be more cut and dried.

There was even a strong drive to create a performance-based culture at the shop floor level. At each production line, there was a real-time monitoring system analysing and displaying the efficiency level of the shift in operation and their efficiency level compared to other manufacturing cells on the same floor. Hence the teams were not only aiming to reach their daily objectives (they were incentivized for going up to 120% of their daily targets), but they also competed among themselves.

One of the secrets of MAS's success with Victoria's Secret was that it never took for granted that the business was assured. The culture was always one of having to compete for business, and therefore the service levels increased sales over the years. To MAS, being reliable in the customer's eyes was key.

Social responsibility

MAS was one of the most admired companies in the country, and was even recognized in the apparel industry worldwide for its social responsibility (a good differentiator in an industry sometimes identified for promoting sweatshops in the developing world). This did not go unnoticed by Nike, Gap, Marks & Spencer, and Victoria's Secret – all of whom valued MAS's work on social policy, labor standards and women's empowerment. (*Refer to **Exhibit 6** for some MAS achievements, awards and testimonials.*)

MAS and its customers: A simultaneous evolution

In the 1990s, there was a rapid shift to consolidate sourcing and production operations for retailers worldwide. The WTO mandate of quota removals in 2005 was expected to herald big changes in the industry. Retailers, seeing the need to rationalize their supply base and respond to an environment of rapidly evolving fashion, thus began to make far-reaching changes in their sourcing and manufacturing strategies.

Retailers also focused on two additional areas. First, there was a pronounced effort to bring innovation into the products with the assistance of suppliers rather than going it alone. Second, there was an increasing use of information technology to make the retail business more efficient.

Victoria's Secret: Managing growth while balancing speed and flexibility

Victoria's Secret, MAS's biggest customer with over 1,000 stores and $4.2 billion in annual revenues, aimed to double its intimate apparel sales without increasing the number of suppliers.[14] To do so, it decided to focus on streamlining its supply chain, shortening the concept-to-market time of products, and greatly improving its information management capabilities.

The goal of the first phase of this three-phase plan was to develop a demand-planning system that would make obsolete the current practice of forecasting demand six months ahead. The aim was to have the right product on the right shelf at the right time. The full-blown ERP solution deployed throughout Limited Brands would evolve over a four-year period and encompass finance, marketing, CRM and supply chain modules. Limited Brands anticipated that this would cost $400 million and be ready by 2008.

The second phase had the goal of reducing the upfront development cycle associated with bringing the product to market. It currently took up to 76 weeks to bring a bra from concept to market. Victoria's Secret had embarked on two different pilots to reduce the time to 38 weeks initially, before ultimately taking it down to as low as 16 weeks!

The third phase revolved around extremely fast reaction speeds to market trends. The goal here was to maximize the top line and minimize markdowns by consistently having in stock the winning styles of the season.

In summary, Victoria's Secret realized that what was most important was to shorten market response times. But future initiatives also included identifying how to minimize its sourcing costs. It was toying with the idea of buying capacity, not units, from its suppliers like MAS, thereby further reducing its overall costs.

Victoria's Secret realized that to successfully implement all of this it would need to change its mindset on working with its partners. The goal: to operate as a single team. The only customer would be the person walking in the store. And with this lofty idea, it believed that it too was a supplier to MAS – a supplier of information on its sales forecasting, store inventory, design changes and more.

To make MAS a successful partner in this process, it would need to get rid of the prevailing blame culture in a typical supplier–customer environment and instead provide the tools for collaboration to happen. The reality was that the center of its business was the stores, and it was going to focus on them over the coming years, leaving much of the back-end supply–demand chain management efforts to its key vendors.

In MAS, Victoria's Secret saw a committed organization and the management ability to pull this off. The old model, in which it asked the vendor to manufacture what it designed, would need to be replaced by a new one, which encouraged collaborative innovation. MAS was invited to the Victoria's Secret Vendor Council and was one of only eight vendors worldwide to participate in the design and development of collaborative processes for the future.[15] Amalean commented:

With Victoria's Secret realigning its business and supply chain, we need to understand what they are doing and what their requirements are and the skills, competencies and infrastructure that we need to support them.

The advent of design and product development solutions at MAS

A combination of factors led MAS to offer design and product development solutions to its customers. First, a survey of the current customer base indicated that at least 60% would welcome and use such a service. There was a significant time lag with concept products and fabrics shuttling back and forth between the customer in Western Europe/US and MAS in Sri Lanka. With speed to market being a key driver in the industry, it became necessary to collaborate with the manufacturer in this area. Some customers saw the need for at least 50% of product development efforts to come directly out of vendors like MAS.

Second, this was an opportunity to build and grow a business across the various group companies and leverage skills across various product categories. MAS's first step toward diversification from being a pure contract manufacturer had been to backward integrate and provide a full spectrum of raw material and component offerings to the customer. This allowed it to hit the right cost base, as the competition post-WTO would become global. Providing concept designs and getting involved in developing the technical aspects of the product was a natural second step.

Third, this was a way to manage the huge growth that MAS's customers anticipated with them. Until the 1980s brand owners were also manufacturers. In the 1990s, they moved away from manufacturing. By 2000, companies were looking to step away from product development and it was only natural that they would soon outsource design in order to focus purely on the brand.[16]

To build its design capabilities, MAS hired several design experts to cover fashion fairs worldwide, since they tended to be the foremost influencers of future product trends. The design specialists walked around these fairs with the MAS customer to understand what kinds of product ranges the customer was interested in developing for the coming season(s). MAS made sure that the product development and design teams were segregated to safeguard the intellectual property and ideas of its various customers.

A long-standing relationship with the customer also allowed MAS to have a flair for understanding their typical requirements. MAS performed a gap analysis of the customer's product range and made proactive recommendations on ideas for new product introductions. By 2010, MAS was targeting to have 30% of its revenues come from the design and product development efforts.

Streamlining the supply chain

The year 2004 saw another major initiative at MAS in response to the growing market trend of a rapidly decreasing time to market for new products, as evidenced by retail competition from the likes of Zara in Europe. Zara's aggressive product development cycle transformed a concept into a product on store shelves in under six weeks. As a result, shoppers at Zara visited a store on average 17 times each year; at Victoria's Secret, the number was 4. The result: MAS needed to help its biggest customer reduce the product development cycle time.

Customers took the product quality as a given. Cost competitiveness was crucial, as was a focus on speed and flexibility. Currently, Victoria's Secret considered over ten designs before one was finally chosen for development. Product concepts were created at the customer site and the samples developed at MAS. The customer then narrowed down the selection before deciding on what would finally be developed.

MAS and its customer agreed on two points. First, MAS would step up its contribution in the design stages. Second, through a more collaborative process, including using CAD systems, the design to development ratio would come down from 10:1 to as low as 2:1.

Third, the possibility of a joint product development center for teams from all the members of Victoria's Secret's Vendor Council was discussed. There was even discussion of a shared production system between several of Victoria's Secret vendors, one which obviously would not fit the current model of profitability and asset utilization for the individual vendors.

In order to meet some of Victoria's Secret's objectives, MAS would require a solution to link its various business units, its customer and its new design center through one cohesive and collaborative information management system to take full advantage of the information flows this could create. If Victoria's Secret were to link its point-of-sale (POS) systems in its 1,000 stores into its supply chain, this would necessitate a very rapid response strategy from MAS. Wal-Mart had achieved this goal over a decade earlier, and other retailers were in the midst of implementing it. It was therefore reasonable to assume that, as a minimum, Victoria's Secret would include this in its performance specifications during the four-year, $400 million ERP project.

As a first step, MAS hired a senior executive to act as a consultant to the various group companies and to help them streamline some of their supply chain activities. This individual, working with a team of four people, acted as a facilitator and advisor to the business units on identifying savings in their value chain activities. This was cleverly designed so that the team only advised and recommended, it did not initiate any changes. And the team's performance was judged purely on the savings it was able to bring into the business unit.

This arrangement paid off! Early on, the team realized that the same supplier had differential pricing agreements for different group companies within MAS. First year savings? $800,000. At the same time, MAS was careful not to trade off the lower costs for the long-term relationships with key suppliers. Still, Gomes said 'If one supplier gives me a competitively priced product and guarantees better lead times, I'll give him the business.'

Still the dilemma remained. How would MAS convince the supplier to invest in the long-term relationship when cost was key? After all, for some of MAS's customers, speed was more important, for others it was price. Rarely was a supplier able to offer both simultaneously.

2005 and beyond

Focusing the 'coalition of companies' around product types

In December 2004, Amalean announced a change in the organizational structure of MAS. The loosely held confederation of companies would be organized by product category around Intimates, Activewear/Leisurewear and Fabrics and would be complemented by a fourth group known as Corporate Solutions. Design and product development would be split between the first two groups.

The goal was to streamline operations, decrease the bureaucracy and bring about a single point of contact for the customer (MAS customers tended to be organized by product and therefore MAS was mirroring the organization of the customer.) This was also intended to increase asset and capacity utilization, bring about a synergy of best practices, and improve communication flows within the group. Amalean commented:

> Different businesses had different standards. Even our HR policies were not consistent across the different business units. Some business unit heads were less particular about processes, systems and methods and these had evolved differently. When the customer talks to us, he sees differing levels of service. There is this dichotomy and we realized the need to bring things together. Our objective here is not to control, but to set the standards and work with the various divisions to reach these standards.

As the organization evolved and grew, it would lose some of the responsiveness to market change. Amalean had instilled a culture that combined an entrepreneurial mindset along with an environment where people felt comfortable challenging the leadership on decisions. With the significant growth possibilities ahead, he realized that the consensus-building and collaborative decision-making process might need to be replaced by a more top-down approach to hasten decision-making processes.

> We need to manage this change process well – work with the managers to have them focus on the benefits of this new process, manage their expectations and concerns, some of the loss of autonomy they will feel, the feeling of having a bureaucratic arm around them.

One of the ways MAS had maintained its competitive edge was to have group companies compete for business among themselves. It was akin to the attitude that the Chinese firms had within the industry – that of first getting the orders, then worrying how to fix the problem. MAS had been able to fend off such problems due to the structure of its organization and the arm's-length transactions between its group companies. Now Amalean needed to restructure MAS in a way to maintain its competitive spirit and still encourage innovation.

Managing information and knowledge flows

The dynamic and flexible nature of the MAS organization had served the company well so far. Yet growth would automatically require more detailed processes, some of which would need to be hardwired into the IT systems. Technology could be used to generate a degree of 'synthetic personalization' – giving the impression of connection by being able to pull up a screen displaying the transactions and details of any one particular customer – but technology could not work at the level of genuine intimacy. The challenge was to know which processes would be best suited for hardwiring into systems vs. which ones should be kept flexible and people-oriented.

As MAS continued to grow, how should it best manage the organization and personnel to promote the culture of people feeling personal ownership in the company? As the number of mid-level managers increased, it was important that they did not feel institutionalized but to instil in them the same levels of passion and enthusiasm that had brought the company to these levels. The last thing MAS wanted to do was to stifle creativity and responsiveness. Could MAS still develop an organization where it could sustain the personal relationships internally and with its customers? Where the people culture was more information-oriented?

Identifying the core business

MAS had moved from being a contract manufacturer to a provider of 'design to delivery' solutions. Many of the competencies it required for design and product development had been acquired through its industry experience over two decades. Yet, there was a significant push to ratchet up its skills in this area by bringing in outside talent.

Simultaneously, there were several discussions within the company about launching a retail brand. And there was always the option of further integrating backwards and managing or owning cotton plantations. Amalean had debated the spread of the organization with his senior management team and it was clear that there were varying perspectives on this subject:

> When we started, we were contract manufacturers. We migrated to being manufacturers providing a total solution to the customer – by having a supply chain to support our manufacturing and by having the product development and design resources. We believe that the next step is to identify how to use the competencies and skill base in-house to establish a brand we can support.

> But this is not an easy step to take. At times I struggle for a suitable and convincing answer. While there is a need for us to look at the opportunity of establishing a brand, how fast do we go in this direction, how much of our resources do we use to drive this? That is a constant dilemma.

Valuing supply chain initiatives

It was increasingly clear that with the customer pushing to reduce lead times and improve efficiencies in its value chain, MAS would need to evaluate its businesses and identify ways to reduce transportation and cycle time costs, thereby reducing lead times from its own suppliers. The problem was how to put a value on this lead time reduction. How should it do so?

The speed and flexibility issue was also worth contemplating. Should MAS add excess capacity and therefore have idle time on its assets to get the speed and flexibility? And how fast was fast?

Or should it focus instead on lean manufacturing techniques that were good for stable volumes but challenging to implement for shifting volumes?

Looking ahead

By December 2004, MAS Holdings had operations in eight countries, sales of over $450 million and 30,000 employees. It had received rave press reviews in the *Wall Street Journal* and *Fortune*, but with over 90% of its exports destined for the EU and the US, it faced significant challenges with the coming abolition of WTO quotas beginning January 2005.

One could look throughout the organization and see that people had faith in and admiration for Amalean and the leadership he had provided for almost 20 years. Amalean now had to decide how to take the company into the post-quota era, which was almost certain to be dominated worldwide by the Chinese.

In the 1950s European and US textile and apparel manufacturing took a hit due to the lower costs of production in countries in Asia. The US, in order to protect its markets, pressed for a global comprehensive agreement. In 1974 the Multifiber Agreement (MFA), establishing the rights of an individual country to set quotas, was signed between exporting and importing countries. Originally intended as a stopgap measure, it lasted till 1994.

In 1995 the WTO member countries instituted the Agreement on Textiles and Clothing (ATC) that would dismantle the MFA over the following ten years. This elimination of quotas between WTO member countries would happen in four gradual phases that suggested a 16%, 33%, 51% and 100% removal of quotas by the beginning of 1995, 1998, 2002 and 2005 respectively.

The United States chose to keep the quotas on the most sensitive product categories for the last stage. This included most cotton and wool apparel, cotton and wool fabrics, bed linens and cotton towels.

There is also a China clause. Countries can unilaterally impose quotas on Chinese imports through 2008 and even restrict quantities in certain categories through 2013. These safeguard mechanisms are intended to support local industry if Chinese imports are seen as disrupting trade.

Exhibit 1 Industry agreements

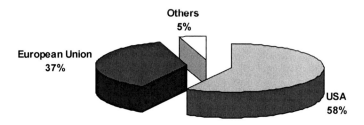

Exhibit 2 The Sri Lankan apparel industry

Source: Internet, Bear Sterns equity research

Some of the brands for which the Sri Lankan apparel industry produces clothes include: Abercrombie & Fitch, BHS, C & A, Calvin Klein, Eddie Bauer, Gap, Marks & Spencer, Nike, Ralph Lauren, Tommy Hilfiger, Victoria's Secret.

Quantity of fabric consumed by the industry annually: 850 million meters.

Number of pieces of apparel produced: 450 million.

SWOT analysis

STRENGTHS	WEAKNESSES
Well-developed and export-oriented industry	A continuing civil war
Low labor costs, varied financial incentives	Needs to import fabric, big lead times required
Focus moving on higher price segments	Some facilities have outdated infrastructure
Young, energetic population	Small domestic market, reliance on exports
High literacy rate, labor standards	Power supply is unreliable
Modern physical and financial infrastructure	Low level of design and product development skill overall
OPPORTUNITIES	THREATS
Global trade in apparel industry growing at 15% annually	Threat of terrorist attacks
Low wages, skilled labor encourages investment into the country	Growing competition after quota regime
	Strict enforcement of health, safety, environmental costs makes it less competitive than China

Exhibit 3 Backward integration

Source: Textile Intelligence Limited

ELASTIC

In 1996, Stretchline, a joint venture between MAS, MAST and Charnwood Elastics (UK) was formed to manufacture elastic. While Stretchline was thankful for the business MAS provided during its teething stages, the company was bent on achieving further growth on its own. To this end, it developed a strategy of investing heavily in R&D to develop a premium offering and set up marketing offices worldwide to be close to the retailers.

The strategy paid off. Some of the innovations included elastic that enhanced the performance of the product and thereby the value it provided for the end customer. The company developed the technology for bras that gave fabric antibacterial properties, a moisture management system and even a micro encapsulation method by which the fabric would include vitamin E or aloe vera[17] capsules that would break open upon contact with the skin.

Other innovations were a patented wire casing fabric system, called Fortitube, and a knitted elastic technology called LockSafe. By setting up marketing offices close to the retailer, Stretchline was able to establish a strong relationship with the retailer and better explain the specific benefits of these innovations.

Once again, its efforts were highly successful. By 2004, all Victoria's Secret underwired bras had changed to include the Fortitube technology. When Marks & Spencer had a massive product issue one year with the elastic unraveling in briefs, LockSafe technology solved it for them. Soon other retailers responded by including the Fortitube and LockSafe insignia as well as the Stretchline label on the packaging. Even the consumer began to recognize and accept this as a premium product.

With an output of over one million meters/day, this operation gradually expanded to meet 75% of MAS's requirements for all its companies except Bodyline.[18] By 2004, Stretchline had expanded its manufacturing operations to Mexico, Indonesia and China.

FABRIC

In 2001 MAS set up a joint venture with Textured Jersey UK to produce knitted fabric for Marks & Spencer. Shortly thereafter, this became a joint venture between MAS and Pacific Textiles. Pacific was the third-largest fabric producer in China, with existing capacities of 1,000 tons/week. Yet it came to Sri Lanka and took a stake in a 50 tons/week operation and managed the technical aspects of the operation while MAS provided the sales and marketing efforts through its relationship with Marks & Spencer and Victoria's Secret.

The rationale behind Pacific's decision? It was one of Victoria's Secret's preferred fabric sourcing vendors. And the co-location of a fabric manufacturing operation with MAS, Victoria's Secret's largest vendor, reduced the lead time between fabric sourcing and product manufacture. In the past five years, Pacific and MAS had seen the lead time requirements from its customer shrink from 12 weeks down to 5 weeks. And this was most certainly going to decrease further over time.

ACCESSORIES

In 2002 Stretchline set up a joint venture with Prym Newey, a major supplier of hooks, eyes and shoulder straps for lingerie. This venture, Prym Intimates, was designed to utilize the elastic from Stretchline to develop components that would ultimately be used in products manufactured in Unichela, Slimline Linea Aqua and other Sri Lankan manufacturers.

LACE

Founded in 2004, Noyon Lanka was a joint venture between Noyon Dentelle, France, and MAS to produce lace for intimate apparel. Discussions between the two sides began in January 2003, and there was immediately a synergy between the values espoused by the two (Noyon was a family enterprise which cherished MAS's long-term growth vision.) Production began barely 20 months later and first year revenues were forecast to exceed $6 million. Within five years, it anticipated contributing $20 million annually to MAS revenues.

Year	Company	Location	Focus	JV partners	Key Customers
1987	Unichela	Sri Lanka	Bras	Sara Lee Courtaulds	Banana Republic, Gap, Jockey, Marks & Spencer, Victoria's Secret Stores
1989	Shadowline	Sri Lanka	Sleepwear, Leisurewear	Brandot	Gap, Nike, Victoria's Secret Stores
1992	Bodyline	Sri Lanka	Bras	MAST and Triumph	Victoria's Secret Stores
1993	Slimline	Maldives, Sri Lanka	Bras, Briefs, Leisurewear	Sara Lee Courtaulds	Marks & Spencer, Victoria's Secret Stores
1996	Linea Clothing	Maldives, Sri Lanka	Briefs	Brandix	Gap, Nike, Victoria's Secret Stores
	Shadeline	Sri Lanka	Sportswear, Leisurewear	MAST	Marks & Spencer, Victoria's Secret Stores
	Stretchline	China, Indonesia, Mexico, Sri Lanka, UK	Elastic	Stretchline UK	BHS, Marks and Spencer, Victoria's Secret Stores
1998	Intimate Fashions	India	Bras	MAST, Triumph	MAST, Triumph
	Linea MAS	Sri Lanka	Marketing	MAS Holdings	
1999	Leisureline	Sri Lanka	Sportswear, Leisurewear	Sara Lee Courtaulds	BHS, Marks & Spencer, Nike, Reebok.
2000	Linea Intimo	Sri Lanka	Sportswear, Intimates	MAS Holdings	Lane Bryant, Nike, Victoria's Secret Stores
	Cottonline	Madagascar	Leisurewear	Brandot	Gap, Tommy Hilfger
	Linea Aqua	Sri Lanka	Swimwear	Speedo, Brandot	Speedo, Victoria's Secret Stores
2001	Textured Jersey	Sri Lanka	Weft-knitted fabrics	Brandix, Pacific Textiles	Marks & Spencer, Gap, Victoria's Secret Stores
	Rapier Consulting	Sri Lanka	Technology services		
	Sabre Technologies	Sri Lanka	Technology services		
2002	Fashionline	Vietnam	Leisurewear	MAS Holdings	Nike, Gap
	Linea Fashions	India	Leisurewear	MAS Holdings	Gap
	Prym Intimates	Sri Lanka, UK	Accessories	Stretchline, William Prym	Intimissimi, Marks & Spencer, Gap, Victoria's Secret Stores
2003	MAS Design Services	Sri Lanka	Design and Product Development Solutions		
2004	Noyon Lanka	Sri Lanka	Lace	Noyon Dentilles	Marks & Spencer, Victoria's Secret Stores
2004	Silueta	Sri Lanka	Moulded products, laminated material	MAS Holdings	Victoria's Secret Stores, Intimissimi, Gap, Dillards, BHS, Vanity Fair

Exhibit 4 Company structure

Source: Company information

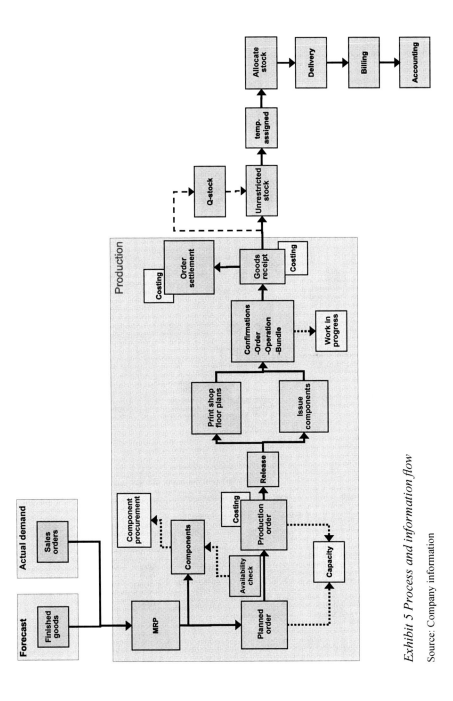

Exhibit 5 Process and information flow

Source: Company information

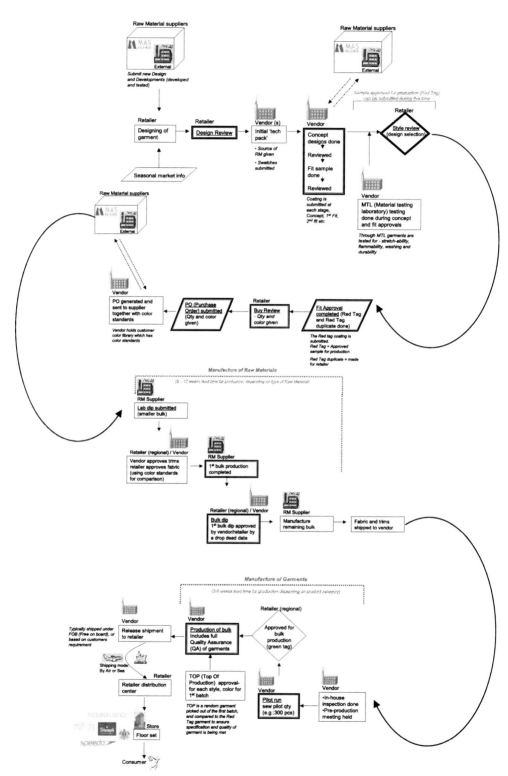

Exhibit 5 (continued)

Source: Company information

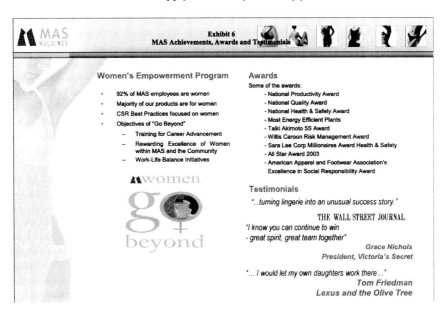

Exhibit 6 MAS achievements, awards and testimonials

Case 2.3
Nestlé: Quality on the boardroom agenda (A)

Petri Lehtivaara, Carlos Cordon and Thomas E. Vollmann

It was a sunny February afternoon in 2001. René-Louis Jaccoud, vice president of quality management at Nestlé, was reading through reports about recent quality issues in well-known companies worldwide. He was stunned. How could these world-class corporations get themselves into this sort of trouble? In particular, with all the changes that had occurred in the last 10 years in the supply chain and business environment, Jaccoud was not confident that the current approach to managing quality had kept pace with them.

When Peter Brabeck took over as CEO he had given a clear message that consumer preference and safe products were a top priority for Nestlé. There was no need to convince Rupert Gasser, executive vice president for technical, production and R&D, who had started his career with Nestlé in quality.

Having quality problems was no longer an issue only for the factory or production unit. It needed to be considered from the top management perspective. With global brands, all the products carried a promise to the consumer. If the promise was not fulfilled, the impact was felt throughout the corporation.

It was typical to hear comments such as 'Oh, quality is a given, you have to have quality or you cannot compete.' The attitude had become too complacent: 'We have achieved quality, so we do not have to worry about it.' Jaccoud believed that many companies had these problems to some extent and knew that he had to see to it that Nestlé did not fall into the same trap.

This was exactly the challenge Jaccoud faced. He wanted to ensure that Nestlé would never be in a bad position because of quality problems. How should the company devote enough attention constantly to the issue of quality inside the company and across the supply chain? What was the best way forward?

Nestlé Corporation

As of April 2001 Nestlé was the world's largest food company. In 2000 its sales were CHF 81.4 billion, with a net profit of CHF 5.8 billion.[19] The largest product groups were beverages (CHF 23 billion); milk products, nutrition and ice cream (CHF 22 billion); and prepared dishes, cooking aids and pet care (CHF 20.6 billion). At the end of 2000 Nestlé had 479 factories worldwide and approximately 230,000 employees.

Its six worldwide brands included Nestlé, Nescafé, Nestea, Maggi, Buitoni and Friskies. The brand portfolio also included other well-known brands like Perrier and Vittel (mineral water), Cailler and KitKat (chocolate).

Nestlé had a quality management team, which set overall quality objectives, policies and guidelines, planned the use of resources for these activities and reviewed the functioning of the quality system. Markets and business divisions had their own quality assurance responsibilities.

Development of quality management

'Quality is consistent conformance to customers' expectations.'[20] Approaches to quality control have evolved over the decades. At first the focus was on inspection (error detection); it was then based on statistical methods and quality standards. Further developments have taken approaches varying from quality assurance and quality systems and planning to total quality management, which includes all company operations.

This has led to a broader view of quality and a more accurate response to basic quality issues. But at the same time quality management issues have dropped off the top management agenda – they are already supposed to be at a high level.

The traditional quality management approach based on statistical methods evaluates the variation from the mean. All processes vary to some extent around the mean. Typically companies have set their acceptable specification range to include three standard deviations (sigmas) on each side of the mean – based on normal distribution, 99.7% of variations lie within this range. As long as a company is able to manufacture its products within its specification range, the products can be deemed to be of acceptable quality. A new quality standard was introduced with Motorola's Six Sigma program. It implied a defect rate of only 3.4 defects per million. In addition to the manufacturing specification, the Six Sigma program included design efforts to remove the latent defects.

Even with this approach there is always a chance of defective products getting through the system. The smaller the filter the better, but even one case in a million could cause a major problem. The improved overall quality standards may also make organizations complacent about quality issues, since defective products are supposedly rarer than ever before.

Statistical methods are typically applied to components of products – and sometimes to the products themselves. But there is another view: quality in use. The concept of 'conformance to customers' expectations' has to include unknown or unexpected phenomena. Customers will use – or abuse – a product in ways that are sometimes difficult to imagine. But if the product fails in this use, it is the product – and its brand – that can suffer.

Impact of recent cases related to quality

Jaccoud wanted to develop a concise report of the evolving set of issues and their implications for Nestlé, as well as a means for the board to provide consistent directions for the Nestlé organization.

Before dealing specifically with Nestlé's situation, Jaccoud wanted to review recent incidents in other companies and reflect on their impact on top management.

The Nestlé quality system was designed to guarantee, when correctly applied, reject rates between six and three sigmas according to the impact of the defect.

Coca-Cola's health scare in Belgium and France in June 1999

WEDNESDAY JUNE 9, 1999

In northern Belgium, 42 schoolchildren complained of nausea, headaches and stomach cramps. Coca-Cola Belgium withdrew about 2.5 million 20 cl glass bottles that had come from the Coca-Cola Enterprises plant in Antwerp.

THURSDAY JUNE 10, 1999

Reuters News Service reported on the health scare with Coca-Cola products in Belgium. A Coca-Cola spokesperson explained the situation:

> We withdrew the product not because of health concerns, but because it did not meet our high quality standards. It takes a lot longer to test what causes an off flavor. There has been speculation, but our scientists have not determined the cause yet.

FRIDAY JUNE 11, 1999

Major news agencies reported the incident in Belgium. Belgian health minister Luc van den Bossche ordered the withdrawal of certain soft drinks as a precautionary measure. Van den Bossche stated 'Neither the Belgian food inspection services nor Coca-Cola know the origin of the problem. Coca-Cola has done all kinds of tests but we cannot say anything sure yet.'

A Coca-Cola spokesperson explained 'Even the Ministry of Public Health still does not know what caused this, but we do know one thing, which is that there is no threat to health comparable to the current dioxin contamination problem.'

SATURDAY JUNE 12, 1999

Maureen O'Sullivan, a spokeswoman for Coca-Cola Belgium said 'The measures are relatively draconian but what is important is that consumers are reassured by the joint decision taken by Coca-Cola and the Belgian government.'

MONDAY JUNE 14, 1999

Another 44 children had suffered with stomach pains. A toxicology center had found signs of hemolysis – a blood disorder that causes the destruction of red blood cells – among people who had drunk Coca-Cola. Health minister Van den Bossche decided to withdraw all Coca-Cola products from the shelves with immediate effect.

TUESDAY JUNE 15, 1999

Luxembourg joined in the ban and France imposed partial restrictions. Coca-Cola said its investigation found that two separate incidents had resulted in below par products. Philippe Lenfant, director-general of Coca-Cola Enterprises Belgium, said that the bottling plant in Antwerp had used the 'wrong' carbon dioxide to add fizz to the drinks. He added that cans for the Belgian market from a canning plant in Dunkirk, France, had been contaminated with a fungicide used to treat 'a small number' of transportation pallets. Coca-Cola said that investigators had found no health concerns.

WEDNESDAY JUNE 16, 1999

More than 80 people fell ill in France after consuming Coca-Cola products. Chairman and CEO Doug Ivester stated from Atlanta: 'The highest priority is the quality of our products.' In Belgium, the health minister Van den Bossche was not pleased: 'Communication [with the health authorities] does not go via news conferences.'

THURSDAY JUNE 17, 1999

The Belgian Health Ministry relaxed its ban on some Coca-Cola products. The ministry ordered Coca-Cola to withdraw and destroy all the banned products and reimburse consumers.

FRIDAY JUNE 18, 1999

French consumer affairs minister Marylise Lebranchu criticized Coca-Cola for taking too long to provide the authorities with a full list of potentially contaminated products.

WEDNESDAY JUNE 23, 1999

Belgium ended the nine-day sales ban on Coca-Cola's drinks and allowed Coca-Cola to resume production at its two plants. 'Quite honestly, I am responsible. Anything that happens with Coca-Cola quality around the world is my responsibility,' said Ivester.

SUNDAY JUNE 27, 1999

Lenfant acknowledged that Coca-Cola had mishandled the scare.

> I admit that we perhaps lost control of the situation to a certain extent. We have a crisis management strategy… But the crisis was bigger than any worst case scenario [we] could have imagined. The first couple of days of the crisis we did not know [the cause] and I humbly admit perhaps we should have said so more clearly… I humbly accept that the image of the company, which is often associated with its products, may have taken a nasty blow.

THURSDAY AUGUST 18, 1999

The European Commission stated that Coca-Cola's explanation of its sale of contaminated drinks in Belgium and France was 'not entirely satisfactory.' The report stated, 'the real reasons for the widespread reports of illness remain unknown.'

MARCH 2000

The Ad Hoc Committee of the High Hygiene Council released its report on the incident. This report stated:

> Its conclusion is that this is not a case of intoxication from the consumption of the soft drinks. The most probable explanation of the observed symptoms is the presence of a bad odor and/or taste which in sensitive people triggered a psychosomatic reaction with real complaints such as a tendency to vomit or actual vomiting and feeling generally ill, as a result… The entire incident has all the characteristics of 'mass sociogenic illness' (MSI).

CONCLUSION

The health crisis had a direct impact on the company. Coca-Cola Enterprises, bottler of Coca-Cola products in Europe and North America, was hit both on sales and costs:

- During the second quarter of 1999, Coca-Cola Enterprises reported one-off product recall costs of $103 million
- The volume of sales in the Benelux countries declined approximately 29% in the second quarter of 1999, with a decline of almost 70% in the month of June.

Bridgestone/Firestone tire recall in August 2000

TUESDAY MAY 2, 2000

The National Highway Traffic Safety Administration (NHTSA) opened a preliminary investigation into possible tread separation in Firestone tires, which were fitted as standard on the Ford Explorer.

MONDAY MAY 22, 2000

Bridgestone/Firestone's prepared statement said, 'We continually monitor the performance of all our tire lines, and the objective data clearly reinforces our belief that these are high-quality tires.'

TUESDAY AUGUST 1, 2000

Two safety groups (Public Citizen and Strategic Safety) asked Ford to recall millions of cars, saying the tread could peel off their Firestone tires. Bridgestone/ Firestone officials could not be reached for comment.

WEDNESDAY AUGUST 2, 2000

Major news agencies carried the story of the NHTSA investigation. A federal agency had received complaints that 21 deaths had resulted from accidents alleg- edly caused by Firestone tires. Earlier in the summer, the NHTSA had said that it knew of only four cases. Bridgestone/Firestone said in its statement that properly inflated and maintained Firestone ATX, ATX II and Wilderness tires were among the safest on the road. The company also urged concerned owners to go to local service centers for a free inspection.

THURSDAY AUGUST 3, 2000

Ford announced that it had launched an intensive investigation.

FRIDAY AUGUST 4, 2000

Sears Roebuck & Co., the number one tire retailer in the USA stopped selling certain Firestone tires. Bridgestone/Firestone reiterated that its tires were safe.

SATURDAY AUGUST 5, 2000

A Bridgestone/Firestone spokesperson said, 'Customers who would like to exchange their tires will be given a credit toward new tires, based on the remaining life of the tires.'

MONDAY AUGUST 7, 2000

The NHTSA spokesperson said, 'At least 46 deaths are potentially related to alleged tire tread separation.' The number of complaints had reached 270, compared with 193 in late July and 90 in May. Bridgestone shares declined by more than 10% on the Tokyo stock market.

WEDNESDAY AUGUST 9, 2000

The executive vice president of Bridgestone/Firestone, Gary Crigger, announced a voluntary recall of 15-inch tires, estimating the number of tires involved to be 6.5 million.

> We have been working around the clock with the NHTSA and Ford to understand the issues at hand and to determine the best path forward. Given the preponder-

ance of incidents in four southern states, and the limited supply of replacement tires at this time, we will be undertaking a three-phase recall [by state].

MONDAY AUGUST 14, 2000

Bridgestone/Firestone released a statement including the following, 'We are working as hard as we can to determine what, if any, problem there may have been with the design or manufacture of these tires...We remain confident that the Decatur plant is and has been world-class.'

TUESDAY AUGUST 15, 2000

An NHTSA official said, 'We continue to investigate whether 16-inch tires should have been in the recall.'

THURSDAY AUGUST 24, 2000

Masatoshi Ono, chief executive of Bridgestone/Firestone, stated, 'All our plants meet QS9000 standards. I do not know the details of what particular workers said they did, but I have complete confidence in our products' quality.'

CONCLUSION

During the fall, the investigation continued. It found that the factories where Firestone tires were produced met standards set by the US authorities and Ford, but the tires produced there varied in quality.

At the beginning of 2001 the impact for Bridgestone/Firestone included:

- Profit for the financial year ending in December 2000 was far below the company's projection (¥13 billion vs. ¥85 billion[21])
- By January 2001 Bridgestone had lost about ¥1.2 trillion in market value
- The company announced that president Yoichiro Kaizaki was to step down in March 2001.

Food poisoning in Japan due to Snow Brand milk products in June 2000

TUESDAY JUNE 27, 2000

Before noon, the company received a call from a consumer claiming to have vomited after drinking Snow Brand low-fat milk. Other members of the public made similar complaints during the day to the Osaka municipal government. All the board members of Snow Brand Milk Products were attending the annual shareholders meeting in Tokyo.

WEDNESDAY JUNE 28, 2000

The municipal government ordered Snow Brand to recall all its low-fat milk. However, the company did not comply, maintaining there was nothing wrong with its products. That evening the board members at the annual shareholders meeting discussed whether or not the company should recall the products. The president Tetsuro Ishikawa was not consulted at this time.

THURSDAY JUNE 29, 2000

Snow Brand informed the Osaka municipal government of its decision to recall the products at 9:00, almost two days after the first call. Snow Brand conducted its first inspection by taking samples from 95 places in the production line.

SATURDAY JULY 1, 2000

Snow Brand president Ishikawa said at a press conference, 'I could have acted more promptly if I had been involved in the discussion... Low-fat milk is an unprofitable product for our company, so the incident will have little impact on our profitability.'

TUESDAY JULY 4, 2000

A company spokesperson said it could no longer keep track of the number of complaints because there were just too many:

> The whole company is in a state of panic. The management has not told me anything about what they will do next. Our sales staff is in a difficult position because they have not been kept informed of the developments.

THURSDAY JULY 6, 2000

President Ishikawa announced he would resign in September.

WEDNESDAY JULY 12, 2000

Snow Brand announced it would voluntarily suspend operations at its 21 factories.

THURSDAY JULY 13, 2000

Employees of Snow Brand Milk Products were puzzled and concerned by their company's suspension of production at all 21 factories.

FRIDAY JULY 14, 2000

Snow Brand said it was even considering changing its brand – a household name in Japan.

WEDNESDAY JULY 26, 2000

Snow Brand ran an advertisement in about 70 newspapers across the nation, apologizing for the scandal and promising to ensure safety in the future.

FRIDAY JULY 28, 2000

President Ishikawa resigned two months ahead of schedule, along with seven members of the company's executive board.

POST-ANALYSIS OF THE CAUSE OF THE FOOD POISONING

On Friday March 31, 2000 the Snow Brand Taiki Factory in Hokkaido, Japan, experienced a power failure. For about three hours the raw milk in storage at the time was held at temperatures between 20°C and 40°C. The milk in question was not destroyed but used for skimmed milk powder production on April 10. On Tuesday June 20, the skimmed milk powder produced at the Taiki plant on April 10 was shipped to the Snow Brand Osaka factory. On Friday June 23 and Monday June 26 the Osaka factory shipped reconstituted milk produced during the previous week.

CONCLUSION

The health scare lasted for almost two months, causing food poisoning in more than 14,000 people and the death of one person. The end results for Snow Brand included:

- Snow Brand Milk Products was expecting to make its first loss in 50 years due to a steep fall in sales
- Snow Brand's shares lost more than a third of their value in the first two weeks after the news emerged
- About 30 out of 500 sales agents for Snow Brand Milk Products had gone out of business or halted operations as a result of the outbreak
- The new president, Mr Nishi, commented: 'It will take several years before we become what we were prior [to the incident].'

Challenges for managing quality

As he thought about these cases, Jaccoud wondered to what extent Nestlé was immune to such unpleasant surprises. He knew that quality was all too easily taken for granted. Top management often assumed quality was a given and concentrated on other more urgent matters. But was this the right approach? The impact of quality problems, real or perceived, could have far-reaching consequences.

How should top management go about managing quality? How could Nestlé quickly respond to a major quality challenge? Nestlé had had a strict quality system in place for some time, but was such a system the answer? What alternatives or modifications would be needed to ensure the responsiveness of such a system?

Case 2.4
Nestlé: Quality on the boardroom agenda (B)

Petri Lehtivaara, Carlos Cordon and Thomas E. Vollmann

The quality discussion could not stop at the concept level. René-Louis Jaccoud, vice president of quality management at Nestlé, knew it was important to think with real examples. He wanted to look around Nestlé to identify where it could be vulnerable in its supply chain. His main message was:

> Complacency is our enemy. If we rely too much on having quality systems, we will become complacent and then disaster will strike. We need to constantly upgrade our awareness of the quality issues across the supply chain.

Quality was not related only to products or manufacturing. The concept had to include other parts of the supply chain, as well as other parts of the company. The supply chain was now much more complex than it used to be, with focused factories, more suppliers and outsourcing, and complex distribution systems when products were supplied to multiple markets and clients. Moreover, all this had become more significant with quicker communication links and the increased importance of brands. Nestlé could be affected as a result of both the quality of the product and the perceived quality.

Nestlé International Travel Retail: Virtual company

Nestlé International Travel Retail (NITR) was responsible for sales to airports, airlines, ferries/cruises and other duty free shops in either downtown or border areas. Airports and airlines were the two most important channels for NITR.

NITR saw these channels as very high-profile ones for the brands – 'A window on the world' for the group. In 2000 there were some 450 million passenger crossings of international borders, and the number was forecast to increase to 1 billion by 2010.

NITR's sales were CHF 64 million[22] in 2000. Confectionery accounted for 73% of the total business. The growth rate for the confectionery business had been 17% per annum since 1998, and growth was expected to continue in double digits.

As a small unit within Nestlé, NITR had 18 people in its worldwide organization. It coordinated its operations from Châtel-St-Denis in Switzerland, some 20 km away from the corporate headquarters in Vevey. NITR was given the status of an independent Nestlé company in 1999. Previously it had been part of a group at headquarters. As a remnant of its history, it depended on headquarters' support for administrative matters relating to finance, human resources and transactions management. It used the same management and

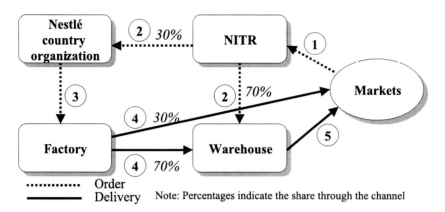

Exhibit 1 Order fulfilment with NITR

information technology systems as the entire corporation, which was sometimes seen as a problem since these systems were designed to satisfy the
requirements of large units.

NITR operated like a virtual company. It sourced its products from different
Nestlé factories around the world. It had about 400 SKUs (shop keeping
units) on its books of which about 25 were specialty packs. The products were
shipped to the third-party logistics provider (warehouse) and then shipped
to the customer when orders were received. Globally about ten operators
controlled 80% of the key airport retail estate and further consolidation was
expected in the sector.

With customers scattered around the world and products shipped to countries
with different standards and conditions, quality was certainly a concern for NITR.
Thomas Iseli, NITR's supply chain manager, explained:

> NITR does not control all the shipments. Our basic shipment conditions
> are to Rotterdam CIF [cost, insurance and freight]. Then our control ends.
> Obviously we need to be able to guarantee a shelf life of seven months
> with the customers. But with different conditions in different parts of the
> world and different handling methods we cannot be sure that the quality
> stays the same.

Another issue facing a global unit was traceability of products. If there was a
quality problem, how could NITR respond? Iseli continued:

> We work on the basis of the expiry date. We can identify the lot number from
> the expiry date. In the warehouse they may assign new numbers. We are able
> to trace the direct customers, but not the secondary customers. For that we
> need the cooperation of our direct customers. If the issue is urgent, we may
> have a problem getting the information quickly.

Nestlé Foodservices Business Unit: Diverse customers

Nestlé Foodservices Business Unit sold both food and beverage products to non-retail customers. The global market for foodservices was estimated to be CHF 600 billion, with an estimated growth rate of 5.4% between 1999 and 2005. Nestlé's sales accounted for CHF 6 billion out of a CHF 60 billion sub-segment.

Customers included fast-food restaurants (McDonald's and Burger King), contract catering companies (Sodexho and Compass) and airline catering (LSG and GateGourmet). These organized customers accounted for 20% of the market and the so-called unorganized part (i.e. small restaurants, cafés, etc.) the rest.

Products in the beverage sector included Nescafé, Nestea and milk-based products, which were typically distributed through the vending machine channel. As long as the drink or the raw materials were in a sealed environment, Nestlé Foodservices was able to provide a very high quality. When the products were mixed with additives, like water, however there could be cause for concern. Depending on the product offering in the machine another area of concern was the maintenance of the machine. As Hugh Hose, quality manager, explained:

> When the product is mixed with local water the hygiene and safety are out of our control. Products may also be mixed in machines that are used for other drinks. Then the cleaning of machines becomes important. We have done risk analysis to identify the critical points in the chain. Now our aim is to develop solutions that would make sure that we are able to control these critical points. For example, in drinks we have developed ready-to-use solutions. The drink is in a closed package until [it is] poured into the cup.

Nestlé wanted to push its brand and build awareness that some of the products consumed as part of a catering service, say, were Nestlé's. This was good for the brand, but if there were quality issues the overall brand could be adversely affected. With large organized customers, Nestlé was more confident about their food-handling training and the hygiene practices in their kitchens. In the unorganized segment, however, it was very difficult to have an impact on the practices. Typically there was a high turnover of personnel and the number of outlets was too numerous for Nestlé to dedicate resources to try to control them. Nestlé worked indirectly on this issue. First, it trained the trainers how to use the machines. Second, it developed solution-based products, as described above. Third, it worked with food and health regulators. Fourth, it worked with several independent food associations to fund and develop training packages on good practices in food outlets. As Hose remarked, 'We have to be active with our customers and the users of our equipment. Quality issues would have a dramatic impact on us. Even if we are not responsible we are accountable.'

If there was a defective product on the market, Foodservices was able to track it back to the factory using lot numbers. The factory was then able to access the records relating to the specific lot and determine the root cause of the problem.

The challenge was going in the other direction: it was difficult to identify where the product was in the distribution channel, especially with the unorganized 80% of outlets which purchased products in small amounts from wholesalers.

Nestlé Leisi: Top class production facility

Nestlé Leisi was a factory based in Wangen, Switzerland, that produced pizza dough and yeast-based products. These products were not shelf stable and were part of the chilled chain because they were extremely vulnerable to temperature changes, which in turn affected their quality. Any break in the chain could cause the yeast to multiply and produce gas, or mold could grow on the surface of the pastry.

Nestlé Leisi produced 24,770 tons of products in 2000. Almost 85% of this amount was exported, mainly to France, Germany and Italy. Nestlé Leisi had a very limited number of suppliers (approximately 40). This factory was a production unit that handed products over to other units for further delivery. Walter Leisi, director of the factory, stated: 'Our responsibility ends at the ramp.'

Clearly, a critical component was the third-party logistics provider. The factory had had some difficulties at the outset but worked closely with the provider and was now satisfied with the quality of their service.

At the factory level the adherence to good manufacturing practices (GMPs), which included very strict hygiene practices, hygienic design of the lines and machinery, pest control programs, training of the operators, etc., was critical to ensure the quality of the goods produced. It was fundamental that the operators understood why the measures were in place so that they were motivated to follow them. The Leisi factory management worked constantly with the operators to improve its quality and hygiene.

The factory obtained ISO 9001-2000 certification in March 2001. In 2000 the factory received 32 complaints from Switzerland and 154 complaints from export markets. To put these in perspective, the factory produced 8.1 million consumer units for the Swiss market and 82.4 million consumer units for export. As Leisi stated, 'We follow all the complaints to understand the reason for them and to be able to improve. Based on our analysis, 90% of the root causes originate outside this factory.'

The case writer was very impressed with the level of GMP exhibited in the Nestlé Leisi factory. But the high level of cleanliness and attention to all aspects of quality led to the question of cost: Did Leisi feel under pressure to reduce his cost structure – or was he able to do whatever he felt was necessary to ensure excellent quality? Leisi responded:

> We are always under great pressure to reduce our costs. Do not forget that 80% of our output is sold into the European Union and common market. We have to have a cost structure that allows us to do so. But it is not easy. Fortunately, we have been able to significantly grow our volumes in recent years, utilize our capacity very effectively, and run with virtually no finished goods inventories. But make no mistake: the costs associated with the quality you have observed are significant – and growing.

Nestlé Switzerland: Managing the supply chain

Nestlé Switzerland had total sales in 2000 of CHF 1,274 million, including exports of products to a value of CHF 406 million. Nestlé Switzerland managed nine factories manufacturing all types of products from chocolate to frozen foods.

As the umbrella organization for all Swiss production, Nestlé Switzerland was concerned with food safety, as well as quality of service. All factories had implemented a quality program to improve the product quality. Most measures taken were directed toward the supply chain inside the company, not toward the total supply chain.

Nestlé Switzerland decided to run an exercise in fall 2000 to track the traceability capabilities in the unit. It was a real-life exercise, since only Philippe Pittet, quality assurance manager, knew it was not genuine. A product had supposedly had a food safety issue and products needed to be tracked down and recalled. The key learning points of this exercise included:

- The factories and downstream distribution units did not use the same language.
- The quality of information varied.
- The discipline of the information flow was not good. Too many people were required to communicate and coordinate.
- There was lack of adequate information systems to make the tracking of products user-friendly.

Pittet summarized the main message as: 'We have the traceability but it takes too long.'

Pittet concluded that Nestlé was able to track its products well inside the company. But once the product left Nestlé and was distributed to retailers it was hard to know where it was. Improvements would require Nestlé to work with its customers on quality issues. However, Nestlé Switzerland felt it needed to have its own quality in top shape. Moreover, it also had to show some benefits to the retailers to make them want to invest in the systems to allow for instant tracking of all products. The retail market in Switzerland was a special one, with two big chains controlling three-quarters of the market. One of these chains did not sell branded products. Because of the near-monopoly situation between the two chains, they dictated the conditions.

Challenges for the quality system

Jaccoud believed that these examples illustrated the diversity of quality issues facing Nestlé, as well as the vulnerability of its suppliers. This, together with a growing awareness of quality overall and the poor reactions of Coca-Cola, Bridgestone/Firestone and Snow Brand, led him to believe that Nestlé needed to take a proactive stance on this issue. In handling a crisis, reacting fast and adequately was the major problem.

Jaccoud also knew that 80% of the quality incidents which cost Nestlé more than CHF 100,000 had something to do with failures in the production area.

Quality had two faces: on one side, the non-negotiable food safety; on the other, consistent quality generating consumer preference.

Jaccoud knew that he would need to work closely with other groups within Nestlé to ensure a truly global approach. One such group was consumer services, which had a presence in over 60 markets worldwide and was instrumental in providing 'perceived added value' to consumers of Nestlé brands and products. Consumer services clearly had a dual role, which it needed to balance: first, it needed to represent the consumer within Nestlé; second, it had to represent Nestlé to the consumer.

From the quality standpoint, consumer services was a vital link as it was often at the frontline when it came to detecting a potential crisis or latent quality deterioration. There could be no global rules on the number of calls that constituted a crisis and the consumer service managers and call operators often responded to a situation based on gut feeling. As one top manager in Nestlé commented, 'We have to give people permission to follow their intuition.'

The more Jaccoud reflected on the challenge before him, the more complex it became. He needed to work with not just the consumer service function but also the purchasing group, the logistics group and the factory performance group. He felt the approach needed to be simple and cut through the complexity if it was to be effective. Targeting reject levels at Six Sigma was only part of the solution. People needed to act with a mindset of quality.

As Jaccoud commented, 'Perhaps, first we have to raise the awareness of the quality issue inside the organization. Then start highlighting the issues and potential solutions for different units and make them start thinking in terms of quality across the supply chain.'

Chapter notes

1 For simplicity we assume that SG&A costs do not change and that supply chain costs are proportional to the number of products produced.
2 Fine, C.H. *Clockspeed: Winning Industry Control in the Age of Temporary Advantage.* New York: Perseus Books, 1998.
3 Chopra, S. and M.S. Sodhi. 'Managing Risk to Avoid Supply-chain Breakdown.' *Sloan Management Review*, Fall 2004: 53–61.
4 For more on this see Norrman, A. and U. Jansson. 'Ericsson's Proactive Supply Chain Risk Management Approach after a Serious Sub-supplier Accident.' *International Journal of Physical Distribution and Logistics Management*, Vol. 34, Iss. 5, 2004: 434–456.
5 Adapted from Stevenson, M. and M. Spring. 'Flexibility from a Supply Chain Perspective: Definition and Review.' *International Journal of Operations & Production Management*, Vol. 27, Iss. 7, 2007: 685–713.

Case study notes

1 Source: Luxottica SEC Form 20-F, *2008*.
2 www.safilo.com
3 Source: The Investext Group, Feb 1994.
4 He was also joined by his brother, Ajay. The third brother, Sharad, joined the company in 1989.

5 In 1986, The Limited Inc. had The Limited, Limited Express, Lane Bryant, Victoria's Secret and Lerner stores. By 1990, Structure and Abercrombie & Fitch had joined its retail portfolio. By 2004, the company was known as Limited Brands.

6 At this time, the company had 50 sewing machines and employed approximately 100 people.

7 Founded in Germany in 1886, the company grew to become the world's number one lingerie manufacturer.

8 By this time MAS had the management skill base to manage a plant of about 500 machines.

9 Speedo was extremely cautious of sharing its intellectual property and know-how with external partners. The MAS Holdings joint venture was its only such foray worldwide.

10 Almost 60% to 70% of the value of the goods was dependent on other suppliers, a cause for concern.

11 Only Reebok, Nike and Vanity Fair had done so till then.

12 Rapier Consulting also began to offer this pre-configured solution to external clients. In 2004 SAP conferred an *All-In-One Partnership* status to this solution.

13 As an example, employees at all levels used the in-house HRMS system at Bodyline, to access personal records or input timecards. Physically designed to look and work like automated tellers, these machines were positioned throughout the shop floor.

14 The annual revenue figure included all sales channels (store and direct sales) and all Victoria's Secret branded products (including lingerie, apparel and beauty products).

15 Similarly, of Nike's 260 worldwide vendors, MAS was one of 8 chosen to participate in its Manufacturers Leadership Forum. Understanding Nike's expectations and building the organization to support these expectations was the greatest challenge that Amalean saw.

16 In 2004, 80% of Victoria's Secret designs were done internally. It expected this figure to reduce significantly in the coming years.

17 Aloe vera was a consumer-accepted trend, with razors, face tissues and other consumer products differentiating themselves by including aloe vera as an ingredient.

18 Bodyline sourced its elastic from one of Stretchline's competitors due to the long-term relationship this supplier had with Triumph.

19 CHF 1.61 = US$1 (December 31, 2000).

20 Slack, Nigel, et al. *Operations Management*. London: Pitman Publishing, 1998.

21 ¥114 = US$1 (December 31, 2000).

22 CHF 1.61 = US$1 (December 31, 2000).

3   Handling dilemmas in the supply chain

Supply chain executives face fundamental dilemmas in the way they configure their global supply chains. A dilemma occurs in situations where there are two goals and pursuing one of them compromises the other. We call them dilemmas rather than trade-offs because there is no optimal solution. They are neither solved nor decided – executives must constantly manage the divergent forces. Among the most important are:

- How flexible vs. how efficient should the supply chain be?
- What is the best global footprint for the supply chain?
- How should capital be allocated in the supply chain?
- How should the processes in the chain be organized?
- What is the best way to accelerate an improvement in the supply chain?

As products transition through different life cycle stages over time, there are no easy answers for how to deal with what in effect constitutes a moving target in terms of supply chain requirements and opposing needs.

The flexibility–efficiency dilemma

In an ideal world, companies would like to have the most flexible as well as the most efficient supply chain. However, as one typically comes at the expense of the other, this has never been realized. Executives must therefore manage the level of flexibility and efficiency of the supply chain based on what fits best with a product's selling proposition.

To illustrate such a dilemma, we can compare a fast-food establishment with a luxury restaurant. The former emphasizes efficiency, and the consumer typically waits to be served until the personnel are available; the latter focuses on flexibility, and the personnel usually wait for the customer to be ready. The second scenario clearly requires more personnel per guest than the first. While both establishments aim to maximize their efficiency and flexibility, they obviously operate in different areas of the respective curves.

Taking as our starting point the objective of meeting the demand of end customers with an aligned supply chain value proposition, we can classify the product or service being sold along a spectrum ranging from functional products (commodities) to differentiated products (innovative).

On the one hand, functional products and services are relatively standardized and satisfy the basic needs of customers, namely businesses (B2B) or end consumers (B2C). Since these needs do not change much, these products and services experience relatively predictable and stable demand, and often have long life cycles or have reached their maturity stage.

On the other hand, differentiated products and services can be distinguished from those of competitors by constantly introducing new features and customizing the service. These products do not have a long sales history on which to base forecasting, and demand is often unpredictable and explosive in nature. In addition, in an effort to constantly be first on the market with new and interesting products and services, their life cycles are often short.

Businesses producing commodities have more functional products compared to other businesses, while enterprises operating in the high-tech and fashion industries, for example, primarily compete on innovative products and services. A well-established framework, such as the one illustrated in Figure 3.1, helps to understand what kind of supply chain is appropriate for different types of products and services.

The supply chain should be as efficient as possible for functional products and services, but responsive for differentiated or innovative products and services.

	Functional Products	Innovative Products
Efficient Supply Chain	match	mismatch
Responsive Supply Chain	mismatch	match

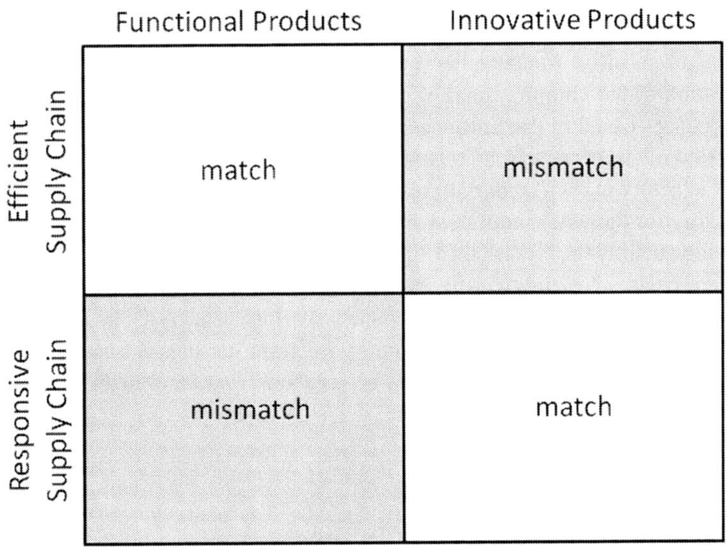

Figure 3.1 Linking product and service characteristics to supply chain design

Source: Fisher, M.L. 'What is the Right Supply Chain for Your Product?' *Harvard Business Review*, March–April 1997.

Our restaurant example again illustrates this point. While it would be a waste of personnel to provide an agile service with staff waiting on customers in the fast-food establishment, a personnel shortage that left guests waiting in the luxury restaurant would seriously downgrade its service proposition. Nonetheless, the fast-food restaurant will obviously still strive to be as responsive as possible within its efficiency constraints, and the luxury restaurant will aim for efficiency but without damaging its service proposition.

Often, however, it is more a question of where and when to be flexible or efficient in a particular supply chain.[1] The dilemma is clearly stated by the supply chain vice president of a global hearing aid producer:

> For our new and innovative products, our top brands, it is in the first half year of their market life, before our competitors catch up, that we earn all our money. Being flexible, fast and responsive in our supply chain operations in this stage is therefore of major importance for us.

The supply chain's global footprint

The global manufacturing footprint of companies today stems from applying several supply chain concepts and managing diverse forces: (1) the 'focused factory' idea; (2) outsourcing vs. insourcing; and (3) offshoring vs. nearshoring.

The focused factory

Over the last few decades many companies have implemented the 'focused factory' concept[2] in an effort to specialize manufacturing plants. For example, following the creation of the common market in Europe, most food companies consolidated their factories based in the European Union, closing small ones and concentrating production of similar products in larger factories. While in the past the concept was to have a factory in each country to serve the national market, this changed to having one factory for the whole continent specialized in a single product.

The idea behind the 'focused factory' is to ensure factory operations are simpler and more productive and that the learning curve is less steep and there are fewer overheads. The downside is that the factory is further away from most markets. For example, the response time of a factory in Spain serving all European markets is usually not going to be fast in terms of feedback from and lead time to Nordic country markets.

Outsourcing vs. insourcing

Outsourcing has been applied extensively in the last few decades. It started slowly with services like the canteen, but today it is widely used across all business functions and processes. An example in the consumer electronics industry is Hewlett-Packard (HP), which completely outsources the manufacturing of many of its products.

A company mainly outsources in order to focus resources such as assets, management and people on the most important aspects of its competitiveness. The motto has been, 'If it is a core competency we develop it in-house, if not we might consider outsourcing.' The other main advantages of outsourcing are that an external supplier serving multiple clients might be more efficient than an internal one, and that competition among potential suppliers might be an incentive for them to improve. Table 3.1 summarizes the main reasons companies give for outsourcing activities to third parties.

The 2008/09 crisis has led companies to re-evaluate their business models and, in particular, their outsourcing and insourcing strategies. In a period of rapid growth, as was the case in the few years before 2008, it makes sense to focus the company's resources on sustaining growth to maintain market share, and outsourcing allowed this. However, in a no-growth period executives may consider owning more of the value chain – or insourcing – to increase profits.

It is important to understand that outsourcing vs. insourcing decisions cannot be made without fully understanding how they will be implemented. We often hear that a decision is strategic but that its implementation is an operational issue. The reality is that implementation and supplier suitability must be considered at the same time as deciding whether to outsource or insource.

Outsourcing only makes sense if appropriate suppliers exist. In the mid-1980s, for example, it would have been unthinkable for global corporations to outsource IT, since no global IT suppliers existed. Similarly, a company must consider the resources and time needed to develop the required competencies prior to insourcing an activity. Over time, decisions to divest certain assets or build in-house capabilities can change industry structures and thus affect the options that need to be considered when making these decisions.

It is also extremely important to understand how risk is spread among different players in the chain. Irrespective of what the contract says about

Table 3.1 The main reasons companies outsource

Expected benefits	Rationale
Cost reduction	Economies of scale, lower labor costs, more effective suppliers.
Flexibility	Economies of scope; supplier can pool demand.
Speed	Smaller size of supplier; supplier expertise with existing technology.
Investment reduction, or to compensate for not having enough resources	Supplier invests and bears the risk.
Making fixed costs variable	Supplier costs are variable.

who carries the responsibility for a particular risk, it always affects all of the companies in the chain. This is particularly evident for companies with big brand names. Take the example of Apple and its Taiwanese supplier Foxconn. Following a series of suicides among factory workers at the supplier's facilities in 2010/11, Apple's COO, Tim Cook, had to personally and immediately step in to calm the huge media storm these incidents had triggered. This action was designed to prevent any further damage arising from Apple's association with the supplier. To deal with the situation, Cook visited the supplier's factory accompanied by suicide prevention specialists. In addition a team worked with Foxconn's management to ensure measures were put in place to prevent more suicides.

Offshoring vs. nearshoring

The offshoring trend has been so forceful that NBC even produced *Outsourced*, a popular TV show about a US company moving its call center operations to India.

One of the fundamental arguments for offshoring manufacturing, services and technological developments is that optimizing global production will result in round-the-clock shifts and lower costs. Other sought-after benefits include opportunities to expand markets, lower consumer prices and create new businesses.[3]

However, after decades of companies going offshore to obtain lower labor costs and gain access to skills they could no longer find in their home countries, we are starting to see a change to nearshoring. The reasons for nearshoring are linked to the complexity and difficulty of making an offshore unit feel close to the business. The benefits mentioned most often are:

- Faster response times.
- Better understanding thanks to cultural similarities (including language).
- Lower environmental impact.
- Major time zone differences are avoided.
- Meeting and establishing trust and long-term relations are facilitated.

The flow and stock of capital in the supply chain

The supply chain has traditionally tied up a large amount of cash, but recently companies have been looking at this in a different way. For example, when Jan Bennink, CEO of Numico, needed several hundred million euros to launch new products, instead of approaching the company banks, he asked his executives to free the capital from the supply chain (see the Numico: King Project case in this chapter).

Today, it is obvious that the way we manage cash flow in the supply chain can result in either a competitive asset or a liability for a company. Traditionally, the company pays its suppliers at 30, 60 or 90 days, following its standard payment terms, and accepts the terms of its customers, in which case it might be subsidizing the competitors' working capital. So if Numico was paying its suppliers earlier than Danone, for example, and they both had the same suppliers, it could be argued that Numico was subsidizing Danone's working capital. Thus, companies are now considering supplier and customer payment terms as well as their working capital needs as an important competitive weapon.

An immediate reaction to the 2008/09 crisis was that larger companies extended their supplier payment terms and pushed their customers to pay earlier. In fact, some big multinationals currently have negative working capital. While this may seem attractive at first sight, the reality is that small companies are financing the whole chain, although it probably costs them more to obtain funds than it does larger firms. The cost for the chain is therefore higher. But if the larger companies do not do this, they could find themselves financing the working capital of their competitors.

To avoid this situation, companies started to implement 'supply chain finance' solutions, which allow suppliers to gain access to preferential rates. While the technique's underlying mechanism is factoring – suppliers selling receivables to factors for immediate cash – there are three important differences. First, since the technique is buyer-centric, factors do not have to evaluate heterogeneous buyer portfolios and can charge lower fees. Second, since buyers are usually investment grade companies, factors carry less risk and can charge lower interest rates. Third, as buyers participate actively, factors obtain better information and can release funds earlier.

Organizing the supply chain processes

Organizing processes to avoid inventory build-up and lack of coordination internally between functions and along complex global supply chains is a daunting task due to the inherent lack of visibility that comes with distance. Two dilemmas need to be resolved: (1) managing the bullwhip effect; and (2) avoiding organizational silos.

The bullwhip effect

The difficulties in managing supply chain processes typically increase as demand variability increases. The famous bullwhip effect – or amplification of variability through the chain – adds to this challenge.[4] The bullwhip effect is due to a distortion in demand and results in excessive inventories in a series of companies supplying each other up the chain. Consider the system depicted in Figure 3.2. In this chain we can see that the retailer faces demand from final consumers and receives products from the wholesaler, which in turn receives products from the manufacturer and delivers them to the retailer. The manufacturer receives materials from the supplier and delivers products to the wholesaler. Finally, the supplier delivers to the manufacturer and, to simplify the exercise, we assume that it has an infinite amount of materials.

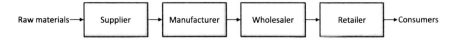

Figure 3.2 Chain of customers and suppliers

Initially, the retailer, wholesaler, manufacturer and supplier make independent decisions about how much inventory to have and how much to order. We assume that each player orders items every Monday morning and receives them the following week, as long as the supplier has sufficient stock. A typical policy for each player is to expect the same demand as the previous week and to keep a week's worth of safety stock. Table 3.2 shows the result.

In this example we can see that the variation in demand is amplified through the chain. A relatively stable consumer demand that increases by just 12.5% in the second week, from 40 to 45, reaches the manufacturer as a 100% increase, from 40 to 80. This is due to each player in the chain creating safety stocks – in addition to replenishing inventory and placing fixed orders – to absorb variations because the orders and inventory are used as signals to estimate future demand. Each player makes its ordering decision on the assumption that the previous order is the best forecast of expected demand. These signals become distorted because the safety stock concept amplifies variability instead of absorbing changes and smoothing demand. If this is what happens when consumer demand is stable, the consequences of consumer promotions can be expected to be far more significant. Variations in the final demand and the bullwhip effect through the chain are huge.

Table 3.2 Evolution of inventory and demand for a chain

Time	Manufacturer		Wholesaler		Retailer	
	Inventory	Demand	Inventory	Demand	Inventory	Demand
Week 1		40		40		40
Monday	40		40		40	
Week 2		40		40		45
Monday	40		40		35	
Week 3		40		55		40
Monday	40		25		50	
Week 4		85		30		40
Monday	0		75		40	
Week 5		0		40		40
Monday	170		35		40	

Organizational silos

The previous example involves several companies, but we see the same effect occurring in different functions within a single company when coordination is not properly managed. If sales do not collaborate with production and purchasing, the same information distortions occur. This is why many companies are trying to eliminate 'silo thinking' within their own organization.

A further and somewhat controversial effect of these silos is related to forecasting, particularly when deciding who should be responsible for it and how to best manage the process. Typically, the sales department produces the forecast because this function is best placed to obtain data directly from the consumer market. This information is then 'agreed' or discussed with the rest of the organization. While this is common practice, companies quite often overdo the forecasting, because it is based on all of the products. Yet the demand for many products is generally stable, so a simple 'straight line' approach is often more accurate than a complex forecast. Many companies find that around 50% of their products do not need complex forecasting to estimate future demand. Consequently, we recommend testing which products could follow a simple forecasting rule and those for which the input of sales executives is required.

An approach that has become widespread today in many industries is consignment stock or vendor managed inventory (VMI[5]) whereby the supplier manages the customer's product stock. This reduces the bullwhip effect by one distortion step, which in turn decreases variability and avoids excessive stocks and obsoletes. Although VMI affords the supplier advantages such as being able to access customer requirements earlier, establish closer ties with important customers, and take advantage of opportunities to level its own production, many suppliers also see VMI as a way for customers to pass the responsibility and financial burden of inventory management on to them.

Innovation through the supply chain

Today, it is increasingly recognized that in many industries innovations are mainly generated through contact with customers and suppliers rather than from within the company. There is a lot of talk about open innovation in consumer-driven companies and inclusive or collaborative innovation in industrial companies. P&G's 'Connect and Develop' initiative (mentioned in Chapter 1) is a good example, but an even more provocative one is the way in which the former VP of purchasing at Numico envisaged innovation expenditures. In 2005 Numico's research budget was around €50 million and purchases from suppliers amounted to €800 million. Based on his analyses, he concluded that Numico's suppliers spend around 6% of their sales on research. Following a somewhat debatable calculation, he stated that Numico paid its suppliers €48 million (€800 million × 0.06) to carry out research on its behalf. He argued that, while Numico controlled the €50 million it spent on research internally, it did not have much influence over the €48 million spent by its suppliers. So if Numico was not willing to listen to its suppliers' ideas it could be subsidizing innovation that would benefit competitors.

Consequently, in many cases, innovation originating through the supply chain is more important than internal innovation, so ensuring an efficient process is in place to facilitate the exchange of ideas is not only relevant but also essential. The cases presented in this chapter provide concrete illustrations of these points and the corresponding decision dilemmas.

Cases in this chapter

3.1 Numico: Delivering innovation through the supply chain (A)

The Numico (A) case illustrates the situation of a company that has traditionally relied entirely on internal innovation and now finds itself in a situation where the last innovation launched was 10 years ago. The only way ahead for the new CEO, Jan Bennink, is to rely on suppliers to develop novel products that consumers and markets will appreciate.

The case also illustrates how standard old procedures for dealing with suppliers and an existing supply chain configuration cannot immediately be used when a completely new source of value from a new type of supplier – here exemplified by Babynov – enters the supply chain. Numico's VP Purchasing had to work hard to solve structural challenges following the selection of a highly innovative external source. Most importantly, the company had to change the way it handled innovations and adopt a new approach for interacting with its new strategic innovative suppliers.

The dilemma was that, previously, Numico's innovation activities had always been internal, but now that it faced the challenge of dealing with an external innovation partner, several questions arose. How should Numico behave towards it? Should it be treated as a normal component supplier? If the normal supplier selection approach had been followed, Numico would never have chosen this partner, but having become an innovative company based on its supplier's innovation, what should Numico do to ensure it is the most attractive customer for its suppliers?

3.2 Numico: Transforming the supply chain to support new realities (B)

While the (A) case looks at the supply chain management requirements of new product development (NPD) and defines a new way of doing things, the (B) case focuses on how to transform the supply chain to support new realities, as the case title indicates. Two large projects are examined: Link! and Focus.

The purpose of Project Link! is to initially provide true visibility of inventories by location and in transit, and to better estimate customer demand. Its primary goal is to improve customer service in the short term and serve as a platform for efficiently providing new, innovative products. The project's focus changes from being on information to being on work, i.e. new ways of doing things or new supply chain approaches.

The primary goals of Project Focus, however, are: (1) short-term and ongoing cost savings; and (2) in the longer term, a different production structure, including the rationalization of distribution points. More specifically, this involves downsizing manufacturing, shifting production to fewer and newer factories in Eastern Europe, and rationalizing product lines and stock-keeping units (SKUs). While Focus entails major changes and operational disruptions, its aim is, unlike that of Link!, to perform the same tasks better.

3.3 Numico: King Project

This case highlights the dilemmas related to the financial flows in the supply chain. When Numico is benchmarked with its direct competitors, it is obvious that the company's use of cash is nowhere near as efficient as the industry average, leading some people in Numico to argue that it has been subsidizing competitors through its supplier and customer payment terms.

The case illustrates the tremendous impact of measures designed to release cash from the supply chain. It is also a significant example of change management across organizations, since the change affected not only Numico but also its customers and suppliers. The dilemmas are as follows: Should the supply chain management focus on financial flows? And who should finance the supply chain (i.e. should small suppliers be financing it)?

3.4 ABB transformers

The ABB case presents best practices in managing the internal supply chain within one unit by the smart use of the theory of constraints to reduce the time required to make a product and deliver it to the client. The reduction of time, the improvement in key performance indicators and the subsequent savings are a logical consequence of the focus on fast manufacturing.

Implementing the focused factory concept triggered the transformation of the factory in Zaragoza from making many products for a few markets to focusing on one line of products for the whole of Europe.

Following the successful implementation of the focused factory strategy, ABB now faces a new challenge, namely how it should supply the Indian market, which is currently small but has great potential. Different strategies could address this, but several of them would be inconsistent with the focused factory strategy.

The dilemma therefore is: Should ABB change its focused factory strategy to adapt to the Indian market? Which of the six options available would be the most appropriate?

3.5 and 3.6 Hewlett-Packard: Creating a virtual supply chain (A and B)

This rich case focuses on outsourcing and supply chain management. It discusses several important issues, from making a pure outsourcing decision to understanding the shift in the industry and how other industries (in this case electronic manufacturing services) will impact the strategic direction of supply chain management.

The case also provides a unique opportunity to follow the situation of the HP tape unit and its outsourcing over the course of two years, from 2001 to 2003. It emphasizes the challenges of implementing an outsourcing agreement while ensuring HP continues to be an attractive customer for suppliers.

It also highlights that the different business models of suppliers will fundamentally affect the way the relationship develops. The case concludes with a dilemma involving three possible routes for HP. Should it outsource to create the ultimate supply chain, enter into a joint venture with a competitor, or follow a more traditional approach?

Case 3.1
Numico: Delivering innovation through the supply chain (A)

Luis Vivanco, Carlos Cordon and Thomas E. Vollmann

In October 2002, Jan Bennink, the recently appointed CEO of Numico, stood before the company shareholders and showed them something he hoped would demonstrate that Numico was becoming the agile company he had set out to create. The audience seemed convinced by the yellow and blue plate-shaped infant food product that he held in his hand. The product, called Ambient Ready Meal (ARM) (*refer to* **Exhibit 1** *for Ambient Ready Meal picture*) and intended for toddlers, was packaged in a revolutionary way that made it substantially more attractive than any product offered by the competition.

ARM products were expected to start out as low-margin items, representing a small, but growing, part of Numico's main market. Babynov, a French company, had developed the ARM. The importance of its introduction to Bennink was to establish a new approach to doing things at Numico. Instead of developing all improvements internally, the company would now partner with key vendors for some major new ideas. There was a catch, however. When Bennink presented the ARM, Numico had neither the legal rights to produce it, nor the committed capacity of Babynov to adequately supply it.

By the beginning of 2004, Numico had received many accolades from some of the Netherlands' main retailers for its introduction of the ARM, by then six months old. This recognition hid the structural problems that could just as easily have made it an embarrassment and that prevented it from being a commercial success. Luc Volatier, VP Purchasing and one of the champions of the ARM, was hard at work solving these problems and, in the process, changing the way Numico dealt with innovation, and worked with strategic suppliers.

Volatier liked working for Bennink. Purchasing jars for the jar factory was not at all the same as developing relationships with key suppliers to support critical new initiatives. Doing so required a transformation in purchasing – doing better things, not just doing the same things better. Volatier saw the ARM as a prime example of the changes required. In essence, he needed to create a purchasing organization that leveraged the brainpower of selected (smart) suppliers who would choose to use their brainpower working with Numico.

Numico: The turnaround

Numico was one of the Netherlands' oldest companies, founded in 1896 by Martinus van der Hagen, when he obtained the exclusive rights to produce infant milk formula from cow's milk. Since then, it had grown to become the second largest player in Western Europe's baby food market after Nestlé, and also had an important presence in parts of Latin America and in the former Dutch colony of Indonesia, where it was by far the largest player.

In 1999, pushed by the decline in birth rates, which directly affected sales of baby foods, Hans van der Wielen, who had been the company's CEO for more than 15 years, took the bold approach of acquiring two major US firms, Rexall and GNC, who manufactured and sold vitamins and nutritional supplements. These acquisitions of both producer and retailer provided a dominant position in the US as well as presence in 29 other countries worldwide. The purchase was intended to diversify and increase the company's revenues and to use the potential synergies to turn Numico into a vitamin powerhouse with worldwide reach.

By early 2002, however, it was clear that synergies were few, and the low-margin vitamin market had taken a turn southward. Numico found itself with a soaring debt of €2.9 billion, and net losses for 2002 were estimated at €1.6 billion, resulting from the provision for the extraordinary loss that would result from the planned sale of GNC and Rexall in 2003. Shares plummeted from a high of €60.10 in 2000 to €4.30 in March 2003. Van der Wielen was gone and a new CEO, Bennink, had been brought in with the mandate to turn the company around. Although both managers were Dutch, the difference in their backgrounds could not be more different. The departing CEO was an engineer by trade whose approach was described by a senior executive as 'have jar factory, will make jars'. Bennink, however, had a marketing background in what was arguably the world's most demanding baby food market: France.

A new ARM product concept

ARMs were a relatively new product concept. Sales growth was primarily due to the decrease in the amount of time parents had to prepare meals for their toddlers. Rather than the pulp-like consistency of products for younger babies, the ARM resembled a home-cooked meal with identifiable pieces of vegetables – the product actually looked edible! The presentation, both in ease of use and perceived value, was extremely important. Mothers who bought ARMs could alleviate feelings of guilt for not cooking the meals themselves. These customers placed great importance in the product being 'as good as if cooked at home'. Typically ARMs had relatively short expiry dates of 9 months compared to 12 months for most infant food products. However, because ARMs had to compete with home-cooked meals, the margins tended to be relatively low. Volatier keenly felt the need to closely control all associated costs but he also understood that extra value could command somewhat higher prices.

In 2002, coinciding with Bennink's appointment as CEO and his decision to focus on infant food, Roger Beguinot, a French entrepreneur, approached Numico's marketing department with a new idea for an ARM. Beguinot was the founder and owner of Babynov, a producer of infant food for many of Europe's main brands as well as for its own Materna brand. Far from being a low-cost producer, Babynov competed through innovative value-adding packaging designs.

In previous years, the idea of producing ARMs at Numico had surfaced a couple of times but was turned down due to a number of factors: Numico was focusing its attention on acquiring Rexall/GNC in the US; Numico's own jar factory was working at 50% capacity and ARMs used plastic packaging that the factory could not handle; and there was an unwritten policy to produce in-house so third party suppliers were not considered. When Beguinot approached Numico's marketing department, the original response was negative. It was only when Bennink refocused the thinking/strategy that Numico became receptive to the idea.

Initially Numico was mildly interested in an ARM comprised of a plate-shaped container, sealed with a removable plastic film, packaged in a printed cardboard box. Babynov already produced such an item as a private label for Carrefour in France. It was only when Beguinot showed Numico a computer-generated image of the product that the Numico people became really excited. 'This is something I'm working on, if you would be interested maybe we can come to an agreement', he told them. A few weeks later, before even reaching a final agreement, Bennink presented it to the board.

Roger Beguinot: The story of an entrepreneur

Beguinot's first job was in the after-sales department of Xerox, from which he eventually moved to the sales post he was to hold for four years. One day, on a sales call to a small yogurt manufacturer north of Paris, he attempted to convince the owner to cancel the contract he had just signed with a competitor and to buy from Xerox. By the end of their lunch together, the owner had agreed to buy the Xerox copier. Furthermore, the man told Beguinot that he was about to retire, that his son was going to be the company's commercial director and that Beguinot was going to be the managing director! 'You are the first person that I can remember that has been able to convince me to go back on a decision I've taken.' Beguinot, barely 26 and with a technical education and four years' experience in copying equipment sales, suddenly found himself responsible for a yogurt company.

A few years later he was approached by the chairman of a milk cooperative in a precarious situation. Its single customer had just cancelled the existing contract. Unless something was done, 110 people in the co-op would find themselves jobless within a few months. The chairman saw Beguinot as the person to help them. Without making any promises, Beguinot set out to save a company with no clients, no money and an old and outdated factory. He succeeded by partnering with a company to provide new technology, and obtaining a customer that required small batches, which larger companies were not interested in producing.

By the time Beguinot was thirty he decided it was time to become his own man. He announced to the co-op board his intention to start a company to buy products from producers and sell them to retailers. The board urged him to stay but Beguinot would not agree unless he became the majority shareholder. He was tired of all the political problems with the co-ops and if the board did not agree to his terms he would leave. However, the board did in fact agree to his conditions. Over the following three years Beguinot developed a 'pôle laitier', a co-op of milk producers, and became the number three in France with 18% market share. His main clients were supermarkets and manufacturers of infant milk formula and infant food.

In 1995 he acquired Materna, a financially strained Swiss manufacturer of milk-based infant food, also from a cooperative. In France, the Materna brand held a slim 0.5% market share. It was to take Beguinot a few years to develop a new strategy for Materna. Between 1995 and 1999 working with baby food producers provided critical insight and experience of the industry. In 1999 Beguinot and his management team went through a brainstorming exercise to find possible ways of entering the baby food market in France. The group estimated that current products had peaked at 60% penetration through typical distribution channels, namely supermarkets. The remaining 40% of baby food products were provided by mothers who prepared baby food at home. Beguinot and the management team viewed this untapped segment as the opportunity. 'Let's think from the mothers' perspective. Why do they prefer to cook the meals rather than buying them?'

Beguinot and his management team concluded that infant meals purchased in a supermarket were perceived as inferior in quality to home-cooked products. They decided to design Materna products that were at least as good as home-prepared baby meals, and to market them through pharmacies and supermarkets as fresh products, rather than traditional baby food. The segment thus defined was new and so was its distribution network. Little by little, Materna was able to develop an important niche in a very competitive market.

Once the market concept had been proven, Beguinot believed it was only a matter of time until his firm would be competing head-to-head with Danone (Bledina) and Nestlé, the dominant players in the French infant food market. This was just not feasible for a small company like Babynov. Furthermore, the activities required for grand-scale brand management, distribution and production did not appeal to him. Beguinot's interest was in continuing to develop innovations, so he decided to approach the big competitors with the intent of forming partnerships.

Babynov thus became a supplier of designs and production for the two companies. The partnerships were product-, market- and channel-specific. In the meantime, Babynov continued to sell its Materna brand through pharmacies and the fresh product section in supermarkets. Beguinot explained:

> We were careful not to compete with our partners. People who bought from us were not the same people who bought from Nestlé or Danone. We were increasing the size of the pie rather than taking a share from our partners.

In 2002, when Beguinot first contacted Numico, Babynov was already an important supplier for both Nestlé and Danone, producing ARMs of unique design for each of them.

November 2002 onwards

Bennink's presentation to the shareholders put the central marketing organization into high gear. The marketing organization did not have a business plan for the ARM, nor did they have a contract or any production capacity allocation from Babynov. Moreover, they did not have the intellectual rights to the ARM packaging design presented by Bennink to the board.

The intellectual rights for the packaging design were of no small importance. Bennink had publicly committed to a product that was very similar to one sold by Danone, Babynov's biggest client – all based on a conversation with Beguinot. When Danone became aware of the proposed arrangement with Numico, they called Beguinot, who had earlier approached them with the design, and offered to buy the patent. Beguinot's response to Danone was: 'I came to you, my existing client, first. You did not show any interest, and now I have given my word to Numico.' Beguinot, expecting Numico to follow through on its end of the bargain, demanded a firm commitment before 31 December 2002. Without it, he would approach other companies with the design. Bennink decided to go with it and the market rollout plans were to introduce it into the Dutch market and then, a few months later, in Belgium. Since Numico was the market leader in these areas, which were also its home markets, the launch would send the desired message of change and innovation to the stockholders, employees and other stakeholders.

Numico's central purchasing team, based in Lausanne, Switzerland, was asked to develop an explicit delivery contract with Babynov after reaching an agreement for Numico to buy the ARM design copyright. The contract for 1.25 million units for the first year, with deliveries starting in May 2003, was based on the sales estimates provided by Central Marketing. It was the first contract with an external supplier in years that was not for raw materials and, in that sense, was no different since it emphasized price over everything else.

With the contract timing and quantities now agreed upon, Central Marketing continued the launch preparations. Central Planning (logistics) was told about the project, but did not see any detailed involvement on their part as necessary. Moreover, their workload was already heavy with normal responsibilities. Shipment specifications were quite straightforward – pallet size, one SKU per pallet, no mixing of batch codes and notice before shipments were to be received.

Numico's main contact at Babynov left the company in December 2002, but he was replaced by an equally good salesperson. This second contact also left the company a couple of months later and was replaced by a person from operations. In May, the detailed planning on the Numico side was handed over to Central Planning. It was only at this time that Volatier, who had joined Numico only two months before, became aware of the situation. When the first shipments were received, there were several problems, for example, the plastic tab that held the ARM's lid shut was not strong enough and was opening occasionally during transport. This problem was influenced by pallet stacking that was not consistent with Numico's specifications. Jan-Jaap ten Hoor, at Numico NL Logistics traveled to Babynov to sort out the problem and change the configuration of the pallets.

Central Planning provided Babynov with forecasts with the specified lead-time of eight to nine weeks. Babynov, however, wanted a longer planning horizon and asked for forecasts for the following three to four months. It also complained that the forecasts it was already receiving changed constantly for no apparent reason. Disagreements over forecast revisions finally led Numico to simply demand that shipments be based on the initial contract rather than updated forecasts.

During this time, Babynov ramped up its production capacity by increasing the production week from two shifts, five days per week in January 2003 to three shifts, seven days per week by November 2003. The Numico contract was not the sole reason for the ramp-up since, in 2003, Babynov had launched similar projects with Nestlé and Danone.

When the orders for September arrived in June, Babynov realized it would have difficulty in filling them. Numico insisted that the orders were in line with forecasts, but Babynov disagreed. Volatier's subsequent analysis showed that the Central Planning forecast was in fact internal and had not been communicated to Babynov. Furthermore, he also discovered that the initial first year estimate by Central Marketing referred to the period between May 2003, when the orders would start to arrive, and December of the same year, while Babynov had taken 'first year' to mean the period from May 2003 to May 2004! Additionally, the marketing forecast represented customer sales but did not include pipeline filling.

Concerned with the situation, Numico decided to postpone the ARM launch in Belgium. In August the numbers for the Netherlands were revised indicating that customer demand (from retailers) was coming earlier – and was higher – than originally predicted. Unless something was done, Numico would run out of stock in three weeks. When this information was communicated to Babynov, it replied that it would have difficulty in supplying the revised requirements.

In order to respond to the additional demands, Babynov decided to do more than increase output to three shifts, seven days per week. A second filling line was installed (*refer to **Exhibit 2** for Babynov's production process*) but capacity was constrained by the earlier parts of the process. Moreover, while total capacity was increased, efficiency in terms of units per hour had actually taken a big dip from 2,300 units to 1,800 units. In the words of a Babynov executive, 'Capacity existed on paper but reality wasn't the same.' To release some pressure from parts of the production process, Babynov created an additional makeshift packaging line where three operators put the final product into cartons. Numico accepted this measure reluctantly since it went completely against its way of doing things.

Concerned with the damage that stock-outs would cause to customer relationships, Numico decided to scale down the planned advertising TV campaign and negotiated for part of the contracted spots to be used on other

Numico products. The actual sales for 2003 reached 850,000 units instead of the forecast of 1.2 million. But in spite of this, Numico received many accolades from its customers for the way it had launched the product.

Throughout the fall of 2003, Babynov worked hard to achieve manufacturing efficiencies and volume increases. In fact, by December, not only had it caught up with requirements but also its output matched the earlier anticipated needs of Numico and the other customers, who had meanwhile reduced their sales to retailers. As a result of the reduced demand, at year-end Babynov stocks were much too high. The large majority of the excess inventories, given their maturing expiry dates, would have to be either sold at a discount or disposed of.

Reflections from both sides

Babynov lacks the experience to launch large campaigns.

Numico

Numico really jerked us around on their forecasted needs.

Babynov

I probably tried to do too much too soon. As a salesman, I had three important leads and expected one, maybe two to go through. I wasn't ready for all three to say yes. We tried to accomplish in one year what would normally take three to four years to learn under normal circumstances.

Roger Beguinot

We were used to dealing with our own factories. We simply lacked the knowledge to deal with third party suppliers.

Numico

Too many contacts, and not the right ones.

Numico

Our marketing/production model is more adequate for our own products.

Numico

It is believed by some that the problem was that things were done too rapidly. Come on! We had from November 2002 to June 2003, there was ample time to do things right.

Numico

Both firms have been hurt by this, and there is plenty of blame to share. We need to focus on how to work as a true partnership in the future.

Luc Volatier

The way ahead

Volatier looked at the blank screen of his computer. It was January 2004 and they were about to re-launch the Ambient Ready Meal. He was determined to avoid the pitfalls of the first time and decided to put his thoughts to how this could be accomplished in writing for everyone involved. He was well aware that the challenge lay not in the success of the re-launch, but on changing the approach that Numico's supply chain had towards third party suppliers.

Volatier shifted in his chair. He felt that the two companies needed to work together more effectively. Moreover, although detailed procedures were important, he felt that at the end of the day there were other issues that needed to be addressed. It was too easy to concentrate solely on the sales, orders and other transactions between Numico and Babynov. Somehow Volatier felt that they needed to develop better networking and shared values. If they could engage in some joint projects the payoffs could be substantial. Perhaps these could focus on how to increase the perceived value of the products as well as ways to improve the linkages/reduce the joint costs in the supply chain. Volatier believed that joint learning and competency development were at the heart of what was needed. As he put it:

> Look, I know we need to make the trains run on time, but if that is all we do with key suppliers, it will not be enough. If we really want to make a difference for our stockholders, we need to find new ways to work in true win–win relationships with the smartest suppliers.

As he looked again at the screen, Volatier began to type.

Exhibit 1 Ambient ready meal

Source: Company information

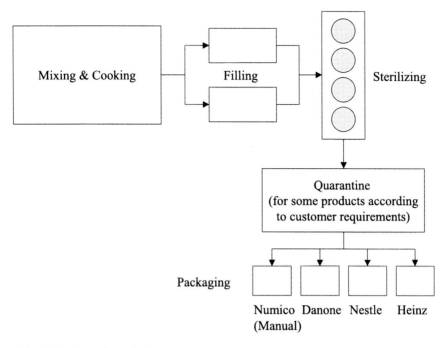

Exhibit 2 Babynov's production process

Source: Company information

This case series won the Supply Chain Management Award in the 2004 European Case Writing Competition organized by the European Foundation for Management Development (efmd).

Case 3.2
Numico: Transforming the supply chain to support new realities (B)

Luis Vivanco, Carlos Cordon and Thomas E. Vollmann

In January 2004 Jan Bennink, the newly appointed CEO of Numico, met with his president of the Operations Division, Niraj Mehra, to discuss the results of what had been one of the largest undertakings the company had embarked on to date. The changes initiated roughly a year before meant an almost complete transformation of the entire supply chain and of the way the company perceived itself in relation to its customers and consumers. It was no exaggeration to say that the future of the company depended directly on the success of this transformation.

After an ill-fated foray into the US health supplement market by his predecessor, Bennink had set a strategy that focused on Numico's historical infant food European market. The strategy embraced both new product innovation and cost reduction. Thereafter, very concrete goals were established to achieve that strategy. Out of a total of 17 baby food factories in Western Europe, eight were to close, and a large amount of the production would be shifted to new factories in Central Europe. Working capital reductions were targeted at €100 million and new product launches were to be stepped up. The reduction in working capital was intended to allow the cash-strained company to finance part of the cost of implementing its new strategy. In a nutshell, for Bennink's strategy to be successful, Numico's supply chain would have to become much more innovative, cost efficient and responsive to changing markets.

At the end of June 2002 Mehra and his team had finalized and communicated a plan to relocate the European baby food production. By January 2004 it was clear that the master plan was working successfully, reducing working capital and manufacturing complexity simultaneously. During the previous nine months Mehra had achieved a reduction in stock levels of 25%, from €204 million to €149 million, without any delay or disruption in the relocation plans. Inside the company, awareness of the challenges they faced was at a high level.

'Awareness is of the essence', explained Mehra. 'One of the first steps was to get everyone to accept a set of clear and common goals. Without these, nothing could be achieved.' He continued, 'While our venture in the US didn't bring the financial benefits we expected, there are a few lessons to be learned from it and that could be used back in Europe. In the US everyone was in one location and a meeting could be called at a moment's notice. In Europe, on the other hand, I have multiple highly independent organizations separated not only by geography and markets, but also by different cultures and histories. All this has resulted in substantially different systems that don't talk to each other. I need to find how to make the people – as well as the systems – work as one.'

Numico in 2003

Numico was one of Holland's oldest companies, founded in 1896 by Martinus van der Hagen, when he attained exclusive rights to produce infant milk formula from cow's milk. Since then, it had grown to become second only to Nestlé in Western Europe's baby food market, with an important presence in Latin America, and as the dominant player in the former Dutch colony of Indonesia.

In 1999, motivated by the decline in birth rates (and therefore sales of baby foods), Hans van der Wielen, who had been the company's CEO for more than 15 years, took the bold approach of acquiring Rexall and GNC, major producer and retailer respectively of vitamins and nutritional supplements. Rexall and GNC had a dominant position in the US as well as significant presence in 29 other countries. The purchase was intended to diversify and increase the company's revenues and to use the synergies to turn Numico into a vitamin powerhouse with worldwide reach.

By early 2002, it was abundantly clear that synergies were few, and the low-margin vitamin market had taken a downturn. Numico found itself with a soaring debt of €2.9 billion. Shares plummeted from a high of €60.10 to €4.30. In May 2002 van der Wielen retired and the new CEO, Jan Bennink, was given the mandate to turn the company around. Although both Bennink and his predecessor were Dutch, the difference in their approaches could not be greater. Van der Wielen was an engineer whose style was described as: 'Have jar factory, will make jars.' Bennink, by contrast, had a marketing background in arguably the world's most demanding baby food market, France.

Jan Bennink and the French example

According to a January 2004 *Forbes* magazine article about Numico, 'Jan Bennink put the company back in high chairs.' A few months after his arrival, the vitamin business was sold, prompting an extraordinary loss in 2002 of €1.6 billion, and any claims to the North American market. The focus was again on Europe, where the infant population continued to decrease. Bennink, who had worked for French food giant Danone before joining Numico, did not see an increase in birth rates as the sole factor for an increase in revenues. He focused the company on boosting baby food sales by 5% per annum over the next three years, based on product innovation, something at which the French were better than anyone else.

Baby food was by and large a substitution product (*refer to* **Exhibit 1** *for dynamics of the baby food and clinical food markets in Europe*). From infant formula to fruit juices, to meals, customers bought prepared products as convenient alternatives to producing them themselves. As children grew, they started eating the same foods as their parents and older siblings. In spite of a decreasing birth rate, the French baby food market experienced a steady growth of 8% per year by developing innovative ways to make convenience more attractive – for a longer period. French baby food companies were creating product categories that did not exist in other markets. This contrasted with countries such as Germany or the Netherlands, where negative growth was expected – and baby food companies acted accordingly.

Numico's US experience

Before it was purchased by Numico, Rexall had gone through a phase of growth, between 1994 and 1998, while the market continued to demand innovations. By the year 2000, however, Rexall's customers were experiencing frequent stock-outs as a result of poor demand planning and coordination of the supply chain. This was despite high inventory levels of more than 70 days. In October 2001 the new Numico management created a department with the specific responsibility for demand planning, a new function in the marketing organization. The objective of the team was to significantly increase customer satisfaction. The team was also given the responsibility of reviewing processes and implementing new ones to restore customer satisfaction targets.

It rapidly became clear that sales and operations were being run separately from each other in 'functional silos'. Although demand planning was located in the 'sell' organization, an experiment was started to bring the entire demand and supply planning under one management in the operations environment. The basic premise was that it was imperative to generate a consistent signal of customer demand that could be used in the 'make' and 'buy' organizations as well. The lack of formalized systems of communication and coherent demand-planning tools caused high inventory levels, sub-optimal product mix and under-par customer satisfaction levels. The bottom line was that customers saw Rexall as unreliable. Internally, the relationship between the sell and make organizations was highly confrontational – when something went wrong, assigning blame often took priority over solving the problem.

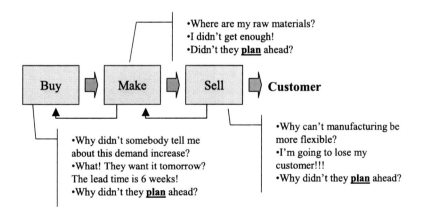

The demand planning team found the process of producing consistent monthly forecasts involving the whole organization frustrating, which also made it difficult to collaborate with key customers based on vendor management inventory (VMI) systems. To address these problems, Mehra established a US-based supply chain team, headed by Eric Koch. This team integrated demand planning with the make/buy operations thus creating a real end-to-end supply chain. The integrated team had gained credibility across the organization by focusing on market information from key customers and driving for manufacturing efficiency at the same time. The information was both objective, directly from the customers' systems, and subjective, such as promotional activities and market intelligence. It was not until Mehra's team gave it top priority that demand planning became an integrated part of the overall supply chain. The logic was, in fact, quite simple – demand planning was seen as part of both operations, i.e., the supply (make/buy) organization, and the sell organization. Demand/supply planning was established as one integrated weekly exercise, with cross-functional representation and multiple management levels. As a result, monthly business planning could be linked to day-to-day processes and routine decision making.

By the end of 2002, Rexall's inventory levels had been reduced from US$150 million to $70 million, some of it obsolete items that had been written off. EDI (electronic data interchange) and VMI had been successfully implemented with several major customers and suppliers, and the overall level of customer satisfaction had improved dramatically. In addition, a rigorous multidisciplinary S&OP process was run.

Shifting the focus to Europe

With exit from the US vitamin operations, Mehra repatriated key members of the US supply chain team to Europe. There, Jan Bennink had established an objective of reaching EBITDA of 20%. To reach this stretch goal, enhancement had to go beyond cutting the costs of doing the same things – a major improvement in supply chain management was essential. By early 2003, Mehra's new team had initiated two major projects to support this goal. The first, Project Link! was an attempt to improve control and reduce inventories. As an example of the situations it aimed to improve, the best estimate that management could get of inventories was on Monday morning from Excel spreadsheets sent in by every unit on Friday afternoon. Products that were not in any of these spreadsheets or in customer systems were simply assumed to be in transit. A senior executive asked, 'If you say you have X number of pallets, is it true? If you and I are talking about product Y, are we talking about the same product? The bad news is that our information systems are full of holes. The good news is that we do not know it.' Mehra and Eric Koch saw Project Link! as a similar effort to that of coordinating the planning in the US: closely connecting demand and supply planning in one integrated structure. It was imperative to quickly obtain some valid data to balance and streamline the forecasting and production planning processes – as a forerunner to making these part of a single exercise.

The second project, code-named Focus, was in the final stages of analysis. Project Focus aimed to simplify the product line and to reduce complexity of the production and distribution network. This was a key means to achieving the cost reductions associated with production rationalization. Project Focus was directly linked to the factory closures, setting up new factories in Central Europe, establishing the right focus in each of these production units, and coordinating the planning across the production units.

The challenges are confirmed

In early 2003, Bennink and his management team were made aware of significant customer service challenges:

> I fail to understand Nutricia's attitude towards service level, which is a fundamental and basic necessity for business with us.
>
> E-mail from UK retailer 1, May 20, 2002

> We have less than one week's stock in depot. If the availability on this line does not improve the line will be discontinued, as it will be unavailable for stores for more than four weeks.
>
> E-mail from UK retailer 2, May 15, 2002

> Your company has a poor record of service to our depots. The current problems with a range of your products and the Cow & Gate biscuit product are affecting our sales and we need urgent action from your teams.
>
> Letter from UK retailer 3, July 9, 2001

In response to these complaints, Numico contracted a study by a renowned strategic consultancy firm. The analysis showed service levels consistently below best practices (*refer to* **Exhibit 2** *for service levels for main markets*). It also showed a fragmented supply chain as the root of the problem. Numico's organization was divided into four main units: the sales units, which worked at a country level; the supply points, basically the factories where the production took place; central planning, which planned production and distribution from supply points to sales units; and Nutraco, a sourcing organization that dealt with all major suppliers. This fragmentation caused conflicting objectives among the units (*refer to* **Exhibit 3** *for non-integrated supply chain responsibilities and incentives*).

The analysis included the following conclusions:

- Live data were seldom available and reports on inventories were unreliable.
- A fragmented forecasting process, largely based on historical data, supported by incompatible systems and databases, caused both high stocks and low service levels.
- Without consistent performance measurements it was difficult to evaluate decisions/actions.

- Alternative channels of communications, which had developed over time, made control of the supply chain more difficult.

In summary, the ability to match demand planning and production planning was hindered by a fragmented structure. Mehra met with Eric Koch, the VP of supply chain management, who had worked for him in the US venture, to discuss his view on the US experience, and realized that 'they had been there before'. Furthermore, since forecasting was seen with suspicion, especially when it came from a different part of the organization, the need for it and the general awareness of it as a tool, were low. Numico had not yet experienced the kind of demand-planning exercise that Rexall had undergone. Link! was a start – but only a start. In April 2003 Koch became responsible for Numico's European supply chain operations.

Raising the awareness level

Mehra was concerned that the fragmented nature of the organization would hinder the potential of Projects Link! and Focus. Momentum would falter unless people bought in on the two projects as part of an integrated plan for the success of the company. In May 2003, with the aid of an external consultant, Koch brought the whole supply chain organization together for a two-day workshop designed to establish a common direction, consensus, and sense of urgency for the task ahead. Participants had to define the practices that they would like to see implemented, describe the expected short- and long-term benefits, as well as suggest the actions and people necessary to ensure their success.

The workshop resulted in specific proposals regarding customer knowledge and integration, supplier integration, responsiveness, flexibility and chain optimization, and control and reporting.

Upgrading Project Link!

Project Link! was ongoing and perceived to be achieving important results, so it was important not to replace this project with another. Instead, based on the workshop results, it was possible to refine its strengths. Moving beyond a focus on inventories was critical, since inventories are essentially the result of other actions. So, the objectives for Link! were expanded to develop a supply chain to fulfil customer requirements with maximum quality, at a service level of over 98.5%, within the lead time requested by the customer, and with minimum supply chain costs (including inventories).

The following guidelines for all parts of the supply chain were agreed upon and endorsed by top management:

- Think from consumer/customer viewpoint.
- Have one common/shared objective and aligned incentives.
- Agree upon clear rules and responsibilities.

- Solidify the simple and robust processes that were designed in the Link! Project.
- Guarantee full transparency, real-time and reliable data/information availability.
- Introduce regular and rigid monitoring, analyse performance root causes and continually refine and improve.
- Adopt a quantitative approach for trade-off decisions and for planning parameters optimization.

The three cornerstones of Link! became: a) the sole ownership of forecasting by the sales units, who were closest to the customer; b) the ownership of the production scheduling by the supply points, who had the capacity to produce; and c) the use of a 'cockpit meeting', run by the supply point, as a tool to match the two. This way, demand planning and production planning flowed from their natural sources.

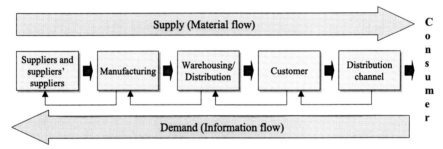

Making Link! operational was achieved through weekly cockpit meetings, run by each supply point with the participation of the sales units that sold any of the SP's products. The objective was to closely couple supply and demand – to track agreed KPI service and stock levels, analyse root causes for out of stocks and KPI deviations, and review process exceptions. A key result would be to define corrective actions and agree upon trade-offs, always based on overall business and economical terms – not on short-term problems.

The weekly meeting facilitated a reduction of the planning period interval from one month to one week. The following diagram shows how this worked in one of the supply units (UK). In essence, every week, the cockpit meeting reviewed the previous week's results, in terms of plans versus actual results – in sales vs. forecasts, actual production vs. planned production, and actual inventories vs. planned inventories. Deviations from plans were examined, root causes isolated, and corrective actions initiated. As the following diagram shows, the plans for the following five weeks were fixed or frozen, since this amount of time was required to order the required materials, plan actual production and move goods through quality control and transport. In essence, the cockpit meeting made weekly adjustments to the plans for the sixth (and subsequent) weeks in the future.

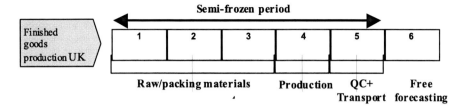

The results of weekly planning with cockpit meetings were almost immediate after its trial introduction in the UK, where it was estimated that €1.5 million, or 6% of sales, had been lost due to mismatches between this sourcing point and the retail customers. By February 2003 the practice was rolled out to three more supply points. Average fill rate went up from 92.5% in the second half of 2002, when the pilot started, to 99.1% by April–May 2003. This significantly exceeded the original goal of 98.5%.

By reducing the planning window from one month to one week, the re-order point and cycle stock also decreased. Weekly planning also highlighted the variations of demand within a month. This was especially true in Southern European countries where promotions were typically at the end of the month. Although smaller (weekly) batches were more difficult to estimate, the weekly replanning compensated since the errors were corrected more frequently and with smaller adjustments. Furthermore, the process brought more visibility to production and demand problems, and the general awareness across the supply chain increased dramatically. This in turn helped to deal with exceptional issues.

Upgrading Project Focus

Mehra and Koch also upgraded the activities in Project Focus. At the outset, this project was seen as a downsizing activity, but Mehra wanted it to be much more encompassing both in terms of activities and in terms of the people involved. The most visible part of Project Focus was the rationalization of production by shifting some capacity from old factories in Western Europe to new and fewer sourcing points in Poland and the Czech Republic. The total number of baby food factories in Western Europe would be reduced from 17 to 9. The rationale for which factories should be closed was largely based on total production cost per product group. Under the existing system, a product could be produced in one site and packaged in another, and similar products were produced in different factories, increasing both complexity and production cost. Once Focus was implemented, products would be placed into logical groups and produced only at one site.

With the reduction in production sites, the same number of products would be produced with less production capacity. It was estimated that as a result of Focus asset utilization would increase from 50%–60% to 80%. 2006 was the target year for all production to come out of the nine assigned factories. A second stage, under the name of Project Laager, would try to reduce the 50 distribution points that currently existed in Europe.

As is often the case in firms like Numico, Mehra and Koch found that a very large number of SKUs existed as a result of traditional decentralized approaches to the multi-market environment in which Numico operated. Sales country units operated more or less independently and created products according to their own market research and seasonal promotions. In many cases the resulting SKUs were kept in the system without further analysis as to profitability. A prime example of this could be seen in Italy with 119 different SKUs for infant milk formula. SKU rationalization was seen as the responsibility of sales and marketing, but this was difficult in a company where results were country-focused. Mehra believed that rationalizing the product line would need to involve both sales units and supply points, working in harmony. It would probably also be necessary to modify compensation systems so that country managers would focus more on overall Numico results.

A related issue (opportunity) existed in the differing formulations used to make the same product, and the resulting large number of items that were purchased. This not only resulted in buying uneconomical quantities of materials but also caused smaller production runs. The ability to harmonize recipes would reduce the complexity of the production scheduling, and also support a significant reduction in the supplier base.

Challenges ahead

Niraj Mehra was reasonably satisfied with the efforts by his team to date. He was confident it would not have been possible without the initial steps taken to get everyone involved. There was no doubt anywhere in the organization that the ball was now rolling and the way of doing things was changing. But the work was certainly not completed and there was always a new set of challenges. Transformation of Numico's supply chain depended not just on good implementation but, more importantly, on continually enhancing the overriding objectives and modifying the direction. It was beyond doubt that the cockpit meetings had brought many benefits, but Mehra was concerned that the continual weekly spotlight on KPIs might be distracting people from going about their job responsibilities, spending too much time worrying about immediate issues. He wondered if it would be better to measure some KPIs on an aggregated monthly basis. Similarly, the Focus project was also yielding good results – but was progress fast enough? Finally, there were new concerns for Eric Koch to address in his role leading the European supply chain operations. As he entered his weekly team meeting on service level performance and forecast accuracy he wondered:

- Was a single supply chain enough to handle all products independently of their demand characteristics?
- Should alternative systems be put in place?
- What were the limits of the production rationalization in the multi-market European environment?
- Were the current initiatives enough to ensure that the organization continued to improve along the established lines without the need for pressure from top management?
- What plans should he present to top management for the immediate future and what would be the implications in terms of things that needed to change?

Segment	Target consumer	Target buyer	Purchasing rationale	Expected consumer growth
Infant food	Babies and toddlers	Mothers	• Ease of use/convenience • 'Guilt' factor reduction (a mother who can't make the food for her baby feels she is giving something as good as) • Nutritional value • Presentation • Digestibility	Negative
Clinical	Sick people with nutritional requirements	Doctors	• Nutritional value • Digestibility • Flavor	Positive
Old people	Old people	Nutritionist	• Nutritional value • Digestibility • Flavor	Positive

Exhibit 1 Dynamics of the baby food and clinical food markets in Europe

Exhibit 2 Service levels for main markets

	Sales Units	**Central Planning**	**Supply Points**	**Nutraco**
Historical focus	• Sales/service level	• Inventory levels	• Total conversion cost (vs. budget)	• Cost price (improvement)
At the cost of:	• Forecast accuracy	• Total supply chain cost	• Production reliability vs. plan • Production flexibility (changeovers, lead times) • Standard unit process cost	• Supplier reliability • Standard material cost (improvement)
Implications	• Excessive orders/forecast changes	• Focus on lower batch sizes/rush orders	• Reduced flexibility • Increased lot sizes	• Focus on cost at the expense of reliability/ quality • Poor supplier support of new initiatives
	No standard Key Performance Indicators			

Exhibit 3 Non-integrated supply chain responsibilities and incentives

This case series won the Supply Chain Management Award in the 2004 European Case Writing Competition organized by the European Foundation for Management Development (efmd).

Case 3.3
Numico: King Project

François Jäger, Carlos Cordon and Luc Volatier

When Jan Bennink was appointed CEO of Numico in 2002, the company was in a dire financial situation. International investments had resulted in poor financial ratios for the company. Trade working capital (TWC), for instance, represented a staggering 18% of annual sales. With a cash flow yield of 0.8%, Numico was lagging behind the competition.

CEOs often focus on cash purely from a financial perspective. They seldom consider the possibility of generating cash by improving operations processes. Initially, Bennink wanted the company to become high growth and high margin by focusing exclusively on baby food and clinical nutrition. However, as top line sales and the share price increased so did the need for cash, and Bennink realized that cash generation had to be part of the equation. Additionally, increasing advertising and promotion expenses, capital expenditures, new product launches and an aggressive acquisition strategy were also requiring more financial resources.

Bennink felt the way forward was to go through a drastic structural reduction of the trade working capital used by the company. Freeing up cash was a new objective, and Project King was born. Yet would this be sufficient to turn the financial results around? And was the company ready for such a drastic move?

Numico

Numico, a specialized nutrition player, sold its products through brands such as Nutricia, Milupa, Cow & Gate and Dumex all over the world. Numico was headquartered in Amsterdam, the Netherlands. For the fiscal year ended December 2006, the company generated revenues of €2,623 million. This resulted in an operating profit of €429 million.

Numico distributed its products in more than 100 countries and operated 27 production facilities around the world. The company was organized around four divisions: baby food, clinical nutrition, operations, and research and development.

The King Project

The King Project was set up to answer Numico's need for free cash flow. When benchmarking the company's financial ratios against the competition, it became clear that Numico was lagging behind in terms of free cash flow yield (*refer to* **Figure 1**).

The Lowest Cash Flow Yield in the Sector

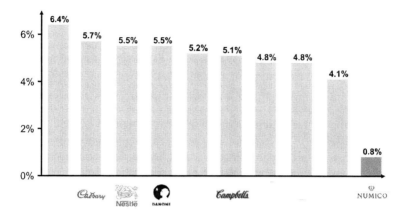

Definition: FCF divided by market capitalisation

Figure 1 The lowest cash flow yield in the sector

The King Project was a transversal project aimed at liberating the cash immobilized in Numico's operations. Cash was actually freed by reducing the need for trade working capital. This was done by focusing on three main areas: accounts payable, accounts receivable and inventory (*refer to* **Figure 2**).

Trade Working Capital

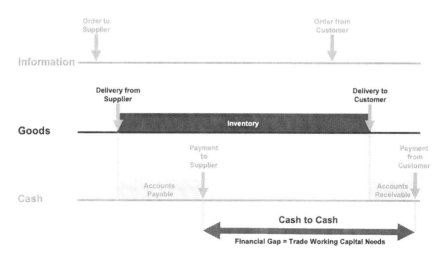

Figure 2 Trade working capital

For instance, by reducing its 2005 trade working capital level (11%) to the Danone level (0%), Numico could actually liberate €220 million in free cash flow (*refer to **Figure 3***).

Trade Working Capital as % Sales

Figure 3 Trade working capital as percentage of sales

The means to an end

The King Project was managed with a top-down approach. Being transversal, it had to be viewed from different angles: generating free cash flow, process set-up and HR management. Everyone in the company was encouraged to comply with the project's target. Yet, many employees did not see the direct relationship between their day-to-day tasks and the reduction of trade working capital.

The cash prophet

Luc Volatier, the Vice President of Global Procurement and 'King Project' project manager had to spread the 'cash is king' message throughout the entire company. People had to understand the difference they could make for the company by embracing this project. Yet the way the message was delivered was as important as the message itself. As he put it, 'You have to talk the same language as the people you speak to; this is the only way to make sure they understand the message.' Cash flow, like trade working capital, can be talked about in terms of money (€), percentage of net sales (basis points), or even in days of sales outstanding (DSO). You just need to adapt to the person with whom you are talking. What people need to understand is the likely impact of all their actions in terms of cash. Therefore, Volatier first had to make people understand the importance of cash flow to the organization, and then help the organization achieve superior returns in its day-to-day work. Finally, he had to show employees how they could personally benefit from reaching the project's goals. Only then would he be sure they would play the game. Understanding is one thing, executing requires some incentive.

This was a mindset revolution, the DNA of the entire company had to mutate. The mutation agent was called 'cash'.

The King toolbox

1. COMPETITION BENCHMARKS WITH REGULAR UPDATES

An easy way to see how well your company is doing is to benchmark its financial performance against the competition. Since publicly traded companies are obliged to publish quarterly and annual reports, it is quite easy to calculate the ratios you feel are relevant to your company.

In the case of Numico, the King Project's focus was cash. Therefore, senior management focused its benchmark on ratios relevant to cash: free cash flow, free cash flow yield, trade working capital, accounts payable, accounts receivable and inventory. (*Refer to **Exhibit 1** for a trade working capital benchmark.*)

With such an approach, employees had to switch from the excuse mode to the how can we do it mode. If competition was able to achieve these results, why couldn't Numico do it?

2. COMPENSATION AND BONUSES

Sometimes, thorough explanations are not enough and individuals need an incentive to perform well. The King Project was set up in such a way that every stakeholder had part of his or her compensation or bonus scheme linked to cash generation. Top management made it happen, therefore, positively influencing the employees' behavior towards the King Project's goals. A significant portion of the executive bonus plan was also dependent upon cash generation.

3. SUPPLYING NEGOTIATION TOOLS TO BOTH SELLERS AND BUYERS

One of the major points that was emphasized to Numico's negotiators was the importance of knowing the partner you are negotiating with. Figure 4 illustrates the relation between information and knowledge and the balance of power when negotiating with either a supplier or a customer. It is a good tool to spot situations where the negotiator can have an advantage over the negotiating partner.

The Negotiation Matrix

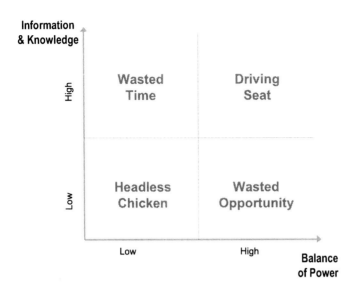

Figure 4 The negotiation matrix

When it comes to dealing with suppliers and customers, annual reports are a great tool in preparing for the negotiations. (*Refer to **Exhibit 2** for examples of annual report analyses.*) Average payment terms, for instance, can easily be calculated by looking at annual reports. They are also useful when preparing a case to request an extension of the payment terms with a supplier or faster payment collection with a customer. In addition to using annual report for negotiation purposes, the King Project management team also relied on regular reporting from the different departments to help them focus their attention where required.

4. SIMPLE MONTHLY PROGRESS REPORTS: INFLUENCE WITHOUT TAKING CREDIT

Volatier made sure to have monthly progress reports that were simple and easy to understand with both numbers and smileys (happy or sometimes sad faces). There were also celebrations acknowledging the results of key performers every three months. Only structural performance improvements were praised. Good performance resulting from external factors was usually not celebrated. He wanted to make sure that the King Project would not become a fad and that it would be structurally embedded within the corporation. It had to become a process that continued regardless of the person in charge. As such, the ongoing progress evaluation was a good way to influence all of the project stakeholders. The organization had to be kept under positive pressure (tension) so that no one would move back to complacency. Still Volatier could only influence and by no means try to actually implement or worse take credit for the job. Stakeholders had to be accountable for the execution and get the credit for the work they did.

Project King outcome

In early 2007, the outcome of the King Project was clear. Over the course of the project, Numico had steadily and, more importantly, structurally decreased the trade working capital from 18% in 2002 to 6.9% at the end of the fourth quarter of 2006 (*refer to* **Figure 5**). The cash 'gene' had been successfully implanted in the corporate DNA. Each and every employee had a good understanding of his or her contribution with regard to cash. The company was on track to achieving the aspirational target of 0% of TWC that was set by the CEO.

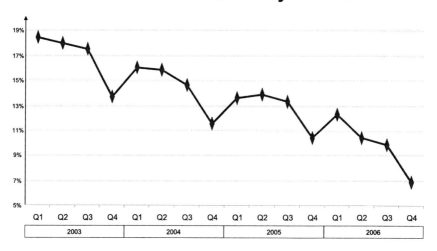

Figure 5 Numico TWC: quarterly results

By all means, the King Project was considered a success and senior management was pleased with such an outstanding result. However, it appeared that competitors were catching up and were also focusing on improving their TWC. In 2006, Paul Polman, the new CFO of Nestlé said to the analyst community that Nestlé's TWC was at an unacceptable level. If much larger competitors were to play the same game, then Numico could lose its edge. Bennink had to think about new ways to capitalize and expand on his success. But how should he proceed? Should he expand the King Project to Numico's supply chain partners? Would they be willing to team up?

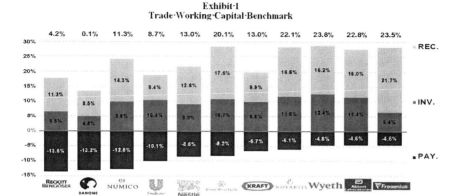

Exhibit 1 Trade working capital benchmark

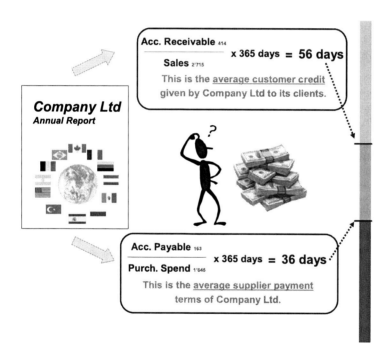

Exhibit 2 Annual report analyses

Case 3.4
ABB transformers

Luis Vivanco, Winter Nie and Carlos Cordon

Zurich, Switzerland, July 2009. In the last ten years, ABB had streamlined its operations through regionalization and globalization of its production facilities, in order to achieve better economies of scale. Prior to 1999, each factory manufactured multiple product lines and served one or more domestic markets. In 1999, the operational strategy shifted to the concept of the focused factory, where each factory would focus on only one product line and serve an entire region composed of several countries.

Simultaneously, during this period, countries like China and India emerged as key players in the global economy. However, the realities of China and India challenged the concept of the focused factory. While they were potentially very big markets, the initial customer base was small and many of the production steps could be outsourced, depending on the customer segment and the suppliers' capabilities. In addition, the economic situation at the time was painting an uncertain picture of the future. Thus, the plans that had initially been drafted in the late 1990s had to be adapted to the reality facing ABB in 2009.

ABB had manufacturing facilities for large, oil-filled transformers in India, but not for dry-type transformers (*refer to **Exhibit 1** for a description of transformer technology and types*). The demand for dry-type transformers in India was met by ABB factories elsewhere. However, as India represented a high-growth market for ABB, it was an integral part of the company's strategy to strengthen and balance its global manufacturing footprint. Tarak Mehta, head of the transformers business unit, was charged with developing a strategic plan that would allow ABB to better serve the Indian market while, at the same time, balancing its manufacturing footprint to the situation.

ABB Transformer Products

ABB Transformer Products was part of the Power Products division, one of five ABB business divisions. The Power Products division included the key components for transmitting and distributing electricity. The division incorporated ABB's manufacturing network for transformers, switchgear, circuit breakers, cables and associated equipment. It also offered all the services needed to ensure product performance and to extend their lifespan. In addition to Transformer Products (TP), the division included two other business units: High Voltage Products and Systems (HV) and Medium Voltage Products and Systems (MV). The Power Products division was divided roughly along the same line as a power grid, with HV covering the needs related to power generation, MV servicing the transport of electricity along power lines, and TP manufacturing all types of transformers needed in the generation, transport and distribution of electricity.

ABB Applications

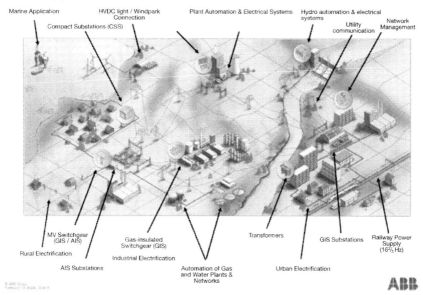

Figure 1 ABB Applications

The transformer market in 2008

In 2008, the global transformer market accounted for $25 billion. For the last five years, it had experienced a year-over-year growth rate of 3%.

In most countries, 65% to 70% of transformer sales go to private or government-owned utility companies, with the remaining 30% to 35% going to industry customers.

Large and medium-size power transformers

Market segmentation was driven by transformer size and their use. Large and medium-size transformers, used in the generation and transmission of electricity, were purchased, almost exclusively, by government- or privately owned utility companies. The purpose of large transformers was to increase the voltage before transmitting the electricity over long distances (from a technical point of view, the higher the voltage the less energy loss, which permits electricity generation to be located far away from the demand points). Medium-size transformers, with capacities ranging from 75.5 kilovolts (kV) to 220 kV, were used in the transport network to lower the voltage along the power grid as the electricity approached cities and other electricity consumption points.

Global market demand for large and medium-size transformers was influenced by both the growth in demand for electricity and the replacement of old infrastructure. Both 2007 and 2008 had seen record sales and, despite worsening economic conditions, demand was expected to remain steady in 2009, mostly due to the need to replace old infrastructure that, for most European countries, dated back to the 1960s and 1970s.

Small power transformers/large distribution transformers

These were used to distribute electricity and bring the voltage down to the level suitable for electric appliances or machinery. Of these small transformers, 20% were dry-type transformers, which could handle a maximum capacity of 53 kV. Utility companies bought them for sustainable energy generation, such as in wind turbines. They were housed at the top of the turbine and reliability and low maintenance were critical. The rest of the dry-type transformers were used in factories, large buildings or other construction complexes, where maintenance and safety were important.

Competition

As of 2008, ABB was the largest transformer manufacturer in the world with a 21% global market share.

Transformer technology had been around for a long time. Companies such as ABB, Siemens and other manufacturers with a global presence focused on manufacturing processes that increased product reliability and longevity in order to reduce total costs for their customers. Because the barriers to market entry were low, there were also many local low-cost competitors that offered transformers with good enough quality. However, large utility companies, especially government-owned ones, were risk averse and valued reliability. Therefore, their purchasing managers preferred well-known global brands like ABB, so if anything went wrong, they could not be blamed for having chosen a product of inferior quality.

Certification of manufacturing sites

It was standard practice in the industry for larger clients to require the certification of production processes of the final assembly to ensure quality. They could also request that the manufacturer certify its suppliers of critical components. However, on some occasions, the larger clients actually audited the vendors. This requirement represented a barrier to new low-cost players wanting to enter the large transformer market for utilities as the certification process often took several years to complete. However, there was nothing stopping them from entering the industrial segment, which comprised 30% of the market and did not usually require certification.

The restructuring of ABB Power

The situation before 1999

Before 1999, if a utility company wanted to acquire all of the products and services that fell under ABB's Power Products and Power Services umbrella, they would have had to contact or be visited by up to five different people, each representing one of the business units.

In the Transformer Products business unit, sales teams were organized around manufacturing sites and they covered the country in which they were located. When a country had no manufacturing facilities, the market was assigned to one of the neighboring countries with a facility. In principle, a manufacturing facility attempted to produce all the technologies that the market demanded, resorting to products manufactured in other facilities only when necessary. The direct link with the sales teams allowed the factories to have a closer relationship with the customers in order to design and manufacture products that responded to their specific needs. As a reflection of this, 10% of Power Product sales in Spain came from products built outside ABB's Zaragoza factory.

Restructuring the Power Products and Power Systems divisions

In 1999 ABB restructured the way it approached its power customers. Under the new strategy, a single sales force, organized along country lines, would sell all the products and services offered by the Power Products and Power Systems divisions. Manufacturing facilities, which previously had their own sales forces, would now have a sales support (back-end sales) team to provide assistance to the new front-end sales force. (*Refer to* **Exhibit 2** *for the organizational structure before and after 1999.*)

The focused factory approach

Rather than each facility producing multiple product lines based on different technological platforms to serve one country, the focused factory specialized on one technological platform and supplied a whole region with the product range allowed by the selected platform. ABB saw several advantages to this approach due to the reduction in complexity of the technology and the processes:

- Higher asset utilization.
- Improved production load.
- More stable and predictable demand as a result of aggregating demand across several countries.
- Lower costs because of fewer 'poor quality' rejects due to specialization.

As a consequence, the existing and forecasted production could be met with fewer factories. By 2009, the focused factory strategy that started in 1999 had reduced ABB Transformer Products' total worldwide manufacturing facilities from 57 plants in 28 countries to 42 plants in 24 countries. Dry-type transformers were produced in only five factories situated in the US, Korea, Germany, China and Zaragoza in Spain.

Difficulties in implementation

The switch to focused factories was internal and relatively straightforward. Once the decision was made, the factories stopped taking new orders for products they were no longer going to produce. After the backlog was completed, lines were taken down and machinery shipped to each respective focused factory.

Switching to the new sales structure proved to be much more difficult. The existing relationships between factory-based sales forces and customers created huge inertia against the change. Switching a contact from one day to the next could alienate clients and put the relationship at risk. Additionally, each country had different levels of resources, both human and monetary, to carry out the required changes. The sales people in the new sales organization needed to learn how to sell multiple products. As a result, it was 2006 before countries like Germany and Italy were able to complete the transformation, while Spain was not completed until the beginning of 2008.

The Zaragoza plant

In February 1999, ABB Transformers' Zaragoza plant in Spain was designed to be the focused factory for dry-type transformers in Europe and challenged with providing positive results in the first year. The plant was to shut down two of its three product lines, dedicated to oil transformers, while increasing the capacity of the remaining line to be able to cope with the demand from the rest of the markets in the region. Zaragoza was also instructed to identify and outsource all non-core processes. For Antonio González, the general manager for the Zaragoza plant, the directive was clear. Since the front-end sales organization could, theoretically speaking, source transformers from any ABB focused factory, Zaragoza was competing with other ABB dry-type transformer plants in the world for internal resources. This put pressure on Zaragoza to become as efficient and fast as possible. As González stated:

> We needed to make our production process more efficient, from the design and engineering to the actual manufacturing of the transformers. We needed to shorten our lead times, so that products manufactured in Asia could not compete with us on delivery times, even if the need for customization of our products made this all the more difficult.

Need for customization

There was no such thing as a 'standard transformer' as there was no standard power grid. Each utility company in each region within a country had their own needs because they had different populations and, therefore, energy needs. Also, rules and regulations regarding the voltage for power lines at the generation, transport and distributions phases were different. The only thing that was standardized was the final voltage for non-industrial services, e.g. 110 volts in the USA and 220 in Europe. Additionally, each client could require specific physical characteristics for each transformer, such as casing or connector placement.

Process improvement in ABB's Zaragoza plant

By the end of 2004, Zaragoza had reduced its total TTPT (total throughput time) from order to shipping by 48%. Production total process time had been reduced by 71% and on-time delivery had increased from 70% in 1999 to 96% in 2004. To accomplish this, extensive outsourcing (almost all outsourcing partners were within 30 kilometers of the factory) was used and production volume had been increased by 245% since 1999.

The improvements had come as a result of the implementation of several projects. One of the most important projects was the scheduling of production to reduce both lead time and down time caused by lack of capacity and the delay of required components. The slowest process, (the bottleneck), determines the capacity of the whole factory. To minimize loss of production, inventory buffers and production schedules are set around such processes. However, the bottleneck can change from one process to another depending on changes to the product mix. Zaragoza was able to identify the changes in the product specifications that could cause the bottleneck to switch back and forth between two processes. As the backlog would normally include a variety of product specifications that could and would make the bottleneck switch, the Zaragoza team designed a software program – Diviner 3.0 – that optimized the production schedule and created buffer inventories in a dynamic way.

In addition, Zaragoza started programs to apply 5S methodology (a Japanese philosophy and way of organizing and managing the workspace and workflow with the intent of improving efficiency by eliminating waste, improving flow and reducing process unevenness). The 5Ss can be translated as: (1) sorting; (2) straightening; (3) sweeping or cleaning; (4) standardizing; and (5) sustaining the discipline. This, they hoped, would help them reach the quality and efficiency levels to compete internally with the dry-type transformers plant in Korea. According to Gonzalez, 'We were able to reduce bad quality rejects down to 2–4%, but once we reached that level, no matter how hard we tried, we could not reduce them any further.'

In 2003, González decided there was more to gain by cooperating with Korea rather than treating them like adversaries. He started an exchange program with them, whereby a team of engineers from one plant would spend a few months working in the other. Throughput time in Spain was better than in Korea, even if process by process both factories were about the same. However, poor quality rejects in Korea were only 0.5% to 1% compared to 2% to 4% in Zaragoza (down from 10% in 2000, when the focused factory approach was first implemented).

Interestingly enough, González, a black belt in Six Sigma, decided to forgo Six Sigma and simply adopt the Korean practices when it made sense. As González explained:

> We still have not been able to reach the quality levels of Korea, but we have learned from them. On one of the visits, we saw they were deep cleaning the high voltage winder and asked how often they did that. 'Daily', was their answer. At the time, we were doing it periodically, maybe every couple of months. Now we perform cleaning on the most critical parts on a daily basis and deep clean it every other week. This is, in effect, a further implementation of the 5S methodology.

Going for India

In 2009, the demand for dry-type transformers in the Indian market was being met by imports from ABB plants in other countries (*refer to* **Exhibit 3** *for the ABB Transformer Products share of the Indian market in 2008*). ABB served the Indian market through a Front End Sales (FES) organization with four regional offices, as it was deemed essential to be near the customer. The FES was composed of marketing engineers who were supported by two sales engineers specialized in dry transformers. The sales engineers could give product-specific presentations to customers as well as providing price and technical advice to the FES.

With a 10% growth rate in the past five years and an average of 100 days of delivery time (from order to delivery), Mehta needed to rethink how to better service the Indian market. It would take $15 million and two years to build a brand new dry-type transformer plant. Therefore, Mehta knew that the decision had to be taken in consideration of not only the cost, risk, time and growth projections, but also how the decision might fit into ABB's global footprint strategy, the future economic outlook and the competitive environment in India. For example, there were several strong local players with high market share and profitability. The prevailing market prices were relatively low and market growth was expected but not a given. How could ABB compete locally while still leveraging its global scale? What was the full range of options available? Mehta started to pencil down his options:[6]

1   Expand existing factories in China and Korea to serve the Indian market. The obvious advantage of this option was cost – it would require a much lower investment. The production scale and the existing supply chain could easily be leveraged. But, was this the best solution for developing the Indian market. There was internal resistance to buying ABB transformers made in China. Would ABB be able to persuade these internal customers to change their minds? Even if this was done, was this solution sustainable in the long run?

2   An ABB hub could be built in India to complete the final assembly of components supplied by ABB factories elsewhere. This factory hub could be an extension of the existing ABB plants, be it the Zaragoza, Korea or even

the China plant. The hub would piggyback not only on ABB's manufacturing facilities, but also on the expertise at these facilities. Transformer components comprised between 50% and 60% of the total cost of a transformer. The role of a hub would be to share the organizational capabilities while reducing the total administrative and other overhead costs.

3 Instead of an ABB hub, find a reputable third party in India to complete the final assembly for ABB. It would still leverage ABB's component manufacturing and further reduce the capital expenditure. In a market downturn, the risk would be transferred to the third party. The practical question was whether it was possible to find a partner who could live up to ABB standards and whether ABB customers would accept products made of ABB components but assembled by another non-ABB party.

4 Use local non-ABB components. This option would allow ABB to compete more effectively in the local market and capture the market segment ABB was unable to compete in due to its high prices. ABB would be the original equipment manufacturer and the local partner would be the contract manufacturer. Similar to Apple and Nike, ABB would be responsible for brand, design, distribution, sales and after-sales service, but manufacturing would be outsourced. The fundamental question for this choice was, 'What is ABB? A brand or a product? What is more important?'

5 Build an ABB factory in India. It was just done in Shanghai. It would be fully loaded in production, R&D, back-end sales and administration. The initial investment would be very high.

6 Acquire an existing player, with an established product line and customer base and turn it into a focused factory. What would ABB be buying? Market? Profits? Time? And what was most important among these and why?

Mehta wondered how these options should be evaluated. Of course, one had to consider both quantitative criteria, such as investment cost, time to market, risk, and qualitative criteria, such as serving the Indian market, growth strategy in India, non-quantifiable risk and the balance of ABB's global footprint.

Another dimension of the decision was the economic uncertainty in 2009, which was clouding the world (no one knew if the global economy had hit bottom or not or how long the recession would last). Would governments resort to protectionism as a response to the crisis? Also, low-cost competition was not going to go away, and given the economic situation, customers were increasingly becoming more cost conscious. Should ABB move increasingly towards the high value-added, high-end segment, or should it consider competing in the mass market? With the wind blowing towards protectionism, should ABB even continue down the focused factory path?

Mehta pondered what the right approach would be for ABB globally and, in particular, for the Indian situation. He wondered if a staged approach would be the best path for ABB to take. And, if so, where should he start and how would he determine when to move from one option to the next?

The function of a transformer is to transfer electricity from one circuit to another while reducing or amplifying the voltage from the incoming circuit to the outgoing circuit through a magnetic process of mutual induction.

ABB transformers could be divided by voltage or by technology type. High voltage transformers were used in power generation, medium voltage transformers were used in the transport of electricity and low voltage transformers were used for the distribution of energy. To better understand this, voltages coming out of a power plant could be as high as 12,000 volts, the typical voltage used in the transmission network is 400 kV and the voltage coming out of an outlet is 220 volts for Europe and 110 volts for most of the Americas. It was the job of the different transformers along the electricity grid, first to scale up the voltage to the required level for the transmission of the energy, with lower losses, and later on to scale down the voltage to the specification for each part of the grid.

In the process of transferring power, a transformer generates heat, which needs to be dispersed. The coil and core (the two main components of a transformer) in large transformers are immersed in transformer oil that both cools and isolates the transformer windings. Those are called the 'oil immersed transformers'. For applications where it is not possible to use transformer oil, there is a technology that provides the insulation by casting the coil in epoxy resin, instead of using oil.

Exhibit 1 Transformer technology and types

Dry-type transformers

Dry-type transformer technology was feasible only for voltages up to 53 kV; thus, they were used mainly for distribution or for low voltage power generation such as that created by wind turbines. Dry-type transformers suffered a cost disadvantage in comparison to wet transformers. Despite being on average 30% more expensive than a wet transformer of similar capacity, dry-type transformers were preferred for indoor use and for mission critical functions, due to the distinct advantages they offered:

- Lower maintenance costs.
- Improved reliability due to the absence of oil that can leak out.
- Impact replacement cost in hard to access housing: skyscrapers, windmills.
- Reduced risk in mission critical functions: nuclear power plants, hospitals.
- Reduced fire hazard.

Handling dilemmas in the supply chain   129

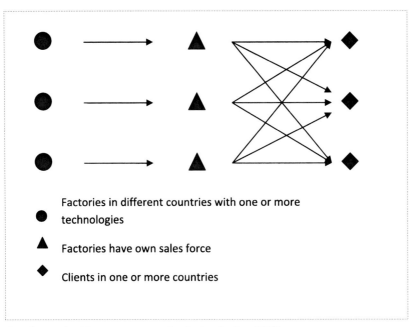

One factory builds one or more technologies (before 1999)

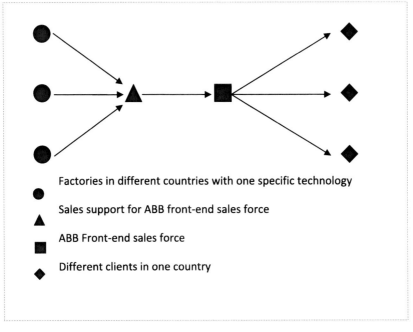

Focused factory (after 1999)

Exhibit 2   Sales structure before and after 1999

Transformer Type	Market Value (MUSD) 2008	ABB share (MUSD) 2008	Approximate number of competitors in India	Market share (%)
Large and Medium Power	495	120	16	24.4 %
Small Power	495	35	40	7.1 %
Distribution	422	18	3000	4.3 %
Dry-Type Transformers	77	4.5	15	5.8 %
TOTAL	**2110**	**177.5**		**12.0 %**

Exhibit 3 ABB transformer products share of Indian market in 2008

Case 3.5
Hewlett-Packard: Creating a virtual supply chain (A)

Petri Lehtivaara, Carlos Cordon, Ralf W. Seifert and Thomas E. Vollmann

'I want Hewlett-Packard to be able to produce and deliver a tape drive in five days, from supplied parts to customers.' The words that Derek Gray, supply chain manager in the tape drive unit of Hewlett-Packard, had uttered just hours earlier to a couple of external visitors echoed in his head.

It was early July 2001. Gray sat down in his cubicle in Hewlett-Packard's open-plan office in Bristol, United Kingdom. He was preparing for the next day's management meeting at which he had to present his recommendations for moving towards virtual manufacturing.

Gray had been managing a project – started some years ago – to create a virtual supply chain. He had gathered vast experience on the way and wanted to use this knowledge to recommend a good solution.

Gray had three alternative routes to choose from:

- Path of least resistance: Outsource the final assembly, testing and configuration to one of the suppliers of a major part (Philips).
- Create the ultimate supply chain: Develop a lowest total cost supply chain; invest in further redesign and resourcing to maximize long-term efficiency.
- Consolidation of the industry: Join forces with a competitor and outsource the final assembly, testing and configuration to it.

HP needed to take manufacturing to the next stage – standing still was not an option.

Hewlett-Packard Company

Hewlett-Packard Company (HP) was a global provider of computing and imaging solutions and services for business and home. In 2000 its sales were $48.8 billion and it employed 89,000 people. HP's three main segments were imaging and printing systems (41%), computing systems (42%) and IT services (14%); other business accounted for 3%.

CEO Carly Fiorina had reorganized HP to become more customer-oriented. The reorganization created a back-end, including product generation units, and a front-end devoted to sales and marketing, delivery channels and the client relationship. In addition, the focus changed from a functional one to a matrix.

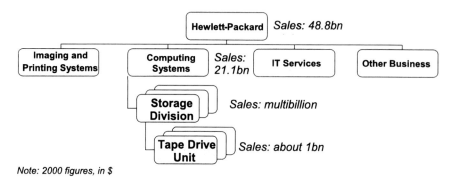

Note: 2000 figures, in $

Figure 1 Tape drive business unit

Tape drives in HP

The tape drive business unit employed 700 people, 550 of them based in Bristol. The headquarters of the unit was in the United States. (*Refer to* **Figure 1** *for the organizational position of tape drives in HP.*)

Products

HP's tape drive business unit had three main areas: digital data storage (DDS), Ultrium and Storage solutions. (*Refer to* **Exhibit 1** *for pictures of tape drives.*) In 2000 sales were just under $1 billion, with DDS generating most of this. Ultrium was the product of the future; it was based on an open standard – called linear tape open (LTO) – developed together with IBM and Seagate.

Tape drive business

The tape drive business was part of the storage market. The storage market in general was expanding due to customers' business transformation. Customers were: (1) taking advantage of opportunities on the internet; (2) increasing their demands and need for information; and (3) evolving IT to meet these unpredictable demands. Storage was potentially a large market – estimated at $46 billion in 2003.

Tapes were an economical way to store large volumes of digital data. Although the market had reached maturity and the time for major growth had passed, tapes still had their advantages compared with disks. As Gray explained, 'The tapes are regularly seven to ten times better than disks in cost/gigabyte stored. They will remain around for at least the next seven years.' The type of tape drives most often used had also started to change, and demand was increasingly for higher capacity, more complex equipment.

The performance and quality of the product were qualifying criteria in the business. The key success factors were time-to-market and cost of the product. The cost was especially important in sales to original equipment manufacturers (OEMs).

The life cycle of a product was typically four years. This meant that getting product to market as quickly as possible was critical for the company, to ensure highest possible sales volumes and margins. In the future merely having a good product would not be good enough; it would have to be part of a system.

The business in transition

Tape technology was in a transitional phase. New technology – LTO and super digital linear tape (SDLT) – had been introduced to upgrade from the traditional technologies of DDS and digital linear tape (DLT). Quantum was the major producer of DLT and was the overall market leader in the tape drive business, particularly the high-end segment. HP had kept its lead in the medium segment. DDS technology-based products were still a profitable product line. (*Refer to* **Figure 2** *for characteristics of tape drive products.*)

Characteristics	Traditional Technology		New Technology
	Medium segment	High-end segment	
Competing products	DDS, AIT	DLT, AIT, Mammoth, 34XX	Super digital linear tape (SDLT), linear tape open (LTO)
Volume (per annum)	1.75 million	400,000	Low
Price comparison	$1,000 (reference price*)	3x to 5x	7x to 10x
Main producers (and market share)	HP (50%–55%), Sony (30%), Seagate	Quantum (80%)	Quantum, IBM, HP, Seagate

Figure 2 Characteristics of tape drive products

One emerging trend in the industry was the link between sales of tape drives and media (tape). The media business was a large and growing one. Gray noted:

> There is less money in the tape drive business. The money is increasingly in media. The business is increasingly like selling razor blades. This is the strategy that many of our key competitors are using with their high-end tape drives.

HP's supply chain in the tape drive business

The supply chain consisted of four phases before final delivery to the customer. (*Refer to* **Figure 3** *for supply chain of DDS product family.*) HP sourced the main components from third parties because they had special technology and expertise that HP did not have in-house.

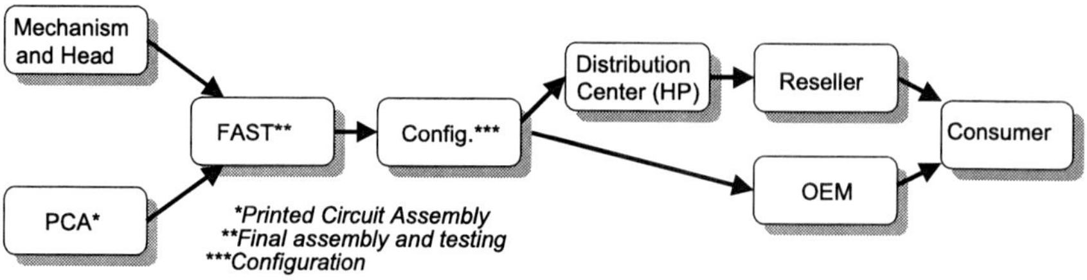

Figure 3 Supply chain for DDS products

Two channels to market

The tape drives were sold to the end consumer either through OEMs or resellers. In volume terms the OEM channel was larger; in sales terms the reseller channel was larger. The reseller channel was pretty profitable for HP, whereas the OEM channel was less so. Danny Berry, OEM supply chain manager, explained, 'OEMs are very demanding. On the other hand, if we deliver it is a good reference. In addition we have a lot of contact with the engineers.'

HP delivered the product to its resellers through three regional warehouses – Asia-Pacific, Europe and the US – which had varying degrees of performance. Gray expressed his views on the deliveries, '[In the reseller channel] we had significant problems with on-time delivery. I am not sure if we need distribution centers in our business. I think we should be able to deliver product directly from production to the reseller.'

The OEM channel received the products directly from the factory. This worked well and HP had even won awards from Sun Microsystems for being a good supplier.

Outsourcing of DDS products

In 1997 HP decided to start developing the LTO standard together with IBM and Seagate. This meant that the requirement for space and investment in the factory increased, but the manufacturing manager indicated there was no more space or investment for manufacturing. Outsourcing of manufacturing was the only option, even if many people had initially been against it.

Between 1997 and 2000 HP outsourced all its models in the DDS product family, one by one. The organization did not have an overall strategy. The solutions were tailored to each individual situation. (*Refer to* **Figure 4** *for evolution of the partners in the supply chain.*) HP always started the manufacturing in its own facilities in Bristol and transferred production to the contract manufacturer after the ramp-up had been done.

OEM customers had an ambivalent reaction to outsourcing. On the one hand, they did not want to go through a new approval process of a new supplier for the product. On the other hand, their attitude to outsourcing was: 'Just make sure that this is invisible to us in terms of quality, delivery performance and cost.'

Players in the Outsourced Supply Chain with Different Models of DDS					
Model	**Start**	**Mechanism and Head**	**PCA**	**FAST**	**Configuration**
DDS1	1990	Sony	CM A	HP Bristol	HP Bristol
DDS2	1997	Mitsumi	CM A	CM A (Scotland)	CM A (Ireland)
DDS3	1998	Mitsumi	CM B	CM A (Scotland)	CM A (Ireland)
DDS4	1999	Mitsumi	CM A	Mitsumi	CM C (Ireland)
Note: CM = Contract manufacturer					

Figure 4 Evolution of the partners in the supply chain

Outsourcing assembly and configuration

HP decided to outsource the final assembly and configuration of DDS2. It chose a contract manufacturer in Scotland to keep the risk of outsourcing low: the contract manufacturer was close to HP, the engineering people liked it and the price was competitive, although not the lowest.

Relatively soon after the deal, it became evident that the contract manufacturer could produce drives at a significantly lower cost than HP, largely because of overhead. Both companies put a lot of effort into managing the relationship. HP had three or four people constantly in Scotland and the companies had regular team meetings. The core team consisted of people from materials, finance, engineering and logistics areas in the two companies. There was also a communications matrix by which HP people talked to their counterparts at the manufacturer. Both companies seemed happy with the situation.

HP also outsourced production of the DDS3 model to the same contract manufacturer. The decision was based on capacity and cost. In this case, HP was concerned about the resourcing of the project. Davey Maclachlan, procurement manager, explained:

> We wanted the contract manufacturer to have a new product introduction team [for DDS3]. It had one team that needed to manage both DDS2 and DDS3. I think the margins were so small that they had to cut resources. We also noted that they were fire fighting. It felt like their departments were not talking to each other. They fixed one problem and the next came up as a consequence. The vendor management, inbound logistics and throughput suffered.

Divisional finance involvement

In 1998 HP's divisional finance function became involved. It had been investigating opportunities for taking advantage of regional benefits. The tape drive unit assessed whether this would work for them and decided on a location in Ireland. This meant that configuration should move there. Legal issues complicated the matter as HP had to have the management of the operation in Ireland, so communication from Bristol went to the factory via the Irish office.

The regional benefits were so significant that the organization was willing to complicate matters operationally. Calculations showed that the financial advantages would be equal to double the normal returns from supply chain savings and efficiencies.

Worsening relations with the contract manufacturer

The relationship with the contract manufacturer deteriorated. Maclachlan explained:

> I went to visit the CM with a colleague in a positive mood. We thought that we would propose some additional business to them. When we met the team we were surprised by their response. Their motivation had clearly diminished and all they could see were problems. We assumed that something had happened to cause their change of heart, potentially in their assessment of the real costs of doing the work. We also felt it necessary to alert them to our needs to consider lower cost geographies (within the same company) and this was not well received.

New outsourcing partner

For the DDS4 model, HP opted to work mainly with Mitsumi and another contract manufacturer. For the new contract manufacturer, which had to configure only one product, this arrangement was not ideal. Also the supply chain had become complex. Gray explained:

> We now had three major deals with different generations of DDS products. The relationships with the earlier contract manufacturers were becoming quite difficult due to the limited future. We had hoped to grow the business with the new CM but were having operational problems. The Mitsumi relationship was working very well, however the overhead to manage all of these various relationships was going through the roof. At this stage we also started to have quite heated debates between the functions (accountants, supply chain and engineering) about the relative benefits of each outsourcing decision.

Launch of the new technology: Ultrium

Work on developing Ultrium started in 1997. HP partnered with IBM and Seagate to develop the standard, which was in competition with the Quantum one. Production of Ultrium began in late 2000. The supply chain looked similar to that for DDS products, with three main components: mechanism, PCA and head (*refer to* **Figure 5**).

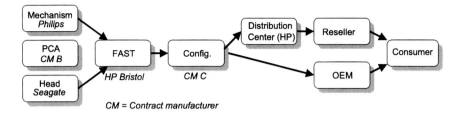

Figure 5 Supply chain for Ultrium

After six months' production of Ultrium, Gray decided to collect data to better understand the ramp-up period. He was amazed to see the level of inventory in the supply chain since production began. (*Refer to **Exhibit 2** for information on the supply chain.*)

The lead time across the supply chain was theoretically 90 days. Gray's ambition was to be able to deliver a tape drive to the customer in five days. He commented, 'It does not take more than a day to manufacture one, and four days are enough for logistics.'

Future alternatives

Gray had come to the conclusion that HP needed to move towards virtual manufacturing and not produce any part of Ultrium. He identified four key issues that should determine the choice of the future alternative:

1   Strategic alignment.
2   Total cost of ownership.
3   Partner choice.
4   Cost of production.

The first two were the most important criteria. Strategic alignment included both supply chain and overall strategy of the storage division and meant that HP's investment would be low with quick returns.

Many other companies in the industry had also moved towards outsourcing or virtual manufacturing. Outsourcing had seen the development of a new industry around contract manufacturers, the largest of which had global operations with high-level manufacturing and supply chain management skills. During 1999 and 2000 the deals had become larger, reaching multibillion levels in 2001.

HP had not been convinced of its contract manufacturers' capabilities in tape engineering. HP's experience was that its fixed cost was not reducing as much as expected, as it had to do the engineering itself. In the future HP wanted to move away from its original practice of ramping up the production in-house for six months and moving the production out after that. Now it wanted to change its manufacturing approach radically and get its partner involved from day one. To this end, it had outlined three main alternatives.

Alternative 1: Path of least resistance

HP would give the final assembly and testing, configuration and distribution to one of its suppliers, Philips. According to Gray this was an easy-to-do alternative. Philips had superb engineers, who understood the tape business. However, Philips was a bit like HP, with high overhead, and the outsourcing deal did not seem to fit with Philips' overall strategy.

The production would be done in Austria and Hungary with five or six HP people always on site. In this case Gray needed to persuade the accountants of the intangible benefits, since the apparent savings were lower. The key issue was: What would it take for Philips to take on this business and what would be left for HP?

Alternative 2: The ultimate supply chain

This would involve designing the supply chain in the right way, from scratch. HP had talked with Mitsumi, which would ultimately have capabilities to manufacture both the head and mechanism and would also take care of final assembly and testing, configuration and – potentially – distribution. Mitsumi would emerge as a major tape drive manufacturer.

Gray assumed the investment would be high, but that the return would also be high. Ultimately this alternative would provide low cost and flexibility. At the moment Mitsumi did not have enough buying power and capabilities to produce the mechanism. HP would need to assist it with technology development for Ultrium. In the past, HP had had positive experiences working with Mitsumi. However, this time HP would need to assist Mitsumi with technology development and was unsure about the implications of moving in this direction.

Alternative 3: Consolidation

The third alternative included collaborating with a competitor. This approach would assume consolidation was necessary in the industry and would concentrate on supply chain efficiency rather than competition. This would be especially true as both companies would be competing against Quantum's standard. The main question would be: Should you help a competitor to survive? The relationship would be complex and troublesome.

Decision looming

Gray also wondered to what extent similar options had come up in other industries. The alternatives were lined up and it was up to him to recommend one. The decision could be a crucial one for the future of the tape drive unit. Gray wanted to achieve efficiency in the supply chain, low cost of products and manageable relationships with HP's future partners. But Gray also acknowledged the fact of the HP culture, 'HP is big on consensus. Any one person can kill the proposal.'

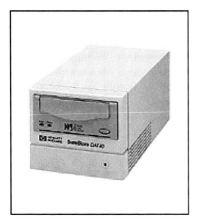

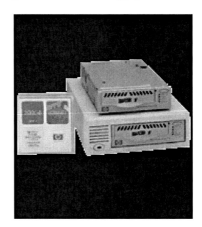

Model DDS4 tape drive   *Ultrium 215 tape drive*

Source: Company information

Exhibit 1   Examples of Hewlett-Packard's tape drives

Month (end)	Supplier to PCA	Head	PCA	Mechanism	FAST	Config.	Sales
Aug 2000	33	9	18	20	4	4	0
Sep 2000	62	26	32	46	13	13	1
Oct 2000	129	34	43	46	21	17	1
Nov 2000	150	70	71	74	42	35	9
Dec 2000	204	100	127	120	73	51	14
Jan 2001	270	136	204	155	96	66	21
Feb 2001	367	185	266	208	130	101	38
Mar 2001	636	237	320	264	174	116	62
Apr 2001	733	294	418	332	220	161	78
May 2001	1,021	343	448	367	265	192	100

Note: The volume information is proportional, with sales in May 2001 being 100 and other volumes proportional to that.

Source: Company information

Exhibit 2   Cumulative volume of parts in the supply chain and sales of Ultrium

This case series won the Supply Chain Management Award in the 2003 European Case Writing Competition organized by the European Foundation for Management Development (efmd).

Case 3.6
Hewlett-Packard: Creating a virtual supply chain (B)

Petri Lehtivaara, Carlos Cordon and Ralf W. Seifert

Another 12 months had passed. Derek Gray took a deep breath and sat back and reflected on the developments that had taken place in this time.

> We took a long time to decide, but now we are ready to move forward. A lot of people were involved in the decision and we also lived through some internal organizational changes. The pending merger with Compaq further complicated the process on our side, but frankly there were also a number of surprises on the part of our potential partners.

Gray was relaxed as the roller-coaster experience of reaching the outsourcing decision was behind him and he could look forward to his new challenge of ramping up production at the supplier. It was July 2002. Gray had just moved to Vienna, Austria. This was not the original intention, but Gray explained:

> In autumn 2001 we decided on a variation of the Mitsumi option. We believed that it was worth winning the battle for the tape drive business and thus wanted to create the ultimate supply chain, removing as many nodes as possible to improve efficiency. The idea with the Mitsumi option was to move our mechanism production, including equipment, technology and tools, from Philips to Mitsumi.

> We discussed our decision with the Philips executive and reached agreement on the matter. Somewhat unexpectedly, however, his team resisted the transfer and [through organizational play] effectively made it impossible for us to proceed.

More time passed and Gray needed to take a fresh look at the Philips option. Philips came back with the alternative suggestion of using Flextronics as a contract manufacturer. Flextronics had an assembly plant in Hungary, a few hours away from Vienna, where the Philips division was based. Gray noted:

> We got quite excited about this option, as it would provide the lower manufacturing cost but with the engineering expertise of Philips. It felt like Christmas to us, it could be a win–win–win situation. The Philips and Flextronics executives were long-time friends and this helped to establish the relationship. We felt that in the circumstances, this would be a deal worth going for. By then we had finally said no to the Mitsumi option, and

our negotiations with Seagate had slowly gone cold. Shortly afterwards, we learned about a management change at Philips. The new executive also subscribed to Philips' strategy, but interpreted it slightly differently: It was no longer desirable for Philips to divest the mechanism manufacturing business to Flextronics as was previously proposed. At that point we had gone through all the options and in view of the significant loss of time decided simply to go ahead with Flextronics anyway. The Flextronics option provided ample opportunity for supply chain integration and was geographically close to Philips. It also provided low cost manufacturing capability in its Hungarian facility.

Gray's learning points from the outsourcing decisions

While reflecting on the ups and downs with the outsourcing, Gray was able to identify four dimensions of learning for himself.

- **'People buy from people'** Individuals make a difference and can alter decisions. A change of individuals will have a huge impact on potential deals.
- **'You get the vendor you deserve'** Vendor management and vendor development are extremely important. A partner who is constantly driven on cost is likely to cut resources to the point of poor performance. The vendor's performance often reflects the poorly developed vendor management practices of the customer, and indeed the other customers that the vendor works with.
- **'We need more accountants and lawyers than engineers'** Regional benefits are extremely significant and can distort people's thinking. The supply chain should still be the primary driver of decisions but there is a great deal of opportunity to be taken through these regional benefits.
- **'Like herding cats'** Large companies have difficulty organizing themselves. Bureaucracy and unclear accountability render decision making difficult. This applies to many multinationals and can be frustrating when two multinational companies try to work together.

Gray described the central learning:

Any team halfway capable but focused could make any of the options work, as long as they want to make things happen and have shared values with the supplier. One should not underestimate the value of the right team and the right skills in making almost any option work.

New challenges

Gray and two other people from HP's Bristol plant moved to Vienna to oversee the transition of manufacturing operations to Flextronics. Gray's challenge was to quickly transfer the manufacturing knowledge to the contract manufacturers. This time he wanted to follow a different approach and work towards a true partnership. With this in mind, Gray had to decide on two issues.

What would be the best approach for knowledge transfer from the HP team to Flextronics?

How should he define success for himself?

This case series won the Supply Chain Management Award in the 2003 European Case Writing Competition organized by the European Foundation for Management Development (efmd).

Chapter notes

1   Childerhouse, P., J. Aitken, and D. Towill. 'Analysis and Design of Focussed Demand Chains.' *Journal of Operations Management*, Vol. 20, Iss. 6, 2002: 675–689.
2   Skinner, W. 'The Focused Factory.' *Harvard Business Review*, Vol. 52, Iss. 3, 1974: 113–121.
3   Fifarek, B.J., F.M. Veloso, and C.I. Davidson. 'Offshoring Technology Innovation: A Case Study of Rare-Earth Technology.' *Journal of Operations Management*, Vol. 26, Iss. 2, 2008: 222–238.
4   Lee, H.L., V. Padmanabhan, and S. Whang. 'Information Distortion in a Supply Chain: The Bullwhip Effect.' *Management Science*, Vol. 50, 2004: 1875–1886.
5   Holmström, J. 'Implementing Vendor-Managed Inventory the Efficient Way: A Case Study of Partnership in the Supply Chain.' *Production & Inventory Management Journal*, Vol. 39, No. 3, 1998: 1–5.
6   For all options, imports would be subject to a 7.5% import tax and 7.5% inland freight, while all locally sourced production inputs (raw material or components) would be subject to 12.2% excise duties and sales tax.

4   Making the supply chain work

While the previous chapters have described a rational view of the supply chain, making the supply chain work is mainly a leadership challenge. It is a particularly difficult one because it requires leading across different companies, and often the people involved tend to be technical and have a somewhat mechanistic view of management. This makes leading the supply chain particularly demanding.

The fundamental learning of Derek Gray – the executive responsible for the supply chain mentioned in the Hewlett-Packard case in Chapter 3 – sums it up neatly, 'Any team halfway capable but focused could make any of the options work, as long as they want to make things happen and have shared values with the supplier.' For Gray, focus, willingness and shared values are more important than capabilities in making the supply chain work.

In this chapter we first review some of the fundamentals of supply management, and then go on to discuss the challenges of managing relations with external partners in the supply chain. Next, we review the difficulties associated with sharing risk and reward with partners, and end with a discussion on the tremendous impact these issues have on the development of new approaches to project management with partners.

Supply chain fundamentals

Previous chapters described the bullwhip effect and the flexibility–efficiency matrix. An additional basic framework worth reviewing is the classification of suppliers using the Kraljic matrix and its variants.

The Kraljic model, as depicted in Figure 4.1, classifies the products or components a company buys according to their profit impact and their supply risk and criticality. Products with low criticality and low profit impact are classified as routine and should be purchased on a transactional basis without spending too much effort on their acquisition. A typical example is buying paper for a photocopier. It does not represent a lot of money for most companies and is not critical, so purchasing it should not consume many resources.

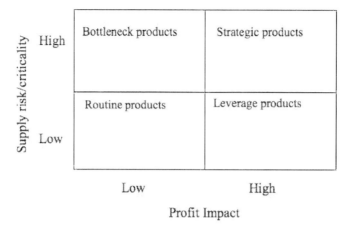

Figure 4.1 The Kraljic portfolio purchasing model

Source: Adapted from Kraljic, P. 'Purchasing Must Become Supply Management.' *Harvard Business Review*, September/October 1983: 109–117.

Products with a high profit impact and low supply risk should be bought at competitive prices. Until recently, commodities were in this quadrant, and large companies tried to leverage their size to obtain the best possible prices. Standard examples here are steel plates and aluminium profiles, which often represent a large share of the end product's cost price, but can be obtained from various suppliers at pre-specified quality grades.

If the profit impact is low but the criticality is high, securing the sourcing of these so-called bottleneck products is important to avoid problems in the supply chain. In the food industry, for example, this is particularly important when sourcing some specific natural flavorings and vitamins.

Products or components with high criticality and a high impact on the profit margin are considered strategic, and their acquisition should be managed accordingly, for example by seeking long-term contracts and close relations with suppliers. A typical example is engine and gearbox suppliers for automobile manufacturers.

There are many variations of this matrix, which mainly involve substituting the profit impact with volume or money spent, and replacing criticality with the complexity of the supplier market or ease of substitution. A significant variant of the matrix would be to apply it to suppliers rather than products, for example the matrix could be used to recommend what type of relations to have with suppliers: (1) transactional relations with suppliers in the routine box; (2) a power-driven relationship with suppliers in the leverage quadrant; (3) a reliable association with those in the bottleneck box; and (4) a partnership with strategic suppliers.

Managing relations across companies

In the last few years there has been a tremendous evolution in the way relations between customers and suppliers are managed. It has been triggered by a simple observation: The best-performing companies enjoy close, collaborative relationships with key customers and key suppliers, or what managers at Honda refer to as 'super suppliers'. We have developed a shorthand term to describe the impact of these deep relationships – we call it the Power of Two.

The Power of Two arises when the customer and the supplier, each recognizing their mutual need, jointly overhaul the way they do business together, and thereby create greater value. As the name implies, we believe it is a powerful way for companies to gain competitive advantage by:

- Eliminating unnecessary work.
- Reducing the costs borne by each side, and achieving considerable cost breakthroughs.
- Increasing market share.
- Attaining significant top-line growth.
- Creating competencies that cannot be copied.

Implementing the plan requires changes to be made in the company, as well as in the companies of the key customers and suppliers, but the payoffs are significant and achievable.

To develop the Power of Two, companies must become attractive customers because they are competing with others for the resources of key suppliers. The question is: What makes a customer more attractive? How can a company convince the smartest supplier to work with them? Ten golden rules for becoming an attractive customer are presented in Table 4.1.

Attraction is understood to be the force that brings a buyer and a supplier closer together in a relationship (see Figure 4.2). To ensure a company is perceived as an attractive partner, it is useful to understand the mechanisms and factors that construct such perceptions.[1]

Attraction between firms is a complex concept consisting of three mutually interacting components: (1) the perceived expected value that the attracted party will achieve from being associated with the other company; (2) the perceived trust in the other company; and (3) the perceived dependence on the other company.

To understand how these three components interact to bring buyers and suppliers together in a dyadic relationship, let us look at a couple of illustrative examples.

Consider a situation where a buyer has almost no supplier alternatives, or where the cost of switching is prohibitive. The buyer will see itself as being highly dependent on that supplier. As long as the buyer's perceived trust is high, the perceived dependence presents no problem to the buyer and the buyer will probably stay in the exchange relationship, expanding the value exchanged over time and therefore enhancing the mutual attraction. However, if the trust is low, the buyer will consider its perceived high dependence on the supplier in question as risky and seek an alternative means of supply.

Table 4.1 Ten golden rules for becoming an attractive customer

	The ten rules	*Details*
1	Be a demanding customer	Challenge your suppliers, but don't crush them. If hard-hitting negotiation is the only tool in your bag, you have problems. Attraction does pay off, but you need to check options with key suppliers: Do they see you as only pushing prices?
2	Determine which suppliers are important	Attraction is not to be spread around like so much peanut butter. Identify which partnerships will pay off in the long term, and invest in them.
3	Recognize explicitly that attraction is double-edged	You will need to work hard to be seen as your key suppliers' most attractive customer. This also implies joint improvement efforts, not unilateral demands for the supplier to make them.
4	Increase the supplier's comfort level	Make sure that the supplier's managers know their ideas are welcomed, acknowledged and implemented. Make it easy for them to provide suggestions. Be fair and scrupulously honor contractual obligations.
5	Help the supplier properly evaluate its expected payoffs	A typical negotiation technique is to hide information. In fact, keeping information from key suppliers leads to poor evaluation and diminished attraction – of both customer and supplier.
6	Manage the misalignment	It is virtually impossible to align the objectives of purchasing, manufacturing, R&D, finance and other functions, so it is even more critical to understand and manage misalignment between the partners.
7	Manage the perceptions	Understand that perceptions are what matter, and that they are often unrelated to reality. Proactively manage the 'stories' and 'feelings' about a supplier.
8	Understand and manage how the supplier allocates resources	Develop a reputation for being the customer most open to new ideas by accepting as many as possible and implementing them. Develop metrics that support implementing suppliers' ideas, and reward those in your company who do so.
9	Help your suppliers leverage the learning	If you not only allow but also deeply encourage your suppliers to use the learning with their other customers, you will increase attraction and be the place where new learning is focused.
10	Sell the opportunities in your company to the supplier	Understand which other customers and initiatives are in the supplier's priority list. You want to be at the top of it.

Source: Cordon, C. and T.E. Vollmann. *The Power of Two: How Smart Companies Create Win–Win Customer–Supplier Partnerships that Outperform the Competition*. Houndmills: Palgrave Macmillan, 2008.

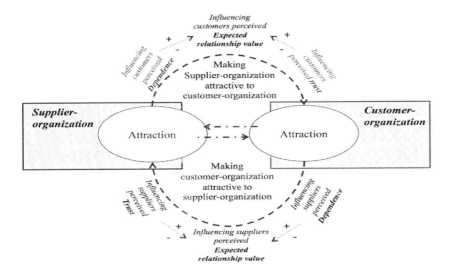

Figure 4.2 Attraction: A force pushing buyers and suppliers closer together

Let us now consider a buyer–supplier dyad from a supplier's perspective. The supplier is known for its innovation capacity and many potential buyers consider it as highly attractive. However, since it can only commit its full innovative capacity to one or a few buyers, which one(s) should it select? One buyer is known as a dominant actor and regularly demands unilateral cost reductions from its suppliers. Another buyer is perceived as a trustworthy actor willing to invest equally with its key suppliers. The choice is obvious, since dependence and benefits are balanced.

These two brief examples illustrate the connection between the three attraction components. Although the perceived expected value is high, the magnitude of both trust and dependence has a major influence on the buyer's perceived attraction. Just as a buyer can see a supplier as attractive and valuable, the buyer's behavior influences the supplier's perceptions of expected value, trust and dependence, which in turn strongly influence whether the supplier will perceive the buyer as attractive. These examples show that perceptions are what count, even though they are difficult to quantify.

Challenging customer demands and reducing supply chain complexities

For many companies the continuous focus on fulfilling customers' wishes and demands leads to a high level of complexity. Firms have to supply a growing mix of products, with features increasingly tailored to customers' individual needs. The relentless effort to satisfy customers has magnified the complexity of the supply chain and led to greater product variety, smaller production lot sizes, more tiers in the supply chain and an increased need to coordinate between the different actors in the supply chain.

Focusing on identifying and eliminating supply chain complexity is often a radical shift in the definition of what supply chain management is. It assumes that the context under which the supply chain operates is malleable. Instead of just blindly executing requests, firms are constructively challenging customers' demands and trying to influence them in order to reduce the complexity of the supply chain. This means cutting back on the different varieties that exist in all the layers of a supply chain system by questioning the need to increase variety and impose stricter deadlines. For example:

- Is the new product or feature absolutely necessary? Does it add enough value for our customers to offset the increased cost of managing the additional supply chain complexity that ensues?
- Is it a real customer demand or is it based on our assumptions?
- Have we been challenging our customers' needs, outlining the real cost/price consequences of their demands?

Sharing risks and rewards with customers and suppliers

Many companies are asking their suppliers to share business risks. In some extreme cases, companies try to pass all of the risk on to the supplier, for example by asking them to invest in production facilities to manufacture specific components. This is quite usual in the car industry where suppliers invest in equipment and tooling that are specific to a certain car model. In the past, the supplier would ask the customer (i.e. the car company) to pay for the tools, which would remain the property of the car company. Today, it is usual for suppliers to invest in tools, even without any guarantees from the car company regarding future purchases of components. The logic is that the market will dictate the amount of products and components that need to be made. In this way, the supplier shares the risk with the car manufacturer in terms of the success of the car on the market. If the car is a success, the supplier will sell more components and, it is hoped, benefit from higher profits.

These developments have reached the extreme situation in which some companies believe they have passed on all the risk to the supplier. However, the reality today is that companies with well-known brands receive extensive media attention and, as a result, they remain vulnerable to the consequences of potential risks. Both the BP case and the Apple case already mentioned in Chapters 1 and 2 of this book are good examples. Thus, the repercussions are much greater for big brand companies, and although risks may be shared with suppliers, in most cases they cannot be entirely transferred to them.

Rewards, by contrast, tend not to be shared with suppliers, who may then be unwilling to take on risks. This type of situation led to a tightening in the supply of some raw materials and components, such as aluminium and memory components for the electronics industry in 2010 and 2011. Although demand for components and raw materials may remain high, many suppliers are not willing to increase capacity because they have no guidance from customers regarding future demand. Also, because customers are reluctant to accept price increases, capacity investments are not considered profitable enough in light of the existing risks.

Fast-track project management with suppliers

Project management is undergoing a fundamental change due to new ways of relating to suppliers and a better understanding of risk. This section reviews these developments and demonstrates how a superior technique for managing the supply chain has allowed some companies to complete projects considerably more quickly.

Most projects involve an implicit trade-off between time, cost and specifications. In the classic engineering-driven project, specifications tend to drive everything else, often resulting in over-designed products that cost too much and appear in the marketplace too late. Current thinking, though, teaches that time is the crucial factor in any of these trade-offs. Delays nearly always mean higher costs, and in many companies costs are now allowed to escalate in the earlier stages, as long as the timing of the overall project is not jeopardized.

Figure 4.3 could represent the traditional paradigm, where project managers have a set of functional specifications that they meet by developing the project in a cost effective way. Some managers would argue that they face a trade-off between development time and the final cost of the project. On the one hand, by increasing time (and probably development costs) it might be possible to reduce the final cost through better development. On the other hand, it might be possible to reduce development time, but the cost could be higher. Where time is a fixed constraint, the trade-off would be between the functional specification and the final cost of the project.

The main argument for designating time as the main driver of the project is that the value of being earlier is often much higher than any additional cost that might be incurred. Additionally, overall development costs tend to be lower because there is less time to spend resources and less opportunity for changes to occur in the market, or for other events to happen due to the short time span.

The concept of the time being fixed, and having the ability to change specifications as the project progresses, requires a high level of trust and risk sharing with suppliers. Changing specifications in the middle of the project means that the contract between the customer and the supplier cannot be entirely defined in detail, so it is necessary to have an understanding among all parties involved in the project that they share the goal of finishing on time and that they are willing

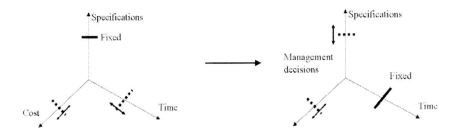

Figure 4.3 From specification-driven to time-driven project management

to be flexible in terms of their role and the work to be done. It also requires the awareness and commitment of each party that they will act for the benefit of the project and not opportunistically.

This implies close cooperation with the customer and the suppliers involved in the project, a high level of trust since the specifications change, and everybody must accept a higher level of uncertainty. Under these conditions, the projects can be more profitable by being completed much faster for the final customers and, logically, the rewards must be shared with the suppliers.

Cases in this chapter

4.1 Novo Nordisk Engineering: Running for fast-track project execution

Novo Nordisk Engineering (NNE) offers a good example of fast-track project management. The firm fundamentally rethought its business and succeeded in reducing the time required to deliver a pharmaceutical factory from over three years to 11 months.

When the new CEO first announced the objective of building a plant in less than 12 months within the next five years, few people in the company believed it was achievable. Indeed, some even publicly questioned the target and the CEO's qualifications.

To reach its objective, the company continually re-evaluated its processes over the next five years, gradually reducing the time needed to build a factory. The key factors for success were:

- Changing the way customers bought facilities, away from the lowest bid approach.
- Changing the project focus from specification-driven to time-driven.
- Creating trust with the customer to leave part of the contract open and share risks.
- Investing in team building and a company culture focused on project execution.
- Including customers and suppliers in the implementation team.
- Adopting a modular design approach, copying modules from previous projects.

The implementation of the last project, which was completed in 11 months, provided many anecdotes about the key factors, such as a team-building exercise that required walking 25 km in the snow, using suggestions from craftsmen to increase the speed of decision making, backward planning and simultaneous execution.

4.2 Building partnerships: Reinventing Oracle's go-to-market strategy

The case charts the strategic shifts in Oracle Corporation's go-to-market strategy through several significant changes in the external environment. Oracle is the second biggest software company in the world, and what makes its channel strategy compelling is that it collaborates with thousands of partners in going to market. Partners vary in size and play different roles. Importantly, several of Oracle's principal partners are also its fiercest competitors.

Larry Ellison, founder and CEO of Oracle, nurtured a culture that encouraged winning at any cost, creating an aggressive, arrogant sales force that closed deals for top-end enterprise solutions worth hundreds of thousands or even millions of dollars each. This strategy had resulted in Oracle's domination of the database software market.

Having saturated the large businesses market, in order to continue gaining market share, Oracle decided to broaden its focus to serve the hundreds of thousands of small and medium-sized enterprises globally, while maintaining its hold on its traditional Fortune 500 customers. To reach these new customers and respond to changing industry dynamics, Oracle had to rethink its go-to-market strategy – and this increasingly emphasized partnerships and marketing efforts. The company's next stage of growth would have to be fueled by its strategy to develop and nurture tens of thousands of partnerships worldwide.

4.3 and 4.4 LEGO: Consolidating distribution (A and B)

In October 2008, LEGO won the prestigious European Supply Chain Excellence Award in the 'Logistics and Fulfilment' category. The award recognized the supply chain changes that had been accomplished and which were seen as one of the key enablers of LEGO's astonishing turnaround. Yet, the company's restructuring and the realignment of its supply chain capabilities did not have an auspicious starting point: LEGO had lost money for four out of seven years from 1998 to 2004, and with only 62% of orders being delivered on time, its logistics capability had been shattered. The two LEGO cases presented here highlight both the organizational and the operational issues that arose while the company was reviving its distribution system and turning its supply chain operations into a distinct competitive advantage.

The LEGO (A) case follows the well-known Danish toy manufacturer through its dramatic restructuring effort. LEGO's turnaround strategy of 'going back to the core, back to the basics', meant that supply chain executives had to proactively question every aspect of the company's operations – including re-examining real vs. perceived customer service requirements. Cutting back significantly on the number of SKUs and moving from daily to weekly deliveries were among the critical changes that propelled the vision of a fully consolidated distribution set-up that would simultaneously lower costs and dramatically improve delivery performance.

The LEGO (B) case considers the challenges of the relationship with the logistics supplier. It describes how a 'closed-door meeting' became the turning point for stepping away from the established 'blame game' and creating instead a 'four musketeers' commitment among the top management of both companies to advance the transformation project.

4.5 Freqon: Buyer–supplier evolution?

This case focuses on the need for a winning competitor to proactively bring together the best set of suppliers, which can only be achieved if the suppliers view this customer as one of their most attractive.

The case follows Freqon's relationship with its supplier NordAlu over a period of 13 years. During this time the relationship had its ups and downs. Studying this supply chain evolution helps to understand the impact of various actions and subsequent developments. Both customer and supplier share the responsibility of continually transforming the supply chain without parochial distinctions as to who must do what.

The case begins in 1987 when Freqon started to develop the relationship with its supplier, and the fundamental focus was on new product development. It shows how early successes were not sufficiently followed up with improvement efforts later on. Finally, by 2000 the relationship had reached a situation of limited joint interest and tension between the two companies.

4.6 and 4.7 Unaxis: Going Asia (A and B)

These two cases explain the dilemma faced by Unaxis Data Storage, a branch of Unaxis, a large European high-tech company. The data storage division was the only one that did not yet have a manufacturing footprint in Asia, and top management was pushing for such an implementation. A bold move such as this seemed worthwhile in view of the expected benefits: faster customer response, more flexibility and lower costs.

Before reaping the benefits of outsourcing, the company faced several major issues. First, no one in the division had any experience of outsourcing in low cost countries. Second, no company had ever moved such a complex production system to Asia.

Localizing the right partner proved difficult. Most Chinese factories lacked the necessary capabilities but fast technical development was feasible. Unaxis eventually decided to source from factories based in mainland China but owned by companies in Taiwan, Singapore or Hong Kong. Still, management was not confident and feared a potential loss of intellectual property. Local patent protections were not considered trustworthy, and counterfeiters were known for moving pretty fast. Furthermore, Unaxis could not afford to risk having quality issues as this would have a negative impact on its currently excellent reputation.

In order to retain control of its supply chain and avoid such issues, management chose to conserve two separate supply chains. This offered several benefits: (1) reduced risk from balancing production over two lines; (2) two supply chains competing against each other for maximum efficiency; and (3) lower costs and proximity to customers, making it possible to meet their demands in the most appropriate way.

Case 4.1
Novo Nordisk Engineering: Running for fast-track project execution

François Jäger, Carlos Cordon and Ralf Seifert

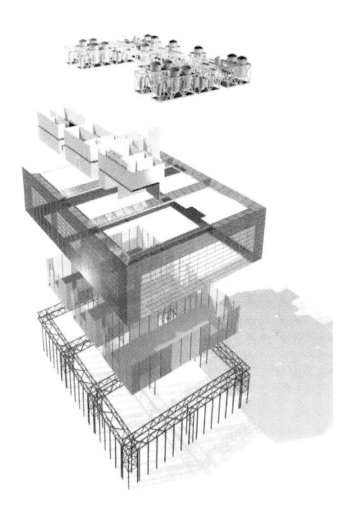

Novo Nordisk Engineering (NNE) had achieved the impossible! In July 2005 it finished building a new vaccine production facility in the record-breaking time of 11 months.

Six years earlier, in 1999, Hans Ole Voigt had taken over as CEO of NNE, a Danish company primarily involved in the construction of turnkey pharmaceutical facilities. Not an engineer himself, he was surprised to learn that it took 30 to 36 months to build a facility.

With the objective of differentiating NNE, Voigt got his management team together and introduced the idea of fast-track project execution. He set a challenging objective, 'Within five years we will have to be able to build a plant in less than 12 months!'

The meeting room went silent. Those present thought it was not an achievable target. Considering themselves to be the engineering specialists, the employees were quite reluctant to be challenged by this 'outsider'.

Voigt needed to motivate NNE's employees and maintain their focus to achieve this goal without sacrificing quality. They would have to fundamentally reengineer many company processes.

Background

In 1991 Novo Nordisk A/S, a leading pharmaceutical company, spun off its engineering arm as NNE. The new company had considerable expertise in engineering projects for the pharmaceutical industry. For nearly ten years, it executed projects solely for customers in the Novo Nordisk 'galaxy'. By 1999, NNE had close to 1,000 employees and was active in Denmark, China, France, Sweden and the USA.

Setting the challenge

When he joined the company, Voigt realized that its only customer was increasingly focusing on reducing the cost of engineering. Novo Nordisk would probably seek alternative suppliers for 'commoditized' services. NNE's value proposition as a high-value-added pharma engineering specialist was not sustainable.

Also, relying on a single customer was risky. Yet, unlike other construction companies, NNE came from the highly regulated pharmaceutical industry. Few competitors in the world understood that industry as well as NNE.

Voigt looked for ways to appeal to other customers and set a challenge for the whole organization. He called it the Big Overarching Goal: To be able to build a complete plant in less than a year by 2005. Voigt explained, 'I wanted a vision to differentiate NNE and allow it to create a profile of its own.'

The challenge was received with a great deal of scepticism. Coming from Novo Nordisk, where he was vice president of business support, Voigt had a good understanding of the pharmaceutical industry, but he was not an engineer. Some employees were willing to try, but the majority thought differently. As Klaus Illum, NNE's engineering director, recalled, the saying was, 'This guy is totally crazy! We are the experts, come on!'

At the time, one year seemed like an impossible goal, since plant construction took 30 to 36 months on average. As Voigt put it, 'I was certain we could reduce the time – I wasn't sure about the one year goal!'

Finding a customer to work with

Speed to market was decisive in the pharmaceutical industry. Patents protected drugs for 20 years. Yet, taking into account discovery, development and clinical trial time, the period of market exclusivity could go down to less than one year in some cases (*refer to* **Exhibit 1**).

On the plus side, a blockbuster drug – one with a turnover of more than US$1 billion per year – could make $1 million profit per day. Not all drugs required the construction of a new plant, but when necessary, gaining two years because of shorter construction time offered significant financial returns. Nevertheless, realizing such short construction time meant to overcome longstanding industry norms.

Building a pharmaceutical plant involved many long and interlocked processes that required extensive construction planning. In the US, the Food and Drug Administration (FDA) requirements were stringent and had to be closely followed. Just focusing on NNE's internal processes and organization would not be enough. The involvement of both suppliers and the client would also be necessary. Carsten Bech, VP of project management, explained: 'You can only optimize if clients and suppliers are involved. You need to have a common goal. You need to change processes also on their side, not just within NNE.'

NNE had to find a company willing to invest in a fast-track project. There were substantial risks, since both NNE and its client would be moving into unknown territory. Most pharmaceutical companies had a lowest bidder approach to supplier selection. They were reluctant to engage in fast-track projects, assuming that speed would automatically increase costs. As John Frandsen, VP of sales, noted: 'With a lowest bidder approach, we cannot help a customer build a factory in 12 months.'

There was significant risk. Although the project could go very well, it could also go really badly, which would mean costs up by 20% to 40% or delays in project delivery. NNE could not afford to bear all the risk, the client would have to share it. Frandsen explained: 'We are working against a [cost-cutting] culture. We need to challenge the purchasing behavior of our clients. Their purchasing managers need to learn about risk management.'

The first step

In 1999 Novo Nordisk needed more insulin production capacity fast in order to supply growing market demand. Because of their long relationship, Novo Nordisk agreed to partner with NNE for the first fast-track project. Construction began in Denmark in June 2000.

A modular approach

Modular technology was used to simplify and speed up the project. By breaking a plant down into modules constructed in parallel and tested at the supplier's premises, NNE could be more efficient and get around some of the time- and space-related constraints arising at a construction site.

Modular design also helped measure the project's progress – when a module was installed and tested, a milestone was reached. All members of the team could visualize it. It was a fact. There was no target in terms of time reduction. As Bech explained: 'We tried to push the project managers and see what we could obtain.'

Ensuring consistency and quality

To be consistent in all its projects, NNE had set up a project activity model (PAM) and a quality management system (QMS). PAM was based on three domains – project management, engineering disciplines and procurement (contract management) – and included documents and activities that were relevant for engineering purposes (*refer to **Figure 1***).

PAM described NNE's critical business processes associated with engineering activities. It provided all members and interested parties with a clear picture of each project and detailed guidance for its execution.

By combining PAM and modular design, engineers could reuse previous knowledge and thus reduce engineering time and cost. As Voigt put it: 'Engineers have a tendency to engineer, to make inventions! Most of the time you can take 80% of a plant that has been made before.'

Figure 1 Project activity model

Source: NNE

Although speed was crucial, it was not to be achieved at the expense of quality. Every single project that NNE worked on had a quality activity plan, describing the quality goals agreed with the client, as well as the methods by which to achieve the goals. This allowed things to be standardized where possible, while still allowing flexibility.

NNE successfully completed the facility – the world's largest bulk insulin plant – in 24 months. People in the company started to change their mindset. Management was excited to see such a change.

The second step: Learn and accelerate

While it was still engaged in the first fast-track project, NNE started a second one with Novo Nordisk: the Novo Seven facility. Resource conflicts emerged, and managers had to negotiate to find mutually acceptable solutions. Voigt explained: 'Managing resource conflicts is the most difficult part of running an engineering company.'

New approach to human resources

The need for speed left no time for politics, and NNE adjusted its HR strategy accordingly. Different project management teams (PMTs) managed each project within the fast-track process. Teams were cross-functional, with individuals coming from departments throughout the company. From the beginning, project managers had to identify employees who could make a difference. Then the company would start to identify individuals everyone could rely on to drive projects – the project managers themselves.

Top management made it clear that PMTs were a special entity. Project managers controlled the team from the start. Once on a project, employees belonged primarily to that team and functional hierarchy was far less important. All team members were based in the same building. Teams functioned in a holistic way; there was a sense of 'we're in this together'. If one person had a problem, the others would pitch in so the whole project would not be delayed.

Each PMT included an HR person to challenge its way of working. This internal coach even led workshops to simulate critical situations. The focus was mainly on communications training so that people learned to communicate without insulting others and – occasionally – how to cope with being insulted. Michele Gundstrup coach for the Novo Seven PMT explained:

> A lot of time was spent on building a feedback culture. What was difficult was to make a difference between good and constructive feedback versus any old feedback.

> The main idea was to keep all problems behind closed doors within the PMT. Once a decision had been taken, everyone would stick to it.

To reflect the importance of project management, the company created a project management career path, independent of other functional areas. Since NNE was the only company in Denmark that built such big pharmaceutical plants, hiring external project managers with the necessary competencies was almost impossible. Even experienced project managers with a construction background did not fit easily within NNE. The pharmaceutical industry had a culture of its own and a project manager would be poorly regarded by the client if he did not have what was deemed to be the necessary knowledge by industry standards. Hence NNE was looking for project managers with a good understanding of pharmaceutical processes and regulatory aspects rather than basic project management skills.

Changing the client's mindset

Fast-track projects meant a lot of pressure on the client, and some were just not ready to play. From the start, clients had to know what they wanted much earlier, and NNE would challenge a particular client's specifications in order to stick to its processes. It was a new way of doing business in a rather traditional industry, and the client had to adapt to these changes. It was not easy, since many clients associated changing the specifications with an increase in either cost or time. NNE's modular concept allowed for shorter construction time, even if set-up time was a bit longer. As a result, both costs and time remained under control. (*Refer to* ***Figure 4.3*** *in the chapter introduction.*)

Small companies with no internal engineering department were fast adopters. Large pharmaceutical companies with long industry experience were not ready for NNE's approach. Their usual reaction was: 'Don't come and tell us what to do!'

To ensure fast decision making and client agreement on proposed solutions, the PMT included an executive from the client company. Whenever discussions at the PMT level did not lead to a mutually acceptable solution, the problem was elevated to an executive committee with representatives from both NNE and the client company.

From a risk management point of view, since 80% of the contract was specified and 20% was open, the challenge was to build trust between NNE and the customer. This would also make finding and implementing solutions quicker. As Frandsen noted: 'When you go this fast, you cannot do your specifications completely. It's truly about trust!'

Purchasing departments were usually reluctant to sign an open contract, so NNE's sales force had to bypass procurement to reach the final customer within the client. NNE did not have to use such a strategy with Novo Nordisk since both companies trusted each other and worked in total cooperation. As Frandsen recalled: 'There was no contractual consequence on the first fast-track project; Novo Nordisk was the only client so we were together on this.'

NNE eventually completed the Novo Seven facility in just 18 months. Those who had still been sceptical after the first fast-track project were finally convinced. The challenge combined with the new processes and organization made total sense. A major milestone had been achieved.

The last dash

People within the company felt energized by these two major achievements. When Bavarian Nordic A/S, a small pharmaceutical company, approached NNE to build a vaccine production facility in 2004, everyone saw the opportunity to aim for the 12-month goal. With its proven track record, NNE started this project with a good idea of what worked and what did not.

Team building

Before starting work with this new client, NNE organized a one-week team-building exercise for the PMT in the north of Sweden in winter. To kick off the week, the team was thrown out of a bus at night and had to walk 25 km in the snow. The rest of the time they did several outdoor exercises a day, with two hours' sleep if they were lucky. As Nielsen commented: 'After two days like that everything is broken down. There is no politics anymore. People find key value.'

The exercise helped the PMT to create an identity of its own and to talk with one voice. Every employee knew that the voice of one PMT member was the voice of the entire team. But this effort was not limited to the NNE team.

Ole Broch Nielsen, the Bavarian Nordic project manager, sought the best craftsmen for the project and set about creating the best conditions on site to attract them. Craftsmen would find everything that they needed to provide first-class work.

To start with Nielsen organized a one-day seminar with engineers, foremen and craftsmen. They would all get to know each other personally so communication delays could be avoided later on. Then a subcontractor mentioned it would be easier and cheaper to build a temporary office for the engineers on the construction site. Nielsen liked the idea and implemented it. When problems occurred during the construction, craftsmen knew the engineers and it was easy for them to pop into the office and explain what the problem was. It was usually resolved quickly and the engineers would modify their plan then and there. Whenever a milestone was reached, small parties with coffee and cakes were held, and when employees reached one of the interim challenging targets set by Nielsen, he would offer gifts to keep morale high. Nielsen noted: 'It is all about giving people the right working conditions and the possibility to be productive.'

Nielsen organized weekly meetings with offsite subcontractors. There were also monthly meetings with all the subcontractors, held either at the construction site or at one of the subcontractor's premises. These meetings fostered information sharing between all parties involved in the construction. They also helped to set common objectives and to give momentum to the project. Each time, the host organized a social event so people could form bonds with one another.

Rethinking project planning

Unlike the previous fast-track projects, construction took place in an existing building and modules could not be brought in from subcontractors. Bavarian

Nordic wanted the project delivered within nine months. How could NNE deliver a fast-track project if it had to build everything on site, without using modules? What about other potential problems? The success of the project would rely on perfect project planning. Nielsen commented: 'Project planning is like the computer game Tetris – you never know which brick will come down next but you have to find a way to fit it.'

Nielsen went back to Bavarian Nordic with a proposal for 11 months. He would do everything possible to reach the target but could not guarantee it.

Traditional project planning methods emphasized the need to identify all the tasks necessary to complete a project, as well as which ones depended on one another, and see what they added up to in terms of time. By using modular processes and documentation as well as PAM, and based on NNE's experience, Nielsen applied backward planning. He squeezed all the different tasks of the project into autonomous subprojects executed simultaneously to fit the timeline. It was a top-down approach versus a traditional bottom-up approach.

While there was no time buffer, Nielsen knew he could devote additional resources to the project if necessary because of the open contract: 'That's why you have money in your wallet at the airport, to buy things you forgot to pack.'

Nielsen also received full management support. For instance, Bech – who was part of the executive committee for the project – dedicated two days per week to customer management. Construction had its ups and downs, but NNE finally completed the project on time – in the record-breaking space of 11 months.

Not long after this remarkable success, Novo Seven (*pictured here*) – the previous fast-track project – won the 2005 Facility of the Year award at the New York Interfex fair, a major pharmaceutical industry gathering. Bech commented:

> We had a stand at this fair and quite honestly it did not receive lots of attention. That is before we received the award. Right after, our stand was completely crowded with people who wanted to understand why we had won. It was surreal!

What next?

NNE had finally achieved success after five years of continuous efforts. Now the company could rest at last. Or could it? While it had earned its new visibility and reputation by achieving what was previously thought impossible, the world was still moving fast and competitors were far from standing still. Voigt had to prove the sustainability of NNE's business model.

Fast-track projects were certainly a good marketing tool, yet NNE still had many other projects that did not require the fast-track process. By the end of 2005 the company had enjoyed steady growth for more than a decade (*refer to* **Exhibit 2**). It was managing a portfolio of more than a 1,000 projects ranging from simply changing a door in a lab to building an entire new plant. Most of these projects were monodisciplinary; about 80 were truly multidisciplinary, with a turnover of more than DKK 5 million each.[1] Of those, 30 critical projects managed by a senior project manager under the direct scrutiny of top management generated about 80% of the company turnover. How sustainable was the current business model? What were its limitations?

New challenges

Voigt needed to find more customers outside the Novo Nordisk galaxy, who, like Bavarian Nordic, were willing to undertake fast-track projects. This would be challenging but not impossible. NNE had achieved its fastest project to date with a customer outside Novo Nordisk. Since the facility of the year award, NNE had gained exposure in the pharmaceutical industry and many potential clients had seen opportunities for themselves. Yet, many customers were somewhat risk-averse, had incentive schemes that did not reward time savings or were simply using NNE as a benchmark to put pressure on their existing suppliers.

In addition, exporting the fast-track model outside Denmark would prove difficult, but was necessary if the model was to grow. By now NNE had a qualified and trusted supplier base in Denmark with experience in modular technology. Yet many of these suppliers would be too small to follow NNE internationally. NNE would probably have to go through a new learning curve with different partners. Culture was also a factor to take into account – successful strategy in Denmark could be difficult to replicate in other countries.

Finally, Voigt feared employees' motivation would be hard to sustain in the long run. Employees involved in the first fast-track project had already earned their stripes. The others would probably also be keen to achieve such a success, but it had already been done, and gaining a couple of months would not make such a big difference any more. NNE needed new energy to keep up the fast pace of the previous five years and maintain the teamgeist of the top teams.

Reflecting on how far they had come and how they had managed to overcome the employees' initial scepticism, Voigt commented: 'A lot of barriers in peoples' minds are just not real. Our job is to push those barriers.'

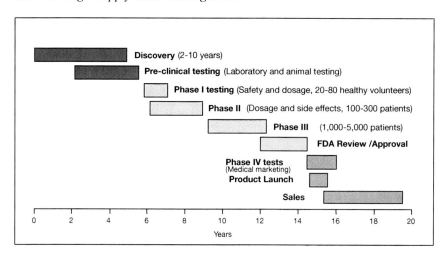

Exhibit 1 Pharmaceutical research and development stages

Sources: Sources: *Scrip Magazine* July/August 2003; PhRMA; Quintiles Transnational company
presentation 2003.

Unconsolidated data	31/12/2004	31/12/2003	31/12/2002	31/12/2001	31/12/2000	Average
	12 months DKK thousands	12 months DKK thousands	12 months DKK thousands	12 months DKK thousands	12 months DKK thousands	5 years DKK thousands
Operating revenue / turnover	1,015,692	959,342	1,304,912	1,090,422	707,422	1,015,558
Profit (loss) before tax	56,408	4,201	91,330	53,953	23,379	45,854
P/L for Period [= Net Income]	39,184	4,105	52,605	37,454	15,004	29,670
Cash flow	51,262	11,421	58,017	43,204	18,594	36,500
Total assets	374,313	320,527	406,152	373,254	229,720	340,793
Shareholders funds	140,023	100,851	123,261	76,153	37,221	95,502
Current ratio (x)	1.56	1.33	1.35	1.25	1.21	1.34
Profit margin (%)	5.55	0.44	7	4.95	3.3	4.25
Return on shareholders funds (%)	40.28	4.17	74.09	70.85	62.81	50.44
Return on capital employed (%)	44.24	n.a.	89.22	62.82	59.53	63.95
Solvency ratio (%)	37.41	31.46	30.35	20.4	16.2	27.17
Employees	816	890	976	769	550	800

Exhibit 2 NNE financial profile

Case 4.2
Building partnerships: Reinventing Oracle's
go-to-market strategy

Donna Everatt, Carlos Cordon and Ralf W. Seifert

For more than 25 years, Oracle Corporation, the second biggest software company on the planet, had created innovative software solutions to help its customers manage critical information. Along the way, Oracle's CEO Larry Ellison and his team had awed analysts and industry watchers with a constant ability to be at the head of the pack in technological development and salesmanship, creating unimaginable wealth for Oracle employees and shareholders.

According to Alfonso Di Ianni, the worldwide head of Alliance and Channels: 'Oracle has a tradition of selling big business to big companies. We drive the market, and our industry.'

With the new millennium, however, Oracle faced several new challenges. These included increased market saturation for the upper-end, enterprise-wide software solutions that Oracle sold; an entrenched slowdown in information technology (IT) spending; and heightened competition.

To capture continued gains in market share, Oracle had thus broadened its focus to serve the hundreds of thousands of small and medium-sized enterprises (SMEs) globally, while maintaining its hold on its traditional customers of Fortune 500 companies. In order to reach this much broader market and to respond to changing industry dynamics, however, Oracle needed to rethink its go-to-market strategy.

Partnerships were increasingly becoming a key component of Oracle's go-to-market strategy. Historically, the company had flourished with a sales force of aggressive high-flyers who were rewarded for winning. This approach had been very successful with Fortune 500 companies. A key success factor in Oracle's next stage of growth would now require reinventing its strategy to develop and nurture tens of thousands of partnerships worldwide.

Oracle snapshot

Within three decades, Oracle, a three-person start-up, had generated revenues that had exceeded $10 billion, with a net profit margin of 23% and 24% in 2001 and 2002 respectively. This was achieved through developing and marketing innovative IT solutions and e-business software at the heart of the information economy. Oracle's sales were classified in two main businesses: database technologies and enterprise applications.

Oracle's 'product' was not the software, but the licenses to use it. Licenses were priced on a per processor unit basis and accounted for about one-third of Oracle's

LICENSE REVENUE

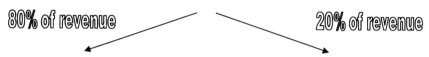

Database Technologies,* including:

- database management software (DBMS), servers and development tools that allowed customers to store, manipulate and retrieve various types of data.

Enterprise Applications, including:

- software programs for financial management, human resources, manufacturing, marketing and sales, order management, supply chain logistics, projects, services, etc.

*With a 42% market share in 2001, Oracle was the undisputed market leader in the database segment – more than ten points ahead of the number two player, IBM, and with more than five times the share of the number three contender, Microsoft. IDC (June, 2000)

overall revenue. The remaining two-thirds of Oracle's *overall* revenue was, again, not the software per se, but the services around the software – Oracle Consulting, Oracle University and Oracle Support.

Services was a very high-margin business for Oracle, generating an overall margin of 61% (the margin in support services in 2002 was 83%). Beyond high margins and revenue,[2] services also provided visibility, brand support and relationship building as a vehicle for increasing Oracle's installed base of over 200,000 customers in over 50 countries.

To service such a broad base, Oracle had transformed itself into an 'e-business', leveraging its own capabilities to provide customer service and support, procurement, expense reporting and reimbursement back in 1999. This had saved billions of dollars. For example, training on a specific topic for a partner who visited the portal cost an average of only $2 via the web, versus $250 before the transformation. Also, desktop support staff were reduced from 500 to 100, saving $60 million annually. Mike Rocha, EVP Oracle Global Support Services, explained his perspective on some key benefits of an online, self-service approach:

> Just two years ago, we were inundated with 170,000 phone calls in North America alone. By creating one call center using Oracle's Business Suite, we've reduced that number to 20,000. Furthermore, once we were able to get online with our customers, we started to know a lot more about them, which allows us to build better knowledge.[3]

Ellison's vision as Oracle's chairman and CEO was to offer a full suite of enterprise applications to leverage its flagship database products – following the industry trend of moving away from modular, best-of-breed IT systems – to become, in theory, a one-stop-shop enterprise application vendor. The suite aimed to support all the business processes of an enterprise's financial management, customer relationships and supply chain management. However, enabling customers to achieve this vision was being slowed by the spending cutbacks in the IT industry, which by 2003 had become entrenched.

Industry snapshot

'This is a brutal slowdown, the worst in the history of America's IT industry', Ellison commented in an interview with the *Financial Times* in 2001. Weak global economic conditions prompted customers to scale back or defer capital spending on IT, resulting in lower new license revenues.

With the bursting of the 'dot.com bubble' and a weakness in the telecommunications and high-technology industries, by 2003 most customers' software procurement was restricted to well-defined needs in the short term. Further, IT solutions were becoming increasingly commoditized, which led to inexorably decreasing prices and a shift in demand to low-cost, high-volume platforms – namely to Microsoft SQL Server/Windows. Oracle experienced a shift from its high-end servers to mid-range ones with fewer features at a lower price. Consequently, the percentage of large transactions[4] for Oracle decreased from 46% of total license revenues in fiscal 2001 to 37% in 2002.[5]

At the same time, the database market was maturing; sustaining double-digit revenue growth would require more emphasis on the larger, fast-growing applications market. In the rush to market, however, Oracle had stumbled. But its commitment to applications since 2000 had brought significant product improvements, and the most recent offerings had been well received by the market and analysts alike.

In relation to well-established competitors, including the market leader SAP AG and niche players such as Siebel, PeopleSoft and i2, Oracle still had an ace up its sleeve – its platform sat under more than 75% of these competitors' applications. Such a massive installed base would be hard for any competitor – even Microsoft – to depose, given the risks and costs of migrating production application systems and data.

Nonetheless, the downturn in the global economy, the maturation of the database market, a more focused attack on the applications market, expansion to the SME market, and increased competition had motivated Oracle to take several actions.

First, the company increased its focus on achieving significant cost savings with its transformation to an e-business. Second, there was a drastic change in the way Oracle priced its products, simplifying its pricing model and making it more affordable. And finally, the key element was the development of a reinvented go-to-market partnership strategy.

High stakes

Oracle, like most software vendors, had a strong direct (internal) sales force – with more than 100 subsidiaries operating in 90 US cities and more than 60 countries. Channel partners, who resold Oracle licenses in combination with their service and software offerings, rounded out sales revenue.

By 2003, partner revenue accounted for a significant part of Oracle's earnings; in Oracle's largest market – the US – partner revenue accounted for about 20% of total revenue. In EMEA[6] this figure was 35%, though the goal was to increase it to 45% in the next couple of years. In some regions, however, including Asia for example, channel partners contributed over 75% of total revenues.[7] Globally, channel revenue was approximately $1.5 billion in 2002,[8] and go-to-market partners represented almost limitless future growth opportunities. For every dollar customers spent on Oracle software, partners could add an additional $3 to $5 of value-added products and services. On average, every $1 of Oracle license revenue sold by partners led to an average of $3 of (high-margin) services revenue.[9]

However, for the thousands of channel partners Oracle engaged, the design, communication and implementation of a partnering strategy were a formidable challenge. Many issues needed to be considered in the context of a fast-moving product cycle in a highly competitive industry, including:

- A myriad of partner types.
- Partners of varying sizes.
- Partners selling different products and services.
- Partners with various levels of competencies and knowledge of Oracle products and services.
- Partners with shifting loyalties.
- Partners often in competition with Oracle.

Developing a go-to-market strategy with partners given its importance and the challenges attached to it was more evolutionary than revolutionary. Oracle was forced to adapt constantly, without losing sight of the business.

The way it was

Historically, Oracle had focused primarily on developing, supporting and incentivizing its own direct sales force. However, over the past few years the company had recognized the value of an optimized distribution model that leveraged all the various channels to maximize market share and profitability goals. Thus an Alliance Division was formed in 1998, as 'one of Oracle's key initiatives in refining its go-to-market strategy with partners' according to Michel Clement, a senior director of partner marketing in EMEA.

Alliance partner types included independent software vendors (ISVs), hardware/infrastructure vendors, systems integrators (SIs), and value-added resellers (VARs) (*refer to **Exhibit 1***). These groups competed every day, not only against each other, but also against Oracle's own sales force, a situation that characterized many of the partnerships of Oracle's competitors. Nonetheless, as Clement explained, each partner played a vital role in generating Oracle sales:

> It's absolutely key that developers with hardware vendors build solutions on Oracle software. The more ISVs adopt your technology, the more universal

Table 1

High-tech industry	PC industry equivalent
Hardware (HP, IBM)	The PC
Database (Oracle 9i)	Windows
Application (Oracle eBusiness Suite)	PowerPoint or RealPlayer
Consultants (Accenture)	A friend
VAR (Morse, Ares)	Media Markt or Wal-Mart
ISV (SAP)	Tax preparation software

it becomes. The SI influence impacts as much as 75% of IT purchasing decisions, so you need their support. And we could never have the kind of depth and breadth of market penetration without the VARs.

An analogy with the PC industry helped explain how these various players worked together.

The structure of the division was decentralized; each region developed its own strategies to foster relationships with channel partners, each with its own profit and loss responsibilities.

Oracle's foray into go-to-market partnerships was initially successful:

- Oracle created the channel, going from having no formal partner relationships to having 10,000 worldwide.
- Partner revenue doubled from 10% to 20%.
- Momentum around the partnership concept was created within Oracle.

However, the model's limitations began to show. For instance, reaching the right contact person within Oracle meant going through a middleman (the partner's Alliance account manager). Likewise, retrieving information online meant going to any one of dozens of websites. Other issues arose, as presented in *Exhibit 2*. According to Di Ianni, feedback from partners summed up a key issue with the Alliance structure: 'We love you when we have a deal, but behind that there's this organization [i.e. Alliance] that's not effective – it's not engaging.'[10] He continued: 'We had a complete separation between the customer and partner world. Nothing about our partners was on our website even just a year ago in 2001 – to our customers, our partners were another world from Oracle.'

These issues were critical to Oracle's future success. Thus Ellison himself spearheaded the next stage of development of Oracle's go-to-market partnership strategy. The question was: Just how would, or should, it evolve?

Towards a new partnering strategy

To ensure that partners were managed in a consistent way throughout the organization, a scaled down and more focused version of Alliance was created.

The new division, Alliance and Channels, connected each business unit in Oracle with partners and vice versa. According to Mark Jarvis, chief marketing officer:

> We broke up our Alliance organization and decentralized it across all the organizations for one simple reason ... to allow the partner to be directly in touch with the people that they actually go to market with, or develop with, or sell with. So, we think it's of benefit to the partners. And actually, it means that every Oracle employee thinks about partnerships. We're really talking about accountability, which is now placed where it should be.

> The Alliance and Channels division's function is very similar to the conductor of an orchestra, making sure that we're playing the right tune, at the right speed, etc. It is a central point of contact that then links partners into the appropriate part of the organization.[11]

Di Ianni explained that it was the newly created Oracle® PartnerNetwork that would act as this unifying force.

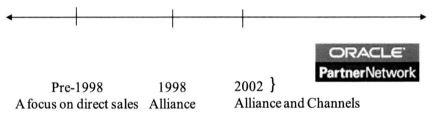

Pre-1998   1998   2002 }
A focus on direct sales   Alliance   Alliance and Channels

Figure 1

Oracle® PartnerNetwork

Alliance and Channels created Oracle PartnerNetwork, which consisted of three key parts: a program, a portal and an interaction center known as Partner ResourceNetwork.[12] Any IT company willing to spend 15 minutes and $1,995 could enroll in Oracle PartnerNetwork and access development, marketing services and sales support through a single portal (*refer to* **Exhibit 3**). Via this portal, content could be personalized based on individual profiles – region, country, language, industry and membership level.

Oracle PartnerNetwork was meant to further the evolution of a customized self-service community and to enable partners to become an extension of Oracle's own sales force, with the same level of efficiency. Though partners were competing with each other and with Oracle sales reps, the intention was to grow revenues for all stakeholders (*refer to* **Exhibit 4**).

With Oracle PartnerNetwork, the company sought to set the stage for the classic win–win scenario that defined successful partnerships, but this was not easy.

One side of the equation: What Oracle thought partners wanted

Oracle clearly drove the process: in a presentation to partners at the EMEA 2002 Executive Partner Forum held in Cannes, a key chart identified 'What You Need from Oracle', outlining development, sales and marketing, and technical tools to increase partner revenue.

By the end of 2002 Oracle PartnerNetwork in EMEA consisted of 6,500 partners, categorized in one of three levels of membership. The majority of partners were in the 'discovery level', as Member Partners. As a partner increased joint revenue and investment in the development of certified Oracle technical and sales 'champs', it advanced through the next level(s) of membership – Certified Partner and Certified Advantage Partner. Benefits increased in tandem with partner commitment to Oracle (*refer to **Exhibit 5***).

The other side of the equation: What Oracle wanted from partners and Oracle PartnerNetwork

Ten per cent of Oracle PartnerNetwork members had qualified for Certified Partner or Certified Advantage Partner status, in part by generating sales revenue exceeding $500,000. Di Ianni referred to this mutual revenue building as 'expanding the Oracle economy', which he estimated was 10 to 20 times bigger than Oracle's $10 billion in revenue, including other services and partner solutions that complemented Oracle technology.

With Oracle PartnerNetwork, partner value would now be based on 'measured business results for *both* parties – not previous relationships or the size of the partner'. He continued:

> We do not partner for partnering's sake; we're not in the business of building 'flower power' and 'free love'. There are no daisies or peace signs on the portal. Partnerships should be based on the value the partner brings to us.

> The messages should be honest.

> We expect partners to buy into our vision, which means building their business around that vision. They should be influencing the marketplace by convincing customers to choose Oracle, and thereby grow Oracle revenue.

The incentive for partners to choose Oracle was expressed in the key message to partners from Sergio Giacoletto, head of Oracle EMEA: 'We are a leader in providing technology applications. We are here to be a long-term provider of leading technology, and therefore, if you stick with us, together we can grow.'[13]

Partners' enthusiasm for 'sticking with' Oracle would depend on several factors, including the attractiveness of incentives and benefits, ease-of-use, a sense of ownership and – importantly – trust.

The three most important success factors of partnerships: Trust, trust and trust

Di Ianni put himself in a partner's shoes, summarizing their feelings with, 'Sure, Oracle competes with us – that we can manage. But sometimes they don't play nice … they take our lunch and run with it.' To put it simply, Giacoletto stated: 'Trust has not always been the case in the past.'[14] Julie Tung, vice president Partner Marketing and Oracle PartnerNetwork, shared her perspective:

> I don't think we can ever eliminate channel conflict, but you can manage it, and the abuse of power. For instance, if an Oracle account manager takes an account from a partner, instead of receiving a slap on the wrist as in the past, there must be consequences.

> Partners need to trust that we're 100% committed – from the top – and that we provide them with the resources to help them get engaged. I think they're starting to see that, but we've got a long way to go. As long as they're making money, they'll be patient.

> In all the surveys we've done with partners, we've heard, 'We stay with Oracle because it's the best technology.' But in the past – certainly before Oracle PartnerNetwork – if they found a better technology, they'd leave us in a New York second. It's the nature of this business.

Oracle redoubled its efforts to gain increased trust from its go-to-market partners in a number of ways by trying to increase bilateral communication via Oracle PartnerNetwork, by changing its attitude and by introducing its Open Market Model[15] (OMM), an initiative to minimize conflict with Oracle Direct Sales.

What would the partners say?

Di Ianni reflected:

> Overall, I think our partners would say they were happier because they are more involved not just on the development side, but on the go-to-market side. I think they would also say that they like our marketing approach (i.e. 100% of our marketing activity is 'with–throughto' partners[16]). However, something we have heard over the years is, 'We want an easier way to contact someone at Oracle if there's a problem', so I think that's still going to be there to a certain extent.

Tung added her viewpoint:

> Our partners would say that they're seeing more engagement and commitment, that the access to information is good, but we still have sales engagement

issues. I think they also may say that it's difficult to communicate with someone directly when they need to.

Happy first anniversary

Oracle executives themselves acknowledged that the company had not always been the strongest of channel allies. However, this was typical of channel partnerships in the IT industry – and for go-to-market partnerships as a whole – to one degree or another because of the difficulty in managing conflicting interests.

With Oracle PartnerNetwork's first anniversary just around the corner, Oracle was breaking new ground in building partnerships as a centerpiece of its go-to-market strategy. Di Ianni confidently stated:

> Partners are at the center of everything we do. Oracle has spent over $130 million on the development of Oracle PartnerNetwork, and training partners. Everybody, from Larry on down, is dedicated to its success.

> But I know it will take more than a year to build trust – to prove Oracle's commitment and consistency. So if I heard from partners at this point, 'It's good progress. We'll see.' I'd be extremely happy.

Independent Software Vendors (ISVs) owned, developed, distributed and supported commercially available application programs that were integrated with Oracle products. They served to broaden and deepen Oracle sales.

Hardware/Infrastructure Vendors provided a wide range of products, technologies and services upon which Oracle products ran, providing the critical link in Oracle's dominant market position. Companies in this category included leading global vendors of hardware, operating systems, telecommunications equipment, storage systems and mobile computing technology.

Systems Integrators (SIs) provided network services, consulting and custom application programs that were integrated with Oracle software. They were critical in influencing purchasing decisions and in building expertise around Oracle software and services, facilitating a broader reach in the market.

Value-Added Resellers (VARs) sold Oracle licenses and thus extended Oracle's sales reach into more regions and companies of all sizes.

Exhibit 1 Main partner types

Segmentation Issues	Michel Clement, a senior director, partner marketing EMEA: "Alliance became a 'company within a company.' There was virtually nothing to stop a salesperson from taking someone else's deal – whether from an Oracle sales rep in another division, or from a channel partner."
Fragmentation Issues	Alain Ozan, a senior marketing director: "Someone from the product line would recruit a number of ISVs in a country, but could not bring them to market in their local market – either the poor chap couldn't find the channel marketing manager to execute, or the recruited partner was not even on the radar screen of the country channel manager."
Channel Conflict	Clement: "The Alliance division created channel conflict both within Oracle's direct sales force *and* between them and their channel partners. Some 'pretty interesting' discussions with partners ensued when a company passed the $200 million threshold and an Oracle sales rep took over the account."
Communication Issues	Alfonso Di Ianni, worldwide head Alliance and Channels: "Oracle was talking only to the people we knew, not those we didn't. Partners had to deal with two worlds at Oracle – the 'Let's do lunch and have a drink, be friends' world and the real world of doing business in the field when they needed something done."

Exhibit 2 Summary of Alliance Division issues

Exhibit 3 Oracle PartnerNetwork sample web page: Home

Source: www.oracle.com

Oracle PartnerNetwork offered its partners:

- Development tools, education, training and support to adopt Oracle technology for their application or service.[17]
- Online marketing services and support, including campaign planning and execution, e-marketing tools, advertising and public relations templates, and more.
- Oracle agreements to simplify the sales process, sales training, partner kits to provide training and collateral materials to assist in selling and delivering Oracle technology, for example.

Oracle's overall strategy to engage partners in a joint go-to-market approach was to:

- **Attract partners** within each industry, region and market segment.
- **Gain commitment** from partners by offering mutually beneficial joint go-to-market plans.
- **Encourage and assist** partners to expand the Oracle economy and to generate incremental opportunities.
- **Promote** internally and externally partner independent software vendor solutions.
- **Drive execution** of sales programs and marketing campaigns.
- **Enhance** partners' sales competencies.
- **Continually increase partners' trust in Oracle** through ongoing support with increased communications through Partner ResourceNetwork and programs such as the Open Market Model (OMM).

Exhibit 4 Oracle PartnerNetwork and Oracle's go-to-market strategy to engage partners

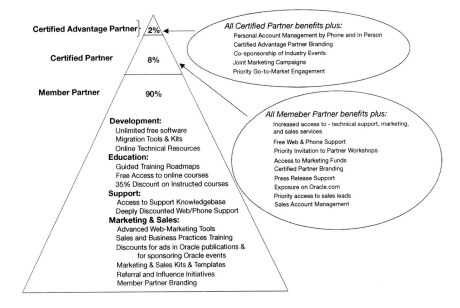

Exhibit 5 Three membership levels and benefits

Source: Company information

Case 4.3
LEGO: Consolidating distribution (A)

Edwin Wellian, Carlos Cordon and Ralf W. Seifert

It was November 2006 and Egil Møller Nielsen, senior director of European/ Asian logistics for the LEGO Group, was undertaking a very challenging logistics transformation. Earlier in the year the company had consolidated distribution from seven operations into a single European distribution center in the Czech Republic. The center was based in Jirny, 10 kilometers outside Prague, and was operated by DHL, the global logistics company.

This had been a stressful year for Møller Nielsen and his team. The implementation had not gone smoothly and there was still much left to do. Fortunately, the 'high season' was over, giving Møller Nielsen some time to breathe and plan his next move. The next phase – the transfer of the remaining operations to Jirny – was meant to start early the following year. But was this still the right thing to do? Should he revise his strategy?

Møller Nielsen had just come out of a meeting with senior executives for a go/ no-go decision on the next phase. He was told: 'Our business is back on track, so we are actually OK if you stop or slow down further consolidation – what do you recommend?'

The company's leadership was looking to Møller Nielsen for a strong recommendation. Should he push his initial, ambitious plan of using a single outsourced central distribution center (DC) in Europe? He had three options:

1   Continue as planned.
2   Keep the status quo – operate with several DCs for a few more years.
3   Explore other alternatives.

Whatever the decision, he would have to move quickly to be ready before the start of the next peak period in about half a year from now.

Financial crisis at the LEGO Group

The LEGO Group was established in 1932 by Ole Kirk Kristiansen in his carpenter shop in Billund, Denmark. For almost 70 years it saw steady growth in both sales and profits until, in 1998, this successful streak came to an abrupt end and the company started losing money. Staff reductions followed for the first time in its history, and LEGO set out on a path of innovative new product development.

By the end of 2002 the company appeared to have turned the corner – net cash flow was positive once again and sales reached record highs. But inventory and receivables were also up, and when retailers' Christmas sales proved to be disappointing – especially in its largest markets – LEGO braced[18] itself for another difficult year. What happened next exceeded even the company's own worst-case scenario: Sales dropped 26% in 2003 alone and another 20% in 2004. This resulted in the largest losses in the company's history over two successive years (*refer to* **Exhibit 1** *for a financial overview*), calling into question the effectiveness of the measures taken in response to the 1998 loss.

2004: A costly and complex supply chain

The company's leadership knew that the supply chain posed the most immediate opportunity for significant improvements. It was selling creative toy products in a competitive and highly seasonal[19] global marketplace. But it did not have a flexible enough supply chain to deal with these great fluctuations. The company's focus on creativity, innovation and superior quality had, over time, created high complexity in the supply chain. LEGO's motto – 'Only the best is good enough' – had contributed to an emphasis on creating, selling and delivering toys at any cost, without regard for practicalities. To rebuild profitability, the company had to re-engineer its supply chain.

Bottlenecks in the supply chain

The company ran one of the largest injection-molding operations in the world, with its own production sites in Denmark and Switzerland, and packing and other facilities in the Czech Republic, the US and Korea. The fully automated factory in Denmark alone had more than 800 machines. Its production people would proudly tell you that LEGO was the largest producer of (toy) tires in the world! The factories produced a staggering 20 billion bricks per year; separate packing facilities assembled them into finished LEGO sets. The logistics flow between each factory and packing location was managed through a complex structure of multiple DCs and warehouses.

Planning remained a constant challenge for LEGO, even after 50 years of experience molding bricks. Sales forecasting was so inaccurate[20] that capacity utilization was just 70%. The company also had to manage a supply chain of over 11,000 suppliers that had grown over time as LEGO sets had become more elaborate, with multiple combinations for the face, body and legs of the main action figures – adding up to a total of 12,500 SKUs in over 100 different colors.

LEGO tried to establish itself as a just-in-time delivery company, but at a cost to itself. It accepted customer orders with immediate or next day delivery. Of these orders, 67% were for less than a full carton and only 62% could actually be delivered 'on time'.

A complex three-level DC structure in Europe

As **Exhibit 2** shows, to be close to the customer, LEGO used four regional DCs: two in France, operated by a third-party logistics provider and serving primarily the UK and southern European markets; one in Germany for the Central and East European markets; and one in Denmark for Scandinavia and Benelux. The last two, also the largest, were operated by LEGO and employed just over 200 people. Almost 14,000 customers received direct deliveries from these four DCs.

The finished LEGO products were stored in a 30,000m² central warehouse in Germany, operated by a third party. Products from this warehouse were delivered on demand to the four regional DCs, two dedicated assortment product lines[21] and LEGO's Shop@Home operation in Denmark as well as DCs located outside Europe.

The factories in Denmark and Switzerland operated their own logistics and distribution centers, storing and consolidating goods from their own production sites as well as from the packing facility in the Czech Republic and other third-party suppliers. From Denmark and Switzerland, finished and complete sets were delivered to the central warehouse in Germany.

Including a separate warehouse and operation for its 'assortment packs',[22] LEGO used **11 different European logistics operations** to manage the flow of products, with more than 60 suppliers of logistics and transport services.

Shared vision

LEGO needed a turnaround. In 2003 and 2004, Kjeld Kirk Kristiansen, CEO and majority shareholder, brought in outsiders and some recent recruits to execute the company's transformation. Jesper Ovesen, from Danske Bank, became the new CFO; Bali Padda, who joined LEGO in 2002, was promoted to VP Global

Logistics; and Jørgen Vig Knudstorp, who joined LEGO in 2001 as a director of strategic development, was tasked with developing a rescue plan. Vig Knudstorp gathered a diverse group of senior executives to develop the strategy and set up a 'war room'. The war room was decorated with process charts, performance data and other project tracking sheets, where senior management and specialists analysed the company's product development, sourcing, manufacturing and logistics process. It was here that LEGO's new 'Shared Vision' strategic plan took shape. In October 2004, Vig Knudstorp replaced Kirk Kristiansen as president and CEO of LEGO, receiving a clear mandate from the company's board to execute this plan. Kirk Kristiansen injected some more of his own cash into the group 'for the last time', but otherwise took a backseat role.

Action plan for survival

The first phase of Shared Vision – 'Stabilize for Survival' – focused on reducing costs, eliminating debt and returning the company to profitability. LEGO sold a 70% share of its four LEGOLAND theme parks to the Blackstone Group in 2004, clearing its debt and reducing direct headcount by approximately 30%. Other assets were also sold or outsourced, such as buildings, land, its own mold-making factory, the Korean packing facility and the corporate jet. The first phase of Shared Vision was achieved in 2005, a year in which LEGO returned to profit. Sales increased also, but this was largely driven by the success of the sixth and final Star Wars™ movie: *Revenge of the Sith*.[23] The second phase – 'Profit from the Core' – would focus on sustainably improving the company's profitability and growth.

Reducing complexity: Breaking with the past

Egil Møller Nielsen had joined LEGO in January 2004 as logistics strategy director, tasked with developing a strategic turnaround plan for the global distribution process. Initially he was given a full year 'away from the frontline' to develop a plan, but this relative period of peace was disturbed after four months, when LEGO made him also responsible for all logistics headcount in Europe and Asia.[24]

Managing the seasonality of LEGO products would be his key challenge. Demand roughly doubled between September and November and so he had to manage almost twice the number of blue-collar workers for a short period of time. His main job would be to find a way to get the right product to the right place, in time – something LEGO had been struggling with for a while. As Padda put it: 'Too much time was spent finding out where a product was at any given time.'

Defining cost drivers and establishing a cost baseline

One of Møller Nielsen's first tasks was to establish a solid logistics cost baseline. It took almost four months to do so and to define key cost drivers and cost ownership. Total yearly costs were estimated at DKK 650 million,[25] or more than 10% of sales. Transportation costs were more than half of total costs.

Understanding the real customer requirements

Another challenge was to convince the people in sales that any cost-cutting changes in the logistics process would not automatically lead to customer dissatisfaction or loss of business. Møller Nielsen knew that he had to establish a direct communication link with LEGO's key customer base, to understand their real – not perceived – requirements. He had a questionnaire sent to the top 20 companies, representing 70% of LEGO's total business, followed by interviews and personal visits. Møller Nielsen learned one very important thing: Most customers did not require daily or next-day deliveries. This was contrary to what he had been told by some of his colleagues. Arguments in favor of immediate delivery were used to justify higher inventory levels and having DCs close to the customer. The direct customer feedback would give Møller Nielsen more credibility in designing the ideal process.

Defining key objectives and targets and developing a high-level strategy

One of the key corporate drivers – to build a sustainable profitable platform – was to make the company more asset light. This was to be achieved through outsourcing and simplified processes. In 2004 LEGO had given its management team a target to cut costs by 20% by the end of 2008. To meet this objective and achieve the cost savings target, Møller Nielsen proposed consolidating all logistics and distribution operations to a single central DC, managed by a third party. This proposal was accepted by the management team at the end of 2004. For economic reasons, this central DC needed to be close[26] to LEGO'S main production facilities and largest single markets (Germany and the UK).

Selecting new partners: Global tendering

In early 2005 a global tendering process started with the company's existing logistics service providers, as well as some new ones. In total, LEGO invited 22 companies to bid on part or all of its global logistics process. The goal was to reduce its 55+ transportation companies to a maximum of 7 global suppliers, bring all finished goods in Europe[27] under one roof and to cut costs by DKK 130 million – including DKK 45 million on transportation.

The central European DC (EDC) would have to have an initial total capacity[28] of 51,000m² – with an option to extend to 62,000m² – and the provider would have to be able to manage the level of the workforce during peak and off seasons. A model created to calculate the ideal location showed that Prague in the Czech Republic was the most central place. However, a distribution center on such a scale 'had never been done before' in an East European country. Møller Nielsen left the choice of final location open, enabling him to evaluate different options, but he urged 'preferred' providers to base their quotation on the assumption that the EDC would be in the Czech Republic.

DHL won the tender. The deciding factor was that DHL, through its global relationship with ProLogis – the world's largest developer of distribution facilities

– was the only company that could quickly construct a facility of the required size close to Prague. DHL-Exel[29] in the Czech Republic, responsible for this EDC, had yearly revenues in 2005 of approximately €30 million (DKK 200 million). The LEGO contract would almost double its annual revenues, so this was 'a big fish' for the company. Building a central DC of this size in the Czech Republic would break new ground, not only for DHL but also for LEGO. The new DHL building in Jirny was intended to be a multi-client operation, with extra office space for DHL's Czech operations.

The contract with DHL was signed for five and a half years and was communicated to all LEGO employees worldwide and to third parties on August 30, 2005. The contractual cost savings were considerable. Reducing the number of transportation companies to seven would result in DKK 40 million savings per year and the consolidation of 10 operations into one another DKK 75 million.

Other changes impacting distribution

Also on August 30, 2005, LEGO announced that it would outsource production from its factory in Switzerland to a contract manufacturer (CM). The same CM would also take over the management and control of LEGO's packing facility in Kladno, in the Czech Republic, which would further be expanded to meet roughly half of the total demand. The Swiss plant mainly produced LEGO's Duplo products and employed 239 people. Production would be transferred to the CM's facility in Hungary during 2006. Other changes were also happening fast on different fronts in an attempt to reduce complexity: The number of different colors was cut by half and SKUs were reduced to 6,500. Of course, the challenge was to reap the full benefit of these changes through excellent execution.

Building the infrastructure

Planning, construction and IT changes

Møller Nielsen and his team had developed a very detailed project plan, but this was tossed out of the window as soon as the team began facing the real day-to-day issues. The construction of the building in Jirny started at the end of 2005, new transport suppliers were introduced, and system changes and transfer to a new SAP platform were in progress, enabling future electronic linkages to DHL's warehouse system. Implementation was planned in a phased approach (*refer to **Exhibit 3***). During 2006, before the start of the peak season, responsibility for the two DCs in France would be transferred to DHL in Jirny. This represented around half of the European sales volume. Goods and responsibilities from the central warehouse in Germany, the two logistics operations managed by the plants in Denmark and Switzerland, and the two Danish assembly lines would transfer the same year as well. During 2007, the remaining two DCs in Billund and Hohenwestedt would follow, and the assortment pack facility in Billund[30] would be phased out completely.

Organization changes

Beyond the standard storage and pick services, DHL also managed the LEGO assortment packs, assembled customer value packs and prepared customized deliveries, described in the 'customer brief'. Having these services under one roof was unique for most large DCs, and to allow it to focus properly on each service, DHL split its organization into three parts: (1) standard orders; (2) value-add services; and (3) customized orders. Not all specific customer requirements were known during 2004 and 2005[31] and thus could not be spelled out in the requirements document. It was, however, mutually agreed between the LEGO Group and DHL that DHL would have to be flexible in adapting to customers' requirements as soon as they became known.

Møller Nielsen created a new 'customer logistics' team. It was his organization's direct link with the customers and responsible for reducing the complexity of customized orders, while also focusing on improving customer delivery satisfaction.

The first warning signs: Cost drivers or cost behaviors?

To simplify the process of accurately allocating the total logistics costs to profit centers, LEGO used 'costs per order' as the main cost driver for logistics. During the tendering process, providers had been asked to quote their prices at the order level, making it easier for LEGO to reallocate their total costs. What DHL did not know at that time was that LEGO was undergoing major changes in its customer ordering process. Large retailers, which had initially placed small daily orders, were requested to place larger orders, at least two months in advance. Most retailers were surprisingly cooperative and in favor of this change; they were used to long lead times from other toy manufacturers, as most toy products arrived by sea from Asia. They preferred to wait for two months, knowing that the LEGO products would at least be delivered within the requested delivery date.

Changes in the cost drivers also changed the behavior of some of the sales offices. With logistics costs allocated at order level, some of them saw this as a reason to shift their focus from smaller to larger retailers. Obviously, as DHL had calculated all costs at the order level, it would lose out when the number of orders started to drop significantly.

2006 implementation

A steep learning curve

During the first transitions before the summer, there were more than the usual start-up issues. The Czech DHL team had never managed an operation of this size before. For starters, there were not enough trained people: 'We even had to teach them how to drive a forklift ...'

DHL's main IT system turned into a bottleneck. It was not designed to handle so many different customer delivery 'rules' and also could not cope with the volume of transactions provided by LEGO. The system ground to a halt more than once, and additional people had to be hired to produce and manually print the different customer labels and shipping instructions.

Also, it took longer than expected[32] to find a big enough skilled temporary workforce for only four or five months. Most of them had to be recruited from Ukraine, but not many spoke English, so they had to be taught how to read the information on the scanners and systems.

LEGO sales teams, anticipating delays and shortages during the transition, had pushed their customers for advance orders. As a result, demand started increasing as early as August, catching everyone 'off-guard', including Møller Nielsen and his team. The first crises started to occur and from then on the teams were in constant firefighting mode.

Soon after it became apparent that DHL did not have the capability to control the flow and communication with the carriers – 'They were not aware that there was a truck-load waiting for 24 hours inside the warehouse' – LEGO decided to take back the management and control of the carriers. To improve this process, it designed and implemented a new web-based tool in less than three weeks.[33]

Misunderstandings and cultural issues

Cultural clashes played an important role, creating an atmosphere of mistrust between both parties. LEGO people blamed the 'Czechs' for not taking enough responsibility, and the Czechs had problems with the Danes' direct approach and their constantly changing requirements. LEGO then started bringing more of its own people into Jirny, something that DHL at first perceived as 'an intrusion on its own territory'. Blame games would start whenever there were issues with deliveries, which were largely caused by the carriers. This situation further escalated when Møller Nielsen was briefly introduced to Leigh Pomlett, the new regional head of DHL-Exel, in August 2006. Pomlett had just come out of a meeting with his Czech team, believing that everything was going smoothly and was in good spirits. This changed abruptly when Møller Nielsen told him provocatively, 'Your people have no clue how to run this warehouse.' Perhaps it was blunt, but Pomlett took the criticism seriously; from then on key issues were addressed and resolved in a more constructive way and a new head of operations, from Pomlett's old team in the UK, was transferred to Jirny two months later.

Misunderstandings[34] and disagreements on the commercial agreement became the main obstacle to establishing a sustainable partnership. LEGO's perspective was that the contract had been signed and it was up to DHL to deliver as promised. In fact, frequently challenged by LEGO on the validity of its quotation, DHL European management confirmed in writing in 2005 in that they were comfortable with their calculations and would deliver as promised. In DHL's view, the contract was very complex and not easy to understand. Long hours were spent arguing over the agreement, as it started to become clear that DHL had underestimated the requirements – especially with regard to the high fluctuations between low and peak periods. For example, in its quotation, DHL estimated a yearly average of 180 full-time equivalent (FTE) employees for 2006, not really believing the projected volume provided by LEGO. The actual average number needed was closer to 500 FTE. DHL was going to pay a high price for the extra costs, which Møller Nielsen was not yet prepared to share, given the initial cost pressure within LEGO.

Capacity constraints

In addition, the warehouse was getting full. It was supposed to be large enough to manage the total European capacity for the next five years, so what had happened?

In June 2006 LEGO announced to employees that most of its production would be outsourced to the CM that had already taken over the production from Switzerland and was also responsible for the packing facility in Kladno. Production at the US-based plant would be phased out completely and relocated to Mexico, affecting about 300 people. Production of the more technically demanding products, such as LEGO Bionicle and LEGO Technic, would stay in Billund, whereas production of the more standard and high volume products would move to Hungary and the Czech Republic. Up to 900 of the 1,200 jobs in Billund would be affected. The relocation would take place between 2006 and 2010. Related to this outsourcing, key changes were made. To mitigate the transition of production from Denmark to Hungary or the Czech Republic, production was ramped up temporarily. Furthermore, the packaging for finished LEGO sets was changed, which decreased the number of sets that could fit on a pallet by almost 20%.

These changes – neither of which was communicated to logistics – created a significantly higher inventory level in terms of pallet positions, not only impacting space but also driving transport and storage costs higher. DHL quickly expanded to use the maximum of the available 62,000m^2 space, but this was still not enough. With the help of ProLogis, more space would ultimately be found in nine additional smaller depots in and around Jirny. The EDC had been built to store 76,000 pallets, but by November 155,000 pallets were being stored in 10 different locations. Once inventory dropped to normal levels again, Møller Nielsen estimated that space for 120,000 pallets – or almost double the size of the current EDC – would be needed.

Assessing the scale of the problem

Even with frequent delivery issues and the tracking of goods seemingly out of control, delivery delays were kept to a minimum. On average, they were limited to less than two days, but only through constant firefighting and long working hours.

By November 2006, it was clear that DHL, which expected to break even during the first year, would finish 2006 with a loss of approximately €3.5 million (DKK 25 million). Møller Nielsen knew that he could not let DHL pick up the whole tab and that he would ultimately have to change the cost drivers in the contract. But how would he explain these increased costs to his management? Perhaps the changes in production and consequent increase in warehouse space would create the opportunity he needed to break this deadlock situation.

Future challenges

The sales organization in Germany was especially critical and vocal as their local DC in Hohenwestedt, managed by the LEGO Group and serving their customers, was next in line to be closed down. They played a large role in trying to convince Vig Knudstorp that this was a bad idea. Vig Knudstorp in return leaned hard on Møller Nielsen and his team, who had expected more support from management back in Billund, but often felt let down by their 'unfair' behavior. Yes, there were many issues related to this transition, but the expected negative customer impact had been marginal.

DHL was losing a lot of money. It was blaming LEGO for a large part and was seeking compensation. DHL and LEGO, despite the fact that they both wanted to make this work, did not trust each other enough and were arguing constantly. The warehouse was full and the situation of using nine additional depots was obviously not an efficient short-term solution. Something had to be done quickly, but what? Build a new warehouse? Where? Of what size and what about the current lease contract?

For the LEGO Group as a whole, sales were up again, and 2006 promised to be the most profitable year of the last decade, so the pressure for massive cost reductions was temporarily off. It was now up to Møller Nielsen to make a decision. Either he should stick to the original concept – transfer the remaining two DCs as planned during 2007 and continue to work with DHL as its main partner, while seeking a larger warehouse. Or, stop further transitions and manage the distribution through three main centers operated by DHL and the LEGO Group in Denmark (Scandinavia and Benelux), Germany (Central Europe) and the Czech Republic (rest of Europe and Asia). There were other alternatives he could explore, like taking over the management from DHL at Jirny or finding an alternative partner, but would this really solve anything?

For Møller Nielsen the answer was clear, but what would you do?

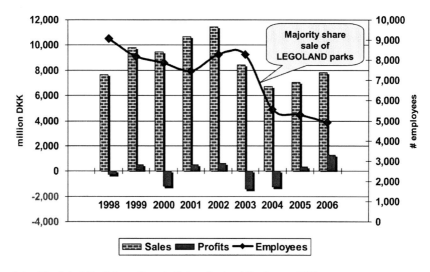

Sales (Net Sales), Profit/Loss (Results Before Tax) and Employees (FTE)
Data from annual reports
Average last 5-year DKK exchange rates: 0.17 US$ and 0.13 €

Exhibit 1   LEGO financial results 1998 to 2006

Source: Company information

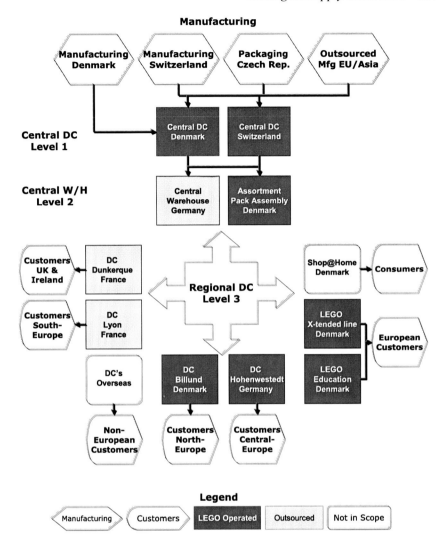

Exhibit 2 Three-level distribution center structure Europe 2004–2005

Source: Company information

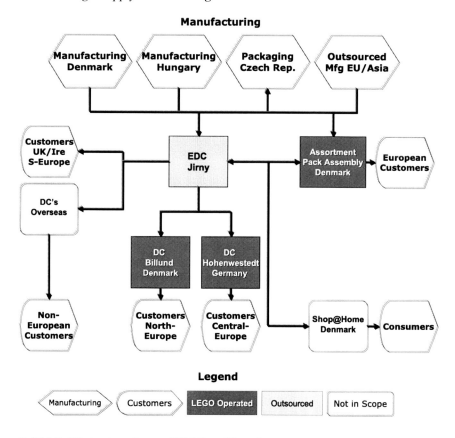

Exhibit 3 DC structure Europe: 2006 Jirny Phase 1

Source: Company information

This case series won the Supply Chain Management Award in the 2009 EFMD Case Writing Competition organized by the European Foundation for Management Development.

This case series won the 2011 ecch Case Award in the category Production and Operations Management.

Case 4.4
LEGO: Consolidating distribution (B)

Edwin Wellian, Carlos Cordon and Ralf W. Seifert

Shortly after the November 2006 meeting, Møller Nielsen had made up his mind. He would stick to his original plan. Retaining two regional DCs on top of a central DC did not make sense. LEGO did not need warehouses close to customers. As long as the company could ensure delivery reliability from a central location, any additional space and workforce would only add complexity and cost. Møller Nielsen knew that he would be held to account for his decision, as some key LEGO executives, including the CEO, were sceptical. But, he was convinced about his strategy: 'The concept is the right one; there is no doubt about that.'

Changing partners at this stage would be even more risky – he somehow had to find a way to make the partnership with DHL work.

This decision proved to be successful. During 2007, the EDC moved to a new and larger site, next to the old building in Jirny. The initial target of 20% cost savings by 2008 had been over-achieved. On-time delivery jumped to 96% and suppliers rated LEGO 'best in class' in terms of logistics. The fixed cost base also reduced significantly, making LEGO less vulnerable to large revenue swings.

The success also brought rewards and recognition. In October 2008, LEGO won the prestigious 2008 European Supply Chain Excellence Awards, in the category 'Logistics and Fulfilment'. In November 2008, Møller Nielsen was promoted to VP Global Distribution & Logistics, reporting directly to Bali Padda, who had been promoted to EVP Global Supply Chain earlier in 2006.

But how did they get there from where they started in November 2006?

Key turning points

The relationship between LEGO and DHL deteriorated as arguments over the contract terms and compensation for DHL's losses continued. One of the parties would have to make the first concession, but which one?

The breakthrough came when Møller Nielsen and his project leader secretly met with their DHL counterparts in a hotel room in Prague at the beginning of 2007. DHL, after the acquisition of Exel, was under pressure from corporate management to demonstrate that the former teams of DHL and Exel were fully integrated and LEGO had no real alternative. They agreed that from then on they would work together on a basis of mutual trust and respect. They took the 'four musketeers' oath – 'all for one and one for all' – and swore not to discuss the outcome of this meeting with anyone. Instead, they undertook to change their behavior towards one another to set an example for the rest of their staff. The stakes were higher than only their personal careers and they knew that if they did not take the driving seat then, someone else would, or in Møller Nielsen's words: 'If one of us dies, everybody will die and the partnership will end in a divorce.'

Within an hour, a gentlemen's agreement was reached on the compensation and high level contract changes. They agreed on a settlement in which LEGO would pay one-third of the total €3.5 million losses that DHL made during 2006. The contract became a working document – the aim was to find a model, fair to both parties, yet challenging enough to keep them focused on working continually on efficiency improvements. The new contract was signed during 2007. It was based on 'open book' calculations with different price levels for fixed and variable costs[35] and KPIs which changed every year and were linked to a bonus/penalty system and a pain/gain[36] sharing agreement.

This change in attitude and behavior was ultimately the turning point in their partnership relationship.

Prior to the hotel meeting – at the end of 2006 – progress was made on finding a larger site. ProLogis accepted a penalty-free, early-termination of the Jirny lease contract[37] and started in early 2007 with the construction of a new 100,000m² complex, next to the old one. This new site – Jirny 2 – was one of DHL's largest buildings in Europe and was operational by mid-2007.

From 'fist fights' to 'rowing the same boat'

LEGO and DHL had moved from a relationship initially characterized by 'fist fights' to 'rowing the same boat'. They had found common ground on which to build a solid platform and could now focus on the final transition. During 2007, the remaining two DCs in Germany and Denmark were closed, as well as the Danish operation responsible for LEGO assortment packs. With the experience gained through previous transfers, these last ones went relatively smoothly.

Continual process improvement

The new building in Jirny was not only one and a half times larger than but also an improved version of the previous building. It had more loading gates[38] and a more economical layout, improving the flow of goods and overall capacity utilization. By then DHL also had a more robust[39] process in place for recruiting temporary and permanent workers, while IT applications were adapted and improved significantly. Based on the success of the 'carrier room', a new 'operations room' was set up. Its walls were covered with reports displaying performance and delivery metrics. Daily planning meetings between LEGO, DHL and the carriers were held here, and on a weekly basis performance issues were analysed and discussed.

Change management

Since the beginning of the whole change process, Møller Nielsen and his team had applied a model example of change management, among other things to allay the fears of salespeople and customers over LEGO's ability to guarantee product availability during the transition. From August 2005 onwards, all LEGO employees were informed of progress via a weekly newsletter, and sales offices and key customers were visited frequently to meet and reassure people face to face. An external HR consultancy was recruited to act as a sparring partner for the employees whose job would change or who would be made redundant. Also, after the 'secret meeting', team-building sessions between LEGO and DHL were organized to help overcome their cultural differences.

More LEGO employees moved to Jirny, including the European head of DC operations. By the end of 2007, 18 LEGO employees worked at Jirny, and DHL employed roughly 900 people during peak season and 450 in the off-peak season.

Change in cost drivers

During 2007, LEGO changed the cost drivers in its accounting, enabling it to measure profitability on a customer and a product level. This allowed Møller Nielsen and his team to better analyse the logistics and transportation costs per market and product line. Through analysis and lean process workshops, LEGO and DHL identified several areas for improvement aimed at reducing costs and waste. With logistics costs visible at a customer level, LEGO could also start charging customers for value-added services, such as customized labels or boxes.

The result of both initiatives contributed significantly to the overall cost savings related to the consolidation of the DCs in Europe.

By the end of 2007, LEGO operated from a central DC (EDC), serving almost 14,000 customers. Deliveries from the LEGO online shop direct to consumers – a continuously growing business for LEGO – were still dispatched from Denmark (*refer to Exhibit 1 for an overview*).

Quantitative results of the distribution consolidation

By the end of 2007 it was not entirely evident that the financial targets would be met in 2008. Costs exploded in 2007 due to the increase in inventory and warehouse space, while changes in the cost drivers and contract prices blurred the whole picture. To improve cost transparency for its top management and key stakeholders, the LEGO Group contracted an independent financial consulting company to dig deep into the logistics data for several weeks. Early in 2008, the external financial controller was able to confirm that the additional space requirements had been caused by the changes in production and also to validate the numbers presented by Møller Nielsen in his business plan. This restored Møller Nielsen's credibility with his own leadership team and led to increased responsibilities on a global level for him and some of his team members.

The real benefits became visible for the first time during 2008. LEGO was in much better shape than it had been three years earlier. Sales increased 35% from 2005 to 2008, and logistics costs dropped 9% over the same period. The logistics costs for 2008 would be DKK 260 million higher if no changes had been made. The risk of large sales fluctuations had been reduced by more than half and was shared with a financially strong third party. Customer satisfaction improved as deliveries were more reliable, while LEGO was also more responsive to requests from customers.[40] To summarize:

1   Total cost savings of about DKK 260 million in 2008. Logistics costs amounted to 7.9% of total sales, down from 10.8%.
2   Fixed cost base reduced from 75% to 33%.
3   On-time customer delivery was 96%. In 2005 this was roughly 62%. Picking and shipping at Jirny was measured by the minute!
4   LEGO is rated 'best in class' supplier in terms of logistics.

LEGO submitted its case to the European Supply Chain Excellence Awards in the 'Logistics and Fulfilment' category. In October it was announced that LEGO had won the 2008 award out of a total of nine shortlisted companies. The jury selected LEGO because it more closely met the five core disciplines than the others, since it:

1   Used its logistics strategy as a strategic asset for meeting business goals.
2   Used process infrastructure to change the way that it was operating.
3   Used collaboration in order to achieve mutual benefits.
4   Used metrics to improve performance.

5   Organized and simplified structure to reflect the new way of working. The judges were also impressed with how supplier performance was measured and presented (available in real time).

Future challenges

LEGO had some catch-up to do with regard to focusing on the demand and requirements of its larger retailers. A good start was made with the creation of a customer logistics group. This opened the door to working with the supply chain contacts at those customers in an attempt to find new and innovative ways to improve the total supply chain process. LEGO started testing a vendor management inventory (VMI) process with one retailer in Switzerland, but could do more in terms of developing more advanced integrated customer solutions, common in the retail sector. This was still new ground for LEGO and the challenge would be to build up the necessary in-house expertise and system infrastructure to roll out different programs and solutions.

The central distribution model with only one external partner had proved to be a successful formula in the current situation, but might not necessarily be the best solution in other circumstances. However, the distribution process was leaner and more flexible than before, which enabled LEGO to adapt more quickly to future changes and developments. This new distribution model would demonstrate its true value during turbulent times, which should be good news for future generations of children (and adults) who enjoy constructing their fantasy world with LEGO bricks.

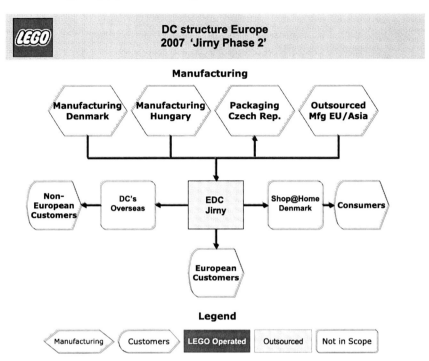

Exhibit 1 DC structure in Europe after 2007 implementation

Source: Company information

Actual rankings provided during high season periods in 2007 and 2008

 EUC LEGO Logistic Quality performance
- From the customers perspective

5=very good, 4=good, 3=fair,
2=bad, 1=very bad.

Quality Performance:		Ranking:						Companies:
	Clarification of the performance:	Week 38	Week 41	Week 43	Week 46			TOYS ЯUS
Packaging Quality	Damage on case packs and pallets, right packaging	3	3,6	3,4	4,0			HOFFMANN SHE MARKY
Packaging Quantity	Right quantity according to order	3,1	3,9	4,2	4,1			GALERIA Müller M
Delivery Precision	On-time, Carrier/Driver behavior	2,8	3,4	3,7	3,5			KARSTADT
Delivery Planning	Documents, booking-in, flexibility in delivery date etc.	3,8	4,8	4,8	4,8			Kaufland
Document Quality	Delivery note, Booking-in, flexibility	3,9	4,3	4,3	4,3			WOOLWORTH
Service Quality	Response time, adapting to customer needs	4,1	4,7	4,7	4,9			myToys
Overall Performance	The whole experience	3,6	4,1	4,1	4,3			

High season 2007

 EUC LEGO Logistic Quality performance
- From the customers perspective

5=very good, 4=good, 3=fair,
2=bad, 1=very bad.

Quality Performance:		Ranking:						Companies:
	Clarification of the performance:	Week 42	Week 44	Week 47				TOYS ЯUS
Packaging Quality	Damage on case packs and pallets, right packaging	4,6	4,8	4,8				HOFFMANN SHE MARKY
Packaging Quantity	Right quantity according to order	4,2	4,5	4,6				GALERIA Müller M
Delivery Precision	On-time, Carrier/Driver behavior	4,0	4,8	4,8				KARSTADT
Delivery Planning	Documents, booking-in, flexibility in delivery date etc.	4,7	4,7	5,0				Kaufland
Document Quality	Delivery note, Booking-in, flexibility	4,7	4,8	4,8				WOOLWORTH
Service Quality	Response time, adapting to customer needs	4,8	5,0	4,9				myToys
Overall Performance	The whole experience	4,5	4,9	4,9				

High season 2008

Exhibit 2 Example balanced scorecard
Source: Company information

This case series won the Supply Chain Management Award in the 2009 EFMD Case Writing Competition organized by the European Foundation for Management Development.

This case series won the 2011 ecch Case Award in the category Production and Operations Management.

Case 4.5
Freqon: Buyer–supplier evolution?

Chris Ellegaard, Thomas E. Vollmann and Carlos Cordon

In November 2000 the buyer–supplier relation between Freqon and its supplier of
extruded aluminium components, NordAlu, was troubled. Hans Meier, purchasing
director of Freqon, wondered how the situation had reached this stage:

> In the early 1990s the relationship between the two companies was seen
> as a benchmark in both organizations. Both sides were highly committed;
> employees collaborated and remarkable improvements were achieved. We
> helped NordAlu improve their performance on process technology and
> delivery time and they helped us optimize our designs. Today the commitment
> is decreasing and the atmosphere is tense. It seems like both parties perceive
> the buyer–supplier business to be unsatisfactory.

Hans Meier had just hired a new purchasing manager for mechanical
components, Helga Becker. One of her primary activities was working with
NordAlu. During the first meetings with the NordAlu employees she quickly felt
the tension in the relations between the two companies. The gap between them
was widening and seemingly minor problems, such as price negotiations, seemed
impossible to solve. She saw the need for NordAlu to improve its performance
but she also perceived that NordAlu people regarded the Freqon business as being
unattractive. Helga realized that only discussing concrete issues such as prices
was not sufficient. She asked herself what she could do to resolve the fundamental
problems between the two firms.

The two companies

Freqon

Freqon was a division of Freqon AG, a German industrial corporation. The
company was the first in the world to produce frequency converters in series and
had been in this business since the 1970s (*refer to **Exhibit 1** for description of a
frequency converter*). Freqon had previously been the only large producer of these
apparatuses but a number of large industrial corporations had entered the market
and competition was now fierce. The competitive situation had caused a decrease
in prices of approximately 10% per year during the last part of the 1990s.

The Freqon brand name for its frequency converter series was FQO. The
frequency converter was a complex construction, containing more than 900 code

numbers. These prefabricated components were assembled into the final product at the main plant in Hamburg, Germany. Freqon was a final assembly company rather than a producer – therefore a large part of the value of the final product originated in the supplier network.

NordAlu supplied a number of different extruded aluminium components to Freqon. The main functions of these components were cooling of power electronics, encapsulation of the apparatus (cover, housing) and reinforcing the construction. The specifications of the cooling components were very important to the functionality and characteristics of the converter and therefore had a direct bearing on the competitiveness of Freqon. The same was true for the encapsulation components, which were important for the design of the apparatus. Of the overall Freqon component purchases of €100 million, almost €5 million or 5% went to NordAlu.

Before the initialization of the relationship with NordAlu, Freqon had used die-cast components for the functions mentioned. (*Refer to **Exhibit 2** for illustration and description of the two component technologies.*)

NordAlu

NordAlu was the Hamburg-based subsidiary of the German corporation AluGermany whose main business was aluminium extrusion. NordAlu did not make extrusions but was specialized in subsequent surface treating and machining of extrusions. The long extruded profiles were delivered from the sister extrusion plants to NordAlu. Here the profiles were cut into the right component sizes, surface treated and machined to the right specifications before they were delivered to Freqon.

NordAlu had developed from a sales company in the early 1980s to a small craftsman-like company with 50 employees in the mid-1980s and from there to an industrial company with 400 employees in 2000.

The 'evolution' of the Freqon–NordAlu industrial relationship

Initiation (1987)

In 1987 Freqon developed a new frequency converter, the FQO 100. For this model, the component technology for the cooling and encapsulation components was changed from die-cast aluminium to extruded aluminium. Therefore a supplier of extruded aluminium components was needed. NordAlu was chosen for two main reasons:

- It had the anodization (surface treatment) process in-house.
- AluGermany's extrusion plants had the large extrusion presses necessary for the production of some of the Freqon components.

Engineers and product development people managed the relationship from the Freqon side. The purchasing managers only handled the more administrative tasks of the relationship from the central corporate purchasing function at Freqon AG headquarters. The product development people managed the detailed relations, with heavy emphasis on technological issues in the initial stages. The product incorporated complex components and Freqon needed NordAlu to master large-scale and technologically complex production. The technological capabilities at NordAlu were not initially sufficient to meet the needs of Freqon.

In the early 1980s NordAlu had expanded from being a sales office to carrying out simple refinement machining operations like shortening, drilling and punching on the extruded profiles.

Integration (1988–1989)

Freqon drove the development during 1988 and the first part of 1989. Within NordAlu, there was not complete enthusiasm for this project, with many people wishing to continue the simpler processing of extruded profiles. But progress continued and with the help of Freqon, NordAlu installed new machinery, hired new people and educated employees. The main actors at NordAlu, director Dieter Schmidt and sales manager Heinz Bauer, were responding to the wishes from Freqon about development; but in 1988 sales of the FQO 100 were still unexpectedly low. NordAlu was not under pressure to perform at that time.

The large degree of joint development without major ramp-up pressures supported good relations and integrated work. The atmosphere was relaxed and employees from both sides developed personal relationships. The understanding and values of the two companies started to merge. The transfer of technology, knowledge and resources from Freqon to NordAlu, the development of new competencies, as well as the commitment of Freqon employees created a strong bond on the part of NordAlu employees in favor of Freqon. Through this common 'project' the relationship grew strong.

INCREASING DEMANDS ON NORDALU

During 1989 NordAlu was able to produce the Freqon components but it needed developments of its production capabilities. One of the Freqon engineers described the problem: 'The NordAlu people were steering the production by hand. The processes and systems were not thoroughly planned and systematized, but rather working in a kind of random state. Some produced components were fine. Others had quality errors.'

At the same time sales of the FQO 100 started rising, resulting in both quality and delivery problems for the NordAlu components. At this point Dieter Schmidt and Heinz Bauer saw the only solution as further investment in infrastructure – supported by AluGermany corporate management. Therefore a trip to the NordAlu corporate headquarters was arranged, where key people from both Freqon and NordAlu presented their case for investment. The delegation succeeded in securing the necessary funds by promoting the Freqon name in the NordAlu organization and creating commitment to the longer-term relationship.

Following this trip NordAlu employees redoubled their efforts to successfully supply Freqon. But this took time. By the end of 1989, NordAlu had developed the last steps in the required technology. However, it still had some problems with quality, delivery time and ramp-up capability; moreover, its prices were seen as higher than those of the competition.

During this developmental period, the two firms worked together to solve whatever problems came up and to better integrate their joint planning. The various actors in the two companies got on well together and in some cases the integration even reached beyond professional relations – with employees from the two companies arranging golf and fishing trips. These social relations reinforced the industrial relationship and helped to resolve problems quickly.

First changes: Further demands on NordAlu for improvements (1989–1992)

By the end of 1989 the relationship was strong, with high levels of commitment on both sides. The NordAlu people treated Freqon problems as their own and vice versa. A product developer at Freqon remembered the strong commitment:

> I called NordAlu on a Thursday to ask for a prototype sample I would need the following Monday. A NordAlu engineer personally arranged for the production of the prototype Friday and Saturday and then drove to our factory to deliver it Sunday afternoon.

Despite this kind of commitment, NordAlu was still not performing to expectations on quality, delivery and price. Freqon had connections to some other suppliers at this time, and in a few instances it moved a component to other suppliers. This was done for benchmarking purposes – and to keep NordAlu up to the mark.

DECENTRALIZATION OF FREQON AG

1989 saw the reorganization of the Freqon AG corporate purchasing function with local purchasing departments at each of the Freqon AG divisions. The Freqon purchasing department started to take charge of managing supplier relations, including the relationship with NordAlu. The purchasing people tended to look differently at both the relationship and the basic performance. They were much more focused on the short-term performance parameters of price, delivery and quality. They started putting pressure on NordAlu for improvements.

During 1990 and 1991 a number of improvement sessions were held at different locations in Germany. Employees from product development, production, logistics, sales and purchasing in the two companies met to discuss possibilities for improvements, including direct cost cutting. The idea was to let the Freqon people communicate their concerns directly to their colleagues from NordAlu and to jointly find the best solutions.

The meetings were held in relaxed settings and there was a pleasant atmosphere, where the participants had a beer and played billiards in the evening. During the day drawings of components and diagrams of production facilities at NordAlu were studied closely with the purpose of creating improvements. The meetings led to successful improvements in costs, quality and especially lead times. (*Refer to* **Exhibit 3** *for development in NordAlu lead times on Freqon components*.)

COST RATIONALIZATION

In 1991 Rainer Hamann, the Freqon director, declared that the company had to cut costs and save 10% per year. The purchasing people responded by demanding increased efforts from NordAlu in the hunt for savings. NordAlu was willing to commit to investments to achieve cost reductions, but in turn asked for a trade agreement with Freqon. The contract provided a guarantee to deliver components for the next three years in return for the improvement efforts. Freqon agreed and the agreement was signed in 1992.

The hunt for cost improvements continued and in 1992 ratio (rationalization) groups were formed. NordAlu and Freqon set up a 'group of technically oriented employees' to work systematically on cost rationalization. Four employees from each company met frequently to work on improvements. Freqon got the savings and NordAlu got the promises of future business. The savings were now coming mainly from product or process changes – especially the removal of machining processes or change of product specifications (material thickness etc.). The meetings were different from the first improvement sessions. They were more formal one-day meetings and Freqon was the main beneficiary of the results. The spirit and atmosphere at the meetings were good – although a purchasing employee from Freqon noted: 'NordAlu probably considered the meetings a kind of arm-twisting – still we achieved great results.'

Divided attention on both sides (1993–1995)

The drive for further savings caused a change in the product architecture in 1993. Freqon designed a new frequency converter model, the FQO 150 for the HVAC (heating, ventilation, air-condition) market. Many of the aluminium components were replaced by steel components. Freqon revealed a prototype of the new model to NordAlu at a meeting in 1993. The NordAlu people were quite shocked to see the product stripped of aluminium, and requested a chance to come up with an even better solution for the cooling and encapsulation components – and they did. Two weeks later they presented their solutions, which impressed the Freqon people. In particular, a remarkable new encapsulation concept made Freqon choose the NordAlu solution. NordAlu was able to make this proposal because it had consulted some of the Freqon engineers, whom it knew well from their working relationship. These engineers helped NordAlu design the new components.

In 1994 component production volumes grew to a considerable degree. NordAlu management decided to divide its organization into a component division and a profile division. The resultant partition of the sales organization meant that some of the key NordAlu people who supported the Freqon relationship were reassigned to the profiles unit – away from the Freqon business.

In 1995 NordAlu was able to attract some major new customers. One of these customers was a very large producer of electronic appliances; the other a producer of windows. Both companies started buying some specialized components at NordAlu. At the same time NordAlu had developed its capabilities to a level where the Freqon components were no longer difficult to produce. The window producer and especially the electronic appliances producer took over the technological developments with NordAlu from this point in time. The electronic appliances producer needed components with very precise tolerances and extremely high quality and NordAlu had to enhance its operations and processing capabilities to meet these challenges.

Freqon developed another new frequency converter in 1995, the FQO 200. This model was to replace the FQO 100, with fewer aluminium components – each with less aluminium. The result would therefore reduce the turnover for NordAlu. Nonetheless, NordAlu participated in joint design, with notable success. Engineers from both Freqon and NordAlu went to the AluGermany extrusion plants to design the extrusion together with employees from these plants. The FQO 200 was introduced in 1996.

Organizational changes at Freqon (1996–1997)

The phasing out of the FQO 100 and introduction of the FQO 200 went smoothly in 1996. NordAlu handled the change very well. For a short while, when the sales of the two models were overlapping, NordAlu had the highest turnover ever with Freqon. After the new product introduction, however, the sales volumes started to fall (*refer to **Exhibit 4** for the turnover development*).

Another event in 1996 was yet another change in the purchasing organization at Freqon. A new purchasing director and new purchasing manager of mechanical components (including the NordAlu relationship) were put in place. The demand for 10% savings per year became even more focused on suppliers, with the purchasing organization pushing for further cost reductions. This was now harder to sell inside NordAlu since the sales volumes were reducing instead of increasing.

The net result was an increasing series of communication and understanding problems. The NordAlu people still managed the relationship in a relaxed, more technologically focused way, whereas the Freqon people were increasingly moving towards a more arm's-length business orientation. In 1997 Freqon introduced Key Performance Indicators (KPIs) as a way of evaluating performance within the company. For the purchasing department the KPIs became price, quality and delivery.

NordAlu found it increasingly difficult to meet the Freqon demands. It started by agreeing to the purchasing manager's objectives – without asking questions or highlighting potential difficulties in meeting these demands. The assumption was always that any problems would be worked out through the familiar joint working relationships. But when problems naturally arose in meeting the concrete objectives, the perception on the Freqon side was that NordAlu performance was unsatisfactory. The NordAlu people found it hard to achieve cost reductions – and the Freqon people pushed for results.

MOVE OF COMPONENTS

In 1997 Freqon moved one third of its extruded aluminium components to Aluex, another German extruded aluminium producer. Aluex presented a good price offer and Freqon purchasing went for the saving. The news came as a shock to NordAlu. The employees felt that the move hurt them personally. The NordAlu people claimed that the Freqon people had not been open about the problems and that they had not given them sufficient warning. The Freqon purchasers on the other hand felt that they had simply reacted to bad performance on the NordAlu side.

Organizational changes at NordAlu (1998)

Dieter Schmidt, the director of NordAlu, who had been one of the mainstays in the relationship and the primary driver inside NordAlu, retired in 1998. His personal friendship with Rainer Hamann of Freqon had played an important role throughout the relationship development.

An assessment of the Freqon account was not very positive: reduced volumes, no longer technologically challenging, heavy price reduction objectives, arbitrary demands and reduced joint working relations. Thereafter, the new NordAlu management team applied a different management style to the relationship, focusing on more professionalism instead of the former relaxed way of working together. The NordAlu people now started presenting their own demands to Freqon. The key account manager responsible for the Freqon account was replaced by Gerd Mahler. He immediately presented a long list of demands to the purchasers at Freqon. Hans Meier of Freqon described the meetings with Gerd Mahler this way: 'He presented many impossible demands. We could not negotiate with him.'

Gerd Mahler's rather aggressive way of presenting the demands upset the Freqon people, but the NordAlu management supported his position. To somewhat ease the conflict, NordAlu reinstated Heinz Bauer who had been working on the relationship in the first years and had experience with Freqon. This move did not, however, change the fact that NordAlu was now more aggressive towards Freqon.

Further divided attention (1998)

The new NordAlu management also motivated the sales people to expand the components business and find new preferred customers. In 1998 another electronic appliances producer and a train producer became key accounts. Serving these customers helped to further develop NordAlu's processing capabilities. These new companies required the complex processes NordAlu had developed through cooperating with the other electronic appliances producer and they also wanted NordAlu to perform assembly at their plant. Therefore NordAlu's focus expanded to include assembly operations.

The year 1998 also marked the introduction of another new Freqon frequency converter, the FQO 300. This apparatus adopted a new design concept and was completely free of extruded aluminium components. The encapsulation was made of plastic and the cooling component was die-cast aluminium (*refer to **Exhibit 2***). The introduction of this product had a further negative impact on the turnover with NordAlu. To deliver these components Freqon contracted with a local German supplier. There were now three suppliers of aluminium components to Freqon.

Recent development of the relationship (1998–2000)

Communication problems were growing and the two parties found it increasingly hard to reach agreements at the end of the 1990s. Helga Becker, the new purchasing manager responsible for the NordAlu relationship at Freqon, was thrown in at the deep end. She had to deal with the problems. Prices, whether or not NordAlu was allowed to produce to inventory and delivery in five days, were some of the more concrete contentions. The problem with agreeing on prices had to do with the fluctuations on the London Metal Exchange (LME) where basic aluminium prices were decided. On the one hand, both parties wanted a steady price level to make purchasing easier. On the other, Freqon wanted price reductions if the LME fell and NordAlu wanted an increase if the LME went up. No compromises seemed possible. More basic was the overall approach to working together – with a shared appreciation for the relationship. It was a vicious circle where one problem and miscommunication sparked the next, and where each disagreement corroded their sense of shared values.

NordAlu found it disagreeable and unfair to be in a competitive set-up with Aluex on the product development projects. This in turn impacted its commitment to the product development projects. The once close and integrated technology collaboration was now almost nonexistent. Development of new NordAlu competencies was driven through working with other customers. Specific joint projects were not very successful and were characterized by less and less commitment from either side. Freqon was no longer among the largest customers for NordAlu. (*Refer to **Exhibit 4** for the development in NordAlu turnover on Freqon components.*) NordAlu performance on delivery time, quality and price was still competitive, but Freqon was not impressed with its performance on development assistance and cost improvement projects. In turn, NordAlu was rebelling against what it saw as unreasonable Freqon demands. Both parties increasingly regarded the business relationship as unfavorable.

The frequency converter is a complex apparatus for regulating and controlling frequencies of electrical motors. Most electrical motors are supplied with a fixed frequency, for example spinning at 60 Hz. The connection of the motor with the frequency converter enables the operator to regulate this frequency. Furthermore the converter comes with a programming unit. The converter can be programed to operate the motor at specific hours or to reduce the acceleration when starting and stopping, among others.

Exhibit 1   Description of a frequency converter

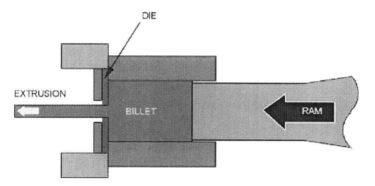

ALUMINIUM EXTRUSION

The extrusion process is analogous to pressing out whipped cream on a cake. Extremely high pressure is applied by the ram to the raw aluminium billet (bar), pushing it against the die with the right geometry for the specific component. The aluminium starts flowing because of the pressure and gets squeezed through the holes in the die. The result is a long extruded profile with a component geometry corresponding to the holes in the die.

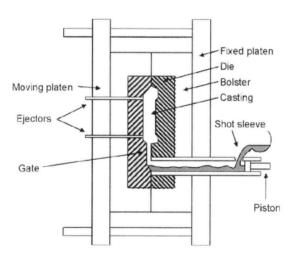

ALUMINIUM DIE-CASTING

Liquid aluminium is poured into the sleeve. From here it is injected rapidly into the die, which holds the geometry of the component. When the component is cooled and solid, the moving platen slides away opening the die from which the component can then be removed.

Exhibit 2   Two aluminium component technologies used so far at Freqon: Extrusion and die-casting

Source: European Aluminium Association website

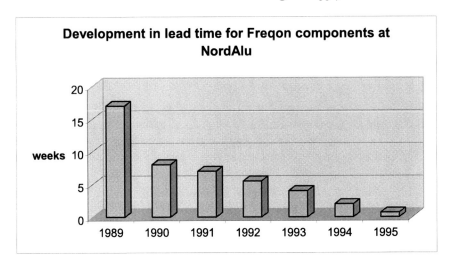

Exhibit 3 The development in NordAlu lead times on Freqon components

Source: Company information

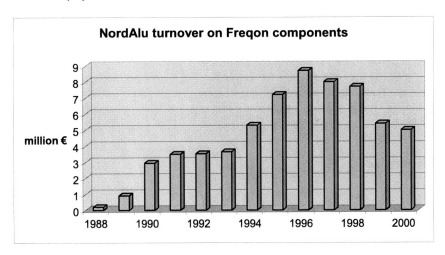

Exhibit 4 Development in NordAlu turnover on Freqon components

Source: Company information

This case won the 2002 Best Case Study award granted by the Decision Sciences Institute.

Case 4.6
Unaxis: Going Asia (A)

Henrik Eklund, Ralf W. Seifert and Carlos Cordon

'So Wilhelm, what are you and your team going to do about Asia?' The question, posed by the CEO at the annual International Management Conference in the fall of 2003, was addressed to Christoph Wilhelm, operations manager for the UNAXIS Data Storage Division. It instantly caught the attention of the hundred or so other managers attending the conference.

A year or so later, at the end of 2004, he could clearly recall the challenge he and his team had been given – it had come as no surprise. The Data Storage Division was one of the few divisions within the company that had not moved its operations to Asia. It was no longer a question of whether to go or not, but rather how to go about it? Wilhelm and his team had suddenly found themselves responsible for the task of moving sourcing and assembly to Asia for one of the most complex production systems ever to be moved to a low-cost region.

Wilhelm also recalled the abundance of questions the team had been pondering during the last year of intensive planning. Was the production line ready to be sourced from China? Were the Chinese suppliers ready to produce modules and components with this level of complexity? To what extent could the production line be outsourced and how should the new sourcing strategy be executed? What impact might it have on existing suppliers, intellectual property protection and delivery lead times? How much time would be required to get things up and running? How would his own organization react to this move and would people still believe it was the right maneuvre if the project were to run into problems?

Background

Unaxis

Formerly known as Oerlikon-Bührle, Unaxis had its headquarters in Pfäffikon, Switzerland and provided production systems, components and services to the information technology industry. The product range included modules and complete automated lines for the production of high-tech products, such as microchips, flat panel displays, optical and magnetic data storage discs, video projectors, solar cells and rocket canopies.

Sales reached SFr 1.85 billion in 2004 and the company had nearly 7,000 employees. The corporation's activities encompassed R&D and production in Asia, Europe and USA, as well as sales and service out of a total of 80 subsidiaries in 24 countries. Since the end of the 1990s, the company had experienced the pronounced up- and downswings of the IT industry. The stock price was down to 30% of the peaks of 2000.

Since 2004, the Unaxis organization had been divided into five different segments: Coating Services, Vacuum Solutions, Data Storage Solutions, Components & Special Systems and Semiconductor Equipment. The core competencies were in thin film, vacuum and precision technology. All organizational units utilized at least one, if not all, of these areas of competency.

During recent years several strategic decisions had been made to increase the production capacity in Asia. Some divisions, such as Display, had already executed an Asia strategy and had taken some hard knocks along the way. Nevertheless, Asia was still a prioritized topic for the corporate strategists, due to cost competitiveness and customer proximity.

Data Storage Solutions

Data Storage Solutions (DSS) was operated out of Balzers, Liechtenstein, and was amongst the world's leading manufacturers of both coating systems (metalizers) and complete replication line solutions for optical data storage media like CDs and DVDs. The division had its origins as a metalizer supplier, delivering these to other manufacturers (so-called integrators) for incorporation into a complete replication line. Such metalizers typically spattered a fine, even coat of metal, e.g. aluminium, on the underside of plastic discs (*refer to Exhibit 1*). The metalizer was considered to be a core component of the line, and sales of this sub-assembly alone still continued to count for more than a third of DSS's total revenues.

In 2000 DSS embarked on a strategy of forward integration. A year later, it started to produce whole DVD production lines, including the metalizer, in order to protect and grow the business. The move further down the value chain was by no means an easy task. A member of the R&D team commented on the implementation of the new strategy: 'We soon realized that vacuum technology and automation required two totally different competencies.'

Nevertheless, the decision to produce the FUSION01, Unaxis's first complete, recordable DVD (DVD-R) production line turned out to be the right one and during 2003, demand rocketed. Optical disc producers literally lined up to buy the new, very reputable line. The ramp-up was fast and furious but as customers urgently needed manufacturing capacity, some 15 prototypes of the FUSION01 were assembled more or less in parallel, to satisfy the demand. While the situation gave the salespeople reason to cheer, it rapidly became a nightmare for production, since there was no time to stabilize the internal processes before beginning to manufacture in volume.

FUSION01 was the 'Rolex' of DVD-R production systems. Consisting of eight modules made of the best materials, it was seen as a masterpiece of Swiss engineering (*refer to Exhibit 2*). However, the demand for less complex and faster machines was a fact. As a member of the sales department pointed out: 'It was laboratory equipment, not something the Asian customers would also want for low-cost mass production!'

The second generation line, the FUSION02 (*refer to Exhibit 3*), was a result of successful product reengineering. The first prototype stood ready in the factory in

Balzers in January 2005, just eight months after the decision to launch a new line was made. The line could produce DVD-R discs faster than its predecessor and was easier to use and maintain. Its structure was much leaner, consisting of only three modules, thereby reducing complexity. The use of materials was optimized and the layout was more efficient. Automation experts had simplified handling wherever possible and FUSION02, although not yet introduced, promised to be a resounding success on its market launch.

Supply chain setup

SUPPLY CHAIN MANAGEMENT BECOMES TOP PRIORITY

As it had become clear that the majority of mass replication customers were located in Asia, the focus turned to operations and especially supply chain management in order to serve them in the most competitive way. In the new circumstances the importance of the function was becoming evident. As Wilhelm remarked: 'We are used to living in an outsourcing world.'

Since 2001 more than 80% of the components for the lines had been sourced from suppliers located in Western Europe. The supply chain was competitive regarding innovation and quality. The increasing competition and the growing demand in Asia, which had been clear trends since 2003, were now forcing the supply chain team at DSS to maneuvre. In addition to value engineering, the focus was now put on the supply base.

In early 2004 the improvement of the supply chain was, for the first time, placed among the three main priorities for DSS. This was a new approach within the company. This change in focus resulted in some organizational changes and new resources.

In July 2004 new manpower was brought to DSS. Carsten Liske was named head of supply chain management and project leader for the Asia project. With support from HQ, a fresh team and a brand new product, the completed supply chain team was now ready to move and set up in Asia.

GOING TO ASIA

The first question was, to what extent should the line be sourced from China? The team took a clear stand on this issue: 'We are not going to do component tourism in China. This would be taking us a huge step backwards, having successfully moved to modular sourcing.'

Therefore they quickly reached the conclusion that it would only be worthwhile if at least an entire bonding module could be made in Asia. Later, if this pilot project were to succeed, the remaining two modules would be sourced from China as well.

Of the three modules in the FUSION02 line, the bonding module was the most complex. The bonding component at its heart was considered to be a core component and would continue to be produced in Balzers. The other components for the module were currently sourced from 15 different tier one suppliers – mainly in Europe.

A deliberate decision was taken to source from Chinese factories owned by companies from Taiwan, Singapore or Hong Kong. Instead of trying to find technically fully capable manufacturing plants, the emphasis was on potential for fast development. The Chinese factories, although currently lacking some capabilities, would be given the opportunity for fast technical development, in order to prove themselves. The selected module supplier would also have to have a differentiated business portfolio, in order to be able to handle the cyclical nature of the demand from DSS.

Due to lead-time requirements, module assembly and testing would also have to be done in Asia. In a series of quick decisions, Unaxis Taiwan was chosen as the location to act as a supply chain hub. DSS already had a large sales and service organization in Taiwan and it was close to customers.

The supply chain team planned to keep purchasing centralized in Balzers. The mission for the purchasing function in Balzers was to act as an orchestrator for two supply chains in the future: one Europe-based and one Asia-based.

FROM SINGLE- TO MULTI-SOURCING

Indeed, the goal was to build a second, entirely separate, supply chain in Asia (*refer to **Figure 1***). Liske explained the benefits: 'By doing this we will have a better understanding of the price and we can create competition between the supply base in both chains.'

DSS had been very open with its current suppliers about its plans to go to Asia. It had clearly expressed that in future it wanted to have two competing chains serving two markets – Europe and Asia. How the balance would evolve would depend on the lead time, capacity and price of the suppliers. The message was clear: 'Stay competitive!' According to a team member, the current suppliers were very understanding and had anticipated the move: 'They understood the reality of today. They also read the newspapers.'

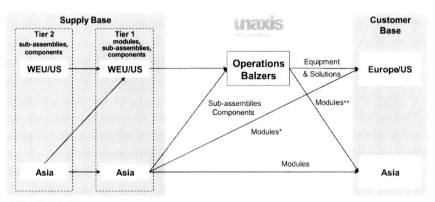

*) Possibly in the future
**) Modules only from Operations Balzers to
 Asian customers until serial production release

Figure 1 Planned supply chain setup
Source: Company information

Implementation

SELECTING THE MODULE SUPPLIER

The supply chain team at DSS had no prior personal experience dealing with Chinese suppliers or moving to Asia in general. Other divisions of Unaxis had mixed experiences and there was no structured approach to supplier selection in place that could readily be adopted for the situation. One solution seemed to be to rely on the services of a third party. Wilhelm commented: 'Regardless of our inexperience, we were very skeptical about using a third party in the selection process.'

However, the team nevertheless explored the option.

In August 2004 a consultant at a third-party consulting company came to the attention of the decision makers at Unaxis. He had a strong solid technical background and more than ten years of sourcing experience in Asia. Peter Tinner, head of DSS, saw an opportunity to jumpstart the project: 'We realized that we didn't want to spend six months doing market research, instead we wanted to have one pilot module of FUSION02 made in Asia in that time.'

The challenge of the whole project was not really clear until the experienced consultant expressed his doubts out loud during a preliminary factory tour: 'Are you guys sure!?! To my knowledge, nobody has ever tried to source a whole module, this technologically complex from China, or any other low-cost countries in Asia.

At DSS however, the decision had already been made. It was the entire module or nothing. The competitors were not standing still and DSS had to push ahead.

During fall 2004, a supplier selection process was developed together with the consultants. The model had four main criteria including total costs, qualifications, financial state and readiness. There were some strong expectations concerning cost savings on a higher managerial level, which put additional weight on the first criterion, but how to approach the tendering process was still a headache, given the nature of the bonding module.

THE CHINESE TENDERS

In late 2004 DSS made a preliminary selection of Chinese companies to whom the quotations would be sent. The goal was to make it as easy as possible for the companies to construct their tenders. The supply chain team also wanted full transparency. For this reason a standard quotation sheet was developed to work as a 'bidding tool' (*refer to Exhibit 4*). It included a detailed Bill of Materials with more than 2,000 lines, as well as drawings and direct links to some second-tier suppliers, etc. The suppliers filled in their prices and costs and the tenders became easily comparable.

The Chinese quickly adopted this new way of making an extremely detailed tender and the potential module suppliers sent their first tenders to Unaxis. The expectations had been for cost savings of approximately 20%, but the reality was different. The received tenders were approximately 20% higher than the current price from the European suppliers! The supply chain team had encountered the first real challenge on the road. What had gone wrong!?! How would the organization react? China was supposed to be cheap!

The goal was still to source all three modules in China by the end of 2005. Senior management also expected costs and lead time to be clearly reduced, FUSION02 to be launched and production to be ramped up at the same time. The supply chain team at DSS was about to have a long meeting ...

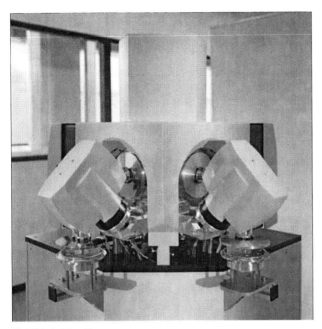

Exhibit 1 Metalizer

Source: Company information

Exhibit 2 FUSION01

Source: Company information

Exhibit 3 FUSION02

Source: Company information

Material (excl. subcontratcted Items) + Labor
+   Material overhead costs
=   **Manufacturing cost**
+   Sales and Administration + Warranty costs
=   **Production costs**
+   Earnings
= **Sub-Total 1 ('Make' Parts)**

  Cost or Subcontracted Items
+ Handling Cost

+ Shipping, Customs
= **Sub-Total 2 ('Buy' Parts)**

Sub-Total 1 + Sub-Total 2 = <u>Sales Price</u>

Exhibit 4 Bidding tool

Source: Company information

Appendix 1 Market development

The optical disc market

The optical disc market developed quickly during the early 2000s. Audio CD technology, with a storage capacity of 650 MB, evolved from prerecorded CDs to write-once discs (CD-R) and further to rewritable discs (CD-RW). The same evolution took place in DVD technology, with storage capacities of up to 9.4 GB. The next step would be so-called HD-DVD and Blu-ray technologies with storage capacities of 15 GB and 25 GB respectively. Such high capacities would allow storage of a three-hour movie on one single disc. New consumer behavior patterns showed that there was a clear need for more disc storage, which would in turn require more complex disc structures, and therefore replication lines with better control of more complex processes at reduced tolerances.

According to recent statistics, worldwide DVD production across all formats had grown in 2003 to approximately 4.7 billion discs including 1 billion DVD-R, and the market continued to expand. Several leading market institutes agreed that DVD production would grow on average at least 25% annually for years to come – even though it had barely affected the heavily populated countries in Asia – reaching 13 billion by 2007, including 4 billion DVD-Rs. However, the demand for DVD-R quality differed from region to region. There were three recognized levels of quality, from A to C. The A-quality, where all the discs in a consumer package worked flawlessly, was the standard used by all brand-leading disc-producing companies. In a pack of ten B-quality discs, on average one disc was faulty. C-quality discs were even referred to as 'the China standard' by some people in the industry: Up to 30% of discs sold had defects! Unaxis was well positioned to compete in the high-quality segment.

The market for replication lines

In contrast to Unaxis and other leading replication line suppliers, the actual production of recordable DVDs had already moved to Asia due to cheaper manufacturing costs. In 2003 more than 75% of DSS's revenues came from Asian customers and there were no signs that the importance of Asian customers would diminish in the future. The biggest group of customers in Asia was located in Taiwan with an 80% share of purchases, followed by Japan, Korea and China. The Chinese market was growing rapidly as the replicating companies were moving directly from CD to DVD-R technology.

Sales by continent 2001–2004

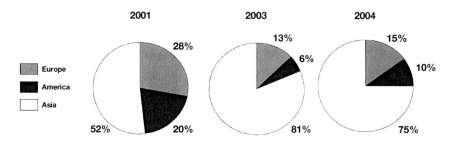

Source: Company information

The demand for replication lines was very cyclical in nature, as DVD-R manufacturers followed investment waves. This put some serious requirements on supply chain flexibility, given the nature of the product. During the first two quarters of 2004, the DSS factory was running at 150% of normal capacity. In two weeks it fell down to 60%, and a month later down to 20%. The world DVD-R replication market was dominated by just a few players (e.g. the top 6 accounted for 70% of total output in 2004), and order postponements and even cancellations for new machines were not uncommon during downfalls. Thus, shortening lead times and risk sharing were key issues.

Case 4.7
Unaxis: Going Asia (B)

François Jäger, Ralf W. Seifert and Carlos Cordon

'What do you mean Chinese prices are 20% higher than the current price from our European supplier?' It was summer 2005, and these words – spoken eight months earlier – were still at the back of Christoph Wilhelm's mind. The team had been totally puzzled when the offers in the tendering process in China had come back much higher than expected. There was a moment of indescribable doubt as everyone tried to figure out what had happened and how to get back on track. This had provided an opportunity for the third-party consultants to play a valuable role.

Price negotiation: Supplier misinterpretation

Instead of Unaxis beginning the price negotiations with a starting price way off the target, the consultants had acted as diplomats. It turned out that from the supplier side, the problem had been more about misperception than real cost issues. The new potential suppliers had no clue of the true market price of such complicated modules and they had assumed that since it was 'Swiss Made' it had to be expensive. Eventually talks between the potential suppliers and the consultants – two long-term business partners – bore fruit and by the second round of offers, received in February 2005, they had been close to the estimated target price for the Asian-made bonding module. In March 2005 the contracts had been signed.

Yet there was still uncertainty for the Data Storage Solutions (DSS) team. What was the real intent of the new suppliers? Would they still keep their promises once selected? What would happen if, once locked in with a supplier, prices were to go back up again? With the planning for a second supply chain well underway, the Chinese modules still had not been tested. But Wilhelm and his team did not have the luxury of time, they had to move forward. They had also taken measures to secure the company's intellectual property (IP), but would they be sufficient?

Securing IP: Copyright doesn't mean right to copy …

Wilhelm had read lots of business articles saying that outsourcing high-tech products in China meant increasing risk of losing IP to Chinese copycats. Also, some colleagues from other divisions with experience in Asia thought that there seemed to be no limit to the complexity that the Chinese were capable of copying nowadays. The supply chain team was well aware of this. Safety measures were taken down to the smallest detail.

The first decision was to use only pure contract manufacturers (CMs), in order to avoid creating new competitors. The CMs were foreign companies with manufacturing plants in mainland China. They would see only part of the final product, making it impossible for them to copy the entire machine. DSS also made sure that the final product would be assembled by its own employees in Taiwan so that no external party would have a complete picture of the FUSION02.

Furthermore, stringent IT controls had been put in place in the Chinese factory to prevent unauthorized distribution of data. For instance, the Chinese factory workers had limited access to e-mail, restricted sizes for outgoing e-mails, etc. Even the USB ports were blocked in the computers, in order to prevent the workers from saving data on private storage devices.

Yet Wilhelm knew that complete data security was not a certainty – even with these stringent IT controls there was the risk that some of the blueprints could be distributed outside the company. However, he knew Unaxis had a significant advantage over potential Chinese competitors – an excellent brand recognition, a good reputation in the industry and, with more than 20 years of successful experience in the field, know-how that would be difficult to match.

Supply chain hub

Headquarters had given the final green light in March 2005 and the first contracts with the chosen supplier were written immediately thereafter. By April 2005 the selected CM had started to manufacture the first module, and the decision had been taken to start manufacturing the other two modules in Asia. But no CM would supply more than one module of the FUSION02. By the end of 2005, the plan was for all three modules to be manufactured in China.

At first, the modules would be tested in Balzers as a complete line assembly, since there was concern that the people in Taiwan would not have the capability to do the necessary fine-tuning.

The first complete Chinese manufactured line assembly was scheduled to arrive in Balzers in October, when DSS teams would be able to check if the quality was up to expectations. If all went well, the testing could move to the Taiwanese hub – a tentative date of early 2006 had been set. Still, a lot could happen before then. What would DSS do if the test results did not meet expectations? There was concern that Chinese-made modules might not match the famous 'Swiss Made' quality. What would Wilhelm do if quality did not match the expected levels?

Moving forward

DSS had already decided to set up a second supply chain in Asia (i.e. close to customers), where both manufacturing and testing would take place (*refer to* **Figure 1**). Localization efforts would start in September in China. This meant that if everything was successful, Unaxis would end up with two supply chains for the FUSION02. In terms of sourcing, commodity parts would be sourced in China, when possible, but certain OEM (original equipment manufacturer) components were only available in Europe, therefore CMs would have to buy those components from the actual European suppliers. The DSS supply chain team was afraid that Chinese suppliers would not be able to match the quality of the OEM suppliers. The final assembly would take place directly at the customer's premises.

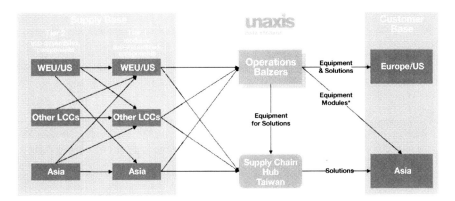

* Modules only from Operations Balzers to Asian Customers until serial production release

Figure 1 Working with two supply chains

Unaxis's management team knew that outsourcing manufacturing would have greater benefits than merely sourcing components in Asia. But should the company keep two separate supply chains? Or should it further push the move to China and only keep the Asian one? Would it be worth the risk? Could it go as far as moving R&D to China as well? On the other hand, what if the test results were not as good as expected? This would delay Unaxis's whole Asia plan. Also, the testing would be carried out on a single unit, so these results would not necessarily be repeated for future lines. This could have a knock-on effect on the upcoming supply chain ramp-up. Some customers were looking forward to having these lines working in their facilities, and failing to deliver could have quite a negative effect in terms of reputation and future revenue generation. The whole DSS Asian plan was dependent upon the success of the FUSION02 ...

Chapter notes

1 Hald, K.S., C. Cordon, and T.E. Vollmann. 'Towards an Understanding of Attraction in Buyer–Supplier Relationships.' *Industrial Marketing Management*, Vol. 38, Iss. 8, 2009: 960–970.

Case study notes

1 Danish krone = US$0.18 (December 4, 2011).
2 Revenue from Oracle software license updates and product support rose 16% as of February 2003 to $1 billion.
3 www.oracle.com
4 Defined as transactions over $500,000.
5 Oracle, 10-K filing, July 29, 2002.
6 Europe, Middle East and Africa.
7 In China 100% of the revenue was generated through partners, due to the vastness of the market.
8 Robert DeMarzo. 'Oracle's Marathon Man: George Roberts Goes the Distance to Bring Channels into the Fold.' VARbusiness, April 1, 2002.
9 Ibid.
10 A reference to involving, or engaging, partners in jointly participating in pre-sales activities.
11 www.oracle.com
12 As of February 2003, Partner ResourceNetwork had conducted almost 1,500 two-hour training sessions, and handled 30,000 inbound calls and 15,000 e-mail requests.
13 www.oracle.com January 2003.
14 www.oracle.com
15 Partners registering sales opportunities on OMM secured Oracle's commitment not to pursue the identified (license) opportunity for a period of time. Further, partners qualified for a referral or initiative fee when they referred an opportunity to Oracle to sell directly or influenced a sale.
16 'With' – to associate Oracle's brand with its partners' brand; 'through' – so partners would reach markets that Oracle could not reach directly; and 'to' – to coordinate a single message.
17 In 2001 Oracle gave away 20,000 training days to its partners.
18 Source: LEGO annual report 2002.
19 New products generated 75% of total sales; 45% of sales took place in the three months before Christmas.
20 The average sales forecasting error was 40%.
21 Assortments of branded non-LEGO products, educational products and loose LEGO bricks.
22 Marketing materials, retail displays, value packs, bundles, one-time products, new SKUs, etc.
23 Total sales of Star Wars products were DKK 980 million in 2005. This was a 190% increase on the previous year. The second last Star Wars movie was in 2002.
24 In 2005 Møller Nielsen was promoted to senior logistics director, Europe and Asia.
25 1 Danish krone DKK 1 = €0.13 = US$0.18 (December 4, 2011).
26 Within 16 to 18 hours' drive.
27 For Møller Nielsen, the focus was on distribution to customers in Europe and Asia. In the US and Canada, a central DC solution already existed and was working well.
28 The calculation was based on the assumption that a maximum space for 76,000 pallets would be required during peak seasons, with additional space for loading, assembly and offices.

29 The name changed from DHL/Danzas Solutions to DHL-Exel after Deutsche Post World Net (owner of DHL & Danzas) acquired Exel in December 2005.

30 Partial transfer would start in 2006, with final closure in 2007.

31 Information about special delivery requirements was either not documented or not provided by the third-party logistics provider that managed the local DCs in France.

32 Up to seven different recruitment agencies were involved in this process.

33 LEGO created the 'carrier room'. In this room, representatives of three different transport companies worked together. They had access to a large monitor showing the turnaround time of trucks being loaded and offloaded – color coded and in real time.

34 After the Exel acquisition, everyone involved in the LEGO deal had either left DHL or moved on. Ironically, the implementation was now being managed by ex-Exel managers – who came second in LEGO's tender – and external consultants. DHL and Exel used to have a different view on how cost calculations should be done. This explained some of this 'lack of understanding'.

35 The fixed/variable cost ratio is roughly 30/70.

36 50/50 on variable costs, e.g. if productivity or prices are better than agreed, the 'gain' is shared 50/50 and vice versa.

37 There was increasing demand for warehouse space in Jirny after DHL made the first move. Following in DHL's footsteps, several other logistics services companies moved there.

38 The EDC has 109 gates; loads for up to 130 trucks can be lined up inside the building.

39 DHL pays bonuses to recruitment agencies for providing qualified, loyal and returning workers.

40 Around 30 customers are called each month by members of the customer logistics group and asked to score LEGO on 6 different tasks. During high season this is increased to twice a month. Refer to Exhibit 2 for an example of how LEGO was rated by customers during 2007 and 2008.

5 Sustaining supply chain alignment

Changes in the business environment in which firms operate have long influenced the relative competitiveness of a supply chain. Consequently, working to sustain supply chain alignment in a dynamic market environment is of utmost importance to any supply chain manager. We define alignment as the fit between the current supply chain set-up and design, and current market requirements. This is a strategic issue for the firm.

Designing supply chains typically involves considerable investments. Building new production facilities and new distribution centers, investing in new equipment, hiring or laying off personnel, and selecting new suppliers are just some of the actions involved in redesigning a supply chain. Yet, maintaining a misaligned supply chain, either as a result of misjudging the changes in business context or responding passively when change happens, can easily be even more costly. It can destroy your business.

How much does change affect your business?

One question is whether your supply chain is currently aligned; another question is whether the company can sustain the alignment over time as market requirements evolve. To do so within their particular business context, executives must understand and react proactively to fundamental changes in demand and consumer expectations. Figure 5.1 provides an overview of potential supply chain change drivers. Changing supply chain costs and quality directly reduces performance. In addition, evolving company strategy and products, changing customer needs, growing competitive pressure, and increasing supply chain benchmarks all place more pressure on the supply chain and thus indirectly erode supply chain competitiveness.

These change drivers apply case by case. For instance, changes in supply chain costs can be caused by increased labor costs or new taxation rules, as Hilti experienced in 2006. Shortly after the firm had shifted part of its production to China, the Chinese government unexpectedly raised VAT, thus challenging the success of the offshoring move. Supply chain quality can erode just as abruptly. Swings in global transportation capacity and transport costs can lead to long and uncertain supply lead times, and may impact customer service levels. Smaller firms with less bargaining power are particularly exposed.

Supply chain quality may change

* Decreasing security (e.g increased interruption risk due to natural disasters)
* Decreasing reliability (e.g. more frequent delays due to increased shortages in global transportation capacity)
○ Increasing average lead time (e.g. due to shifting customer target markets)

Supply chain benchmark increases

* Emerging technologies (e.g. RFID)
* Tightening cost targets (e.g. due to accessibility of new low-cost sourcing countries)
* Emerging distribution channels (e.g. internet, TV shopping, supermarkets)
* Rise of new third-party providers (e.g. contract manufacturing, distribution. logistics)

Supply chain costs may change

* Changing raw material costs (e.g. due to natural resource constraints)
* Increasing labor costs (e.g. due to rising minimum wages in emerging countries)
* Changing transportation costs (e.g. due to growing pressure on natural resources)
* Facing tax incentives
* Currency fluctuations

Firm strategy and products may evolve

○ Evolving firm strategy (e.g. due to new management)
* Changing product demand parameters (e.g. due to commoditization)
* Changing product volumes (e.g. due to evolving life cycles)
○ New product introduction / abandonment
○ Augmenting product variants (e.g. to address more customer segments)

Competitive pressures may increase

* Increasing price pressures
* Emerging value competitors (e.g. Costco, Aldi, competition from developing economies in Asia)
* Radically restructured industries (e.g. cost advantages from economies of scale due to consolidation)
* Increasing rate of firms losing their leadership position

Customer needs may change

* Increasing bargaining power of customers (e.g. retail giants emerged)
○ Geographic shift of main customer target margets (e.g. shift to Asia)
* Changing service level and speed expectations (e.g. due to online competitors)
* New customer segments (e.g. low-cost items in developing countries)
* New distribution channels

SC performance change

SC requirements change

Competitive supply chain setup

■ external factors   ○ (partly) internal factors

Figure 5.1 Drivers of change

Other important change drivers relate to evolving product portfolios. When new innovative products enter the supply chain, volumes are typically low, but the upside growth rate can potentially be enormous. Therefore supply chains for this type of early innovation must be highly adaptable, and fast response times are crucial to avoid undue loss of market share. Selecting adaptable supply chain partners that are both able and willing to raise their capacity allocations overnight is one of the key design parameters in such situations. Later, as time progresses and competitors catch up with similar innovations, the product matures and supply chain efficiency becomes much more important. Finally, as products mature and volumes begin to fall, a vital aspect of supply chain design is the ability to downsize operations. Thus, as products commoditize the supply chain will need to shift from being market responsive to cost efficient. However, when the life cycle evolution occurs over a period of just a few months, as is common in the consumer electronics industry, such supply chain alignment decisions must be taken into account upfront.

In addition to volume-based product commoditization, low cost sourcing has significantly raised cost pressure during recent years as a change driver. Originally regarded as an end-of-product-life cost advantage, low cost sourcing is now a competitive imperative. More and more global players are adopting low cost sourcing from the outset, thereby critically raising supply chain cost benchmarks. In the retail industry, value competitors such as Aldi, Costco and Walmart have clearly changed the game. Their aggressive price policies and enormous size have intensified competition and consequently strengthened the need for cutting-edge supply chain performance.

To keep pace with these trends, firms need to continuously adapt their supply chains to sustain alignment with supply chain costs and quality considerations, evolving product portfolios and customer requirements, as well as competitive price pressures and changing supply chain benchmarks. Consequently, strategic supply chain alignment is the result of a systematic review of the big picture and basic business premises. So, begin by analyzing how the world is changing around you and to what extent this affects your firm.

Business Context Analysis

The next step is to carry out an in-depth business context analysis (see Figure 5.2) addressing four well-structured diagnostic questions:

1   How good is your current supply chain?
2   What are the key determinants of your business today and in the future, and how do they translate into supply chain requirements?
3   What are your supply chain's current main capabilities?
4   What does your supply chain lack?

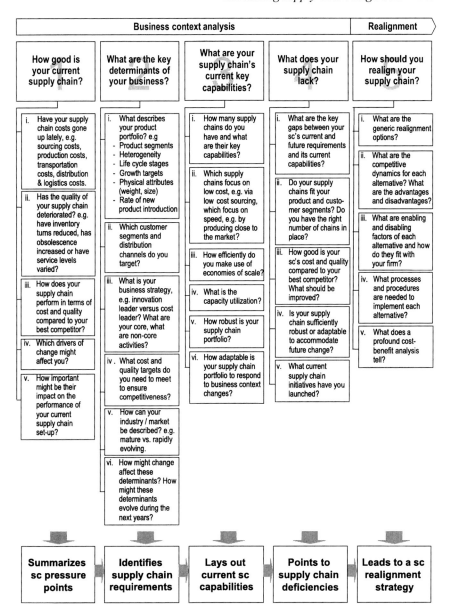

Figure 5.2 The realignment process

While the answers to some of these questions may seem unpalatable, honest responses will reveal which supply chain capabilities best support your business.

Once you have assessed the performance of your current supply chain, address the second question and distil the key determinants of your business, as they will directly translate into supply chain requirements. For example, try to quantify key product segments and key product attributes, such as demand volatility, product devaluation rate and cost constraints, in each segment. Include other internal and external characteristics that affect your business such as customer expectations for product co-creation and alternative distribution channels. The explosion of offers to customers and consumers in terms of variety and customization of products and services can fundamentally change the supply chain capabilities you will require to succeed in the future. Yet, while customization, for example, might be important in some instances, multiple consumer segments will typically coexist. In many industries, price pressures have increased as much as consumers' expectations for co-creation and added services but not necessarily all in the same consumer segment.

In response to the third question in Figure 5.2, note how many distinct supply chains you have established and what their key capabilities are. Clarify which supply chains are most market responsive, which are more physically efficient and how robust or adaptable they are. The analysis of the key determinants and requirements of your business on the one hand and the situational analysis on the other hand provide an excellent platform to address the fourth question and identify the gaps in your present supply chain set-up. Compare your current and future needs with your existing supply chain capabilities. For example, analyse to what extent your supply chain fits with your product and customer segments, and assess whether your supply chain is sufficiently robust or adaptive to accommodate expected change. Scenario-based evaluations may help you to estimate the actual and potential damage these gaps may cause.

Only after conducting such a business context analysis to gain a thorough understanding of your supply chain's deficiencies does the last question become relevant: How should you realign or extend your supply chain capability?

Realigning your supply chain

The next step is to apply the insights from the business context analysis to develop a supply chain strategy capable of sustaining success. We have identified three key strategic dimensions that characterize a firm's supply chain portfolio: the number of supply chains in use, the degree of market responsiveness versus the physical efficiency of each chain, and the degree of stability versus robustness versus adaptability.

Generic options and competitive dynamics

While a single supply chain keeps complexity low and makes it possible to leverage economies of scale, a larger portfolio of different supply chains enables a firm to cater to heterogeneous requirements. Put in simple terms, the more diverse and volatile a firm's supply chain requirements are, the larger the optimal number of different supply chain capabilities (see Table 5.1).

Table 5.1 A few vs. many supply chain capabilities

	A few supply chain capabilities (1–2)	*Many supply chain capabilities (>4)*
Opportunities	Reduces fixed costs (e.g. facility investment & maintenance costs, capacity costs, potentially inventory holding costs due to pooling). Allows economies of scale to be leveraged (e.g. reduced rates for transportation). Reduces complexity costs (e.g. overhead costs, discounted supply chain set-up costs, uncertainty in setting up a supply chain). Makes new product introduction easier.	Allows supply chain customization to meet differing needs (e.g. different target markets, product or customer segments) and thus results in low product-specific costs, such as raw material and other acquisition costs, transportation costs, direct and indirect manufacturing costs, costs of working capital. Spreads risk across many supply chains. Might increase supply chain adaptability (e.g. reassigning products across existing facilities).
Enabling factors	Homogeneous product portfolios (e.g. similar physical products, coefficient of variation, devaluation rates, profit margins, …). Homogeneous customer segments (e.g. in terms of quality requirements or geographic location) and homogeneous distribution channels. High fixed costs and chances for economies of scale (e.g. automotive industry). High complexity costs (e.g. for small firms with little experience in administering a large number of supply chains).	Heterogeneous product portfolios (e.g. products with different physical and demand characteristics, in different life cycle stages, …). Heterogeneous customer segments (e.g. quality customers versus price-sensitive customers) and distribution channels (e.g. retailers versus internet). Highly innovative products that nevertheless differ from one another (as these products benefit most from small changes in the degree of market responsiveness).
Implementation	Clear segmentation of products and customers to identify required supply chain capabilities. Focus on homogeneity (e.g. prune products from the portfolio that do not fit the predefined supply chain).	Clear segmentation of products and customers to design supply chain capabilities for competitive advantage.

Source: Langenberg, K. U. and R. W. Seifert. 'Sustaining Supply Chain Alignment: Step by Step.' Working paper. EPFL, Lausanne, Switzerland: 2008.

At one time, for example, Hewlett-Packard had more than 20 different supply chains. This meant that the supply chains were highly adapted to the characteristics and life cycle of particular product groups. However, the complexity of managing so many supply chains resulted in high administrative costs and prevented gains in terms of cost synergies. At the same time Dell had only one major supply chain capability in place, serving as a radically different supply chain benchmark in the same industry. Yet, while Dell enjoyed stunning success during the 1980s and until the mid-2000s, by the late 2000s personal computers had become much cheaper and, for all its strength in customization, Dell came under increasing pressure from producers tapping into the efficiencies of low-cost sourcing.

In addition, it is also important to understand that it is not easy to change a supply chain or to try to use one for a purpose other than that for which it was designed. Taking the Dell example again, the company tried twice during the 1980s and 1990s to sell its computers using the traditional retail channel. However, both times it failed at heavy cost because its supply chain was not adapted to such a channel. Similarly, Hewlett-Packard tried the mass customization model without substantial success. The lesson is that to shift from one model to another requires a fundamental change and transformation of the company.

Classic examples and their supply chain implications

The landmark example of industrialization was Ford's mass production factory in Rouge River, Michigan which made the famous Model T in the early 20th century. It was also famous because the customer could have the car 'in any color ... so long as it's black'. This is a prime example of make to stock (MTS). The factory produced a car every 24 seconds in a continuous cycle, and sent the cars to dealers who stored them on their parking lots until they were sold. Thus, customers were able to buy a black Model T when the dealer had one available.

BMW offers another classic example of how car companies sell their products in Europe. Customers specify the options they want – such as color and leather seats – and the car is made to order. This means that the customer must wait until the car is assembled and delivered, usually several weeks to a few months.

A fundamental difference between the make to order and the make to stock environment is that usually with the MTS option, variety is greatly reduced, thus allowing economies of scale due to the production of a greater number of standard units. The dilemma for many companies is how to balance the end consumers' wish for variety and individuality with the advantages of mass producing a standard product.

Companies have learned to deal with the variety vs. economies of scale dilemma by applying modularity and pushing the 'postponement' point as far as possible down the supply chain. For example, in the automotive industry, companies have standard platforms for different cars. The Volkswagen Golf, Audi A3 and Skoda Octavia all draw on the same product platform. This means that many components and a substantial part of the supply chain are exactly the same for all three models, thereby allowing economies of scale in production. Toward the end of the supply chain, the products are differentiated (this is the postponement point) and no more economies are obtained. Often the supply chain functions in an MTS environment up to the postponement point, and then switches to make to order.

For many companies, the objective is to push the postponement, or differentiation, point as close to the end of the supply chain as possible. Thus, it is possible to manufacture different products economically in the same supply chain. Pushing this logic to its limit, the concept of mass customization developed in the mid-1990s.[1] The most emblematic example of mass customization at the time was Dell Computers. Customers could order a portable computer to their specifications to such a degree that almost every customer received a different configuration entirely adapted to their needs. The advantage for consumers was that they were not forced to buy a standard configuration such as 256 MB of CPU and 20 GB of hard disk if that was not what they needed. Instead, they could order only a 10 GB hard disk, for example. Other manufacturers did not offer all of these options. Thus, customers might find it was cheaper for them to purchase a Dell computer with the configuration they required, rather than the standard configuration of other manufacturers, with superior – and to them superfluous – features.

Dell was famous for making all its products to order and stating that the minimum order size for manufacturing was one. Many executives visited Dell factories all over the world to see how to make mass customization work. The costs of these factories were only around 4% higher than those of mass production factories. Yet, when the business context evolved, even Dell's highly praised supply chain came under pressure and the company sought to divest its manufacturing assets.

Long-term thinking: Stable vs. robust vs. adaptive design

The final key dimension in sustaining supply chain alignment is long-term planning. We differentiate three generic concepts to ensure supply chains are fit for the future: building a stable, a robust or an adaptive supply chain (see Table 5.2).

In a stable supply chain, all processes are streamlined to best accommodate a firm's current business context. Depending on the firm's requirements, this may mean, for example, configuring a particularly cost-efficient supply set-up. A stable supply chain focuses on current opportunities and challenges and outperforms robust or adaptive supply chains as long as the business context remains stable. Unforeseen changes, however, may result in unexpected deficiencies, since the chain is not prepared to manage them. Firms operating in steady business contexts, such as Swiss chocolate company Lindt & Sprüngli with its strong brand name, might benefit from a stable supply chain.

Likewise, a robust supply chain is designed for the long term and not expected to undergo frequent structural adjustments. It is, however, set up to accommodate change. A permanent multi-sourcing strategy, for example, may hedge against suppliers dropping out or transportation capacity becoming unavailable. Producing with low average capacity utilization rates may help to accommodate demand swings or prepare operations for potential future growth – at the price of higher fixed costs. However, innovative concepts such as making short-term use of idle capacity (e.g. an opportunistic production of secondary brand products) may help diminish such costs.

Table 5.2 Stable vs. robust vs. adaptive design

	Stable design	Robust design	Adaptive design
Opportunities	Eliminates waste (e.g. lean supply chains) and thus reduces static supply chain costs.	Makes the supply chain less vulnerable to expected change and risk. Reduces the need for supply chain adaptation.	Makes the supply chain adaptable and thus enables it to quickly shift gear when necessary. Capability to be ahead of the competition.
Enabling factors	Stable business context, e.g. with respect to: • Product portfolio • Customer needs • Competitive pressures • Supply chain benchmarks • Supply chain costs • Supply chain quality.	(Potentially) dynamic business context. High barriers to supply chain adaptation (e.g. requirement for costly production assets). Soft factors that constrain frequent supply chain adaptation (e.g. hiring/firing people).	(Potentially) dynamic business context. Low barriers to supply chain adaptation (e.g. relying on contract manufacturers). Exposure to unpredictable change, which cannot be accommodated by robust design. Industries with high cost pressures where robustness is not an alternative.
Implementation	Stability analysis of the firm's business context and industry analysis. Measures to further increase business context stability, such as: • Considered new product introduction • Product portfolio renovation • Careful supplier selection.	Possible design elements are: Multi-sourcing (from different regions and suppliers) Dispersed manufacturing footprint (geographically) Excess capacity Multi-channel distribution Multiple logistics providers Short-term capacity utilization (e.g. refurbished products).	Possible design elements are: Outsourcing of sourcing, manufacturing, logistics, distribution, e.g. use of contract manufacturers Flexible machine set-ups (e.g. possibility to shift production of a product across facilities) Short-term contracts despite potentially higher prices.

Source: Langenberg, K. U. and R. W. Seifert. 'Sustaining Supply Chain Alignment: Step by Step.' Working paper. EPFL, Lausanne, Switzerland: 2008.

In an environment of ongoing change, the challenge is to build highly adaptive supply chains,[2] in which all processes are designed for the short term. Fixed long-term assets, such as production facilities that require considerable investments, should thus be minimized and replaced by more flexible alternatives, such as short-term contract manufacturing. Although adaptive supply chains are extremely difficult to attain and maintain, they are a competitive imperative in many fast-moving industries. Lucent, for example, lost ground in the Asian market for digital switches when it neglected to redesign its supply chain in the late 1990s. To match the speed of its rivals Siemens and Alcatel, Lucent had successfully set up regional production facilities in Taiwan and China. However, as the technology for digital switches matured, a number of medium-sized manufacturers built up the capability to manufacture the product for a fraction of Lucent's development costs. While its competitors immediately outsourced their production to capitalize on the lower prices, Lucent was tied to its production facilities, in which it had invested heavily. By the time Lucent finally realized that it had no choice but to follow the trend if it wanted to stand its ground, the firm had already lost the battle for market leadership.[3]

The right choice between stability, robustness and adaptability is based on the exposure to change, on the one hand, and on barriers to adaptation, on the other hand (see Table 5.2). Identifying the optimal design requires a careful business context analysis.

Outlook

A sustained supply chain strategy is about managing change and constant adaptation. It requires tough choices, alignment and execution across partnering organizations in the supply chain. An initial supply chain realignment project is thus only the starting point. The far bigger challenge is to preserve alignment in the future in the face of the internal and external changes that a firm constantly undergoes. During one of its realignment projects, Hilti estimated its growth rate at 3% for the years to come and was surprised when an annual growth rate of 8% later materialized. The firm reacted quickly and set up an additional production facility in South America to meet local demand. Sustaining alignment entails constantly reviewing potential change drivers, assessing their impact on your firm's supply chain strategy, and acting accordingly. In essence, you have to constantly challenge your firm's supply chain strategy, which requires company-wide efforts and stringent commitment but also ongoing communication with supply chain partners. This goes beyond functional excellence in logistics, and there is a lot more at stake than simply viewing the supply chain as an afterthought to strategy formulation. Anticipating change is critical in building an institution capable of sustaining success. Neglecting it might put your firm's prosperity at risk. Supply chain realignment should thus be an integral part of strategy making, and it should be informed by careful market analysis, competitor benchmarks, and product and technology roadmaps.

Cases in this chapter

5.1 The 'mi adidas' mass customization initiative

Many companies are exploring mass customization (MC) as a way to demonstrate market leadership and capture price premiums. This case examines adidas' 'mi adidas' initiative, aimed at delivering customized athletic footwear to retail customers. It discusses the practical implications associated with expanding the initiative from a small pilot to a wider operation with a retail presence and within an existing supply chain set-up. The mi adidas case illustrates several implications of trying to reach new customers, but two major challenges in particular emerged:

1   Was it possible to leverage existing mass production principles in the new customized set-up without disturbing the smooth, efficient flow when combining two distinct product concepts? The case illustrates how this was near impossible since the two different production forms required distinct performance criteria for them to work as intended.
2   Was it possible to use the existing IT platform with its current data structure designed for mass production to accommodate the customization initiative? The case illustrates how this was challenging since the data requirements for individualized products were much higher than for regular mass production products.

The case also highlights the importance of considering the supply chain implications of sales and marketing initiatives or new product innovations such as the one launched by adidas. Normally, a mass production flow is steady, but when they incorporated event-based discrete flows in small quantities, it challenged the adidas supply chain. Variability and the ability to handle many different product configurations fast and in parallel were simply not easily incorporated into the adidas supply chain.

5.2 and 5.3 Hilti: Gearing the supply chain for the future (A and B)

The Hilti case series illustrates how a proactive future-oriented approach to supply chain design can help ensure the supply chain is constantly aligned with a global market portfolio of customers. The key approach to adjustments at Hilti is focusing on small incremental redesigns of the supply chain. The case series demonstrates how supply chain design at Hilti is about constantly challenging the current global manufacturing footprint by asking and answering questions such as:

* Which product components should be made in-house and which should be sourced externally?
* Where to produce which products, leading into considerations of where to invest in new production facilities and where to close down factories?

The case further demonstrates how Hilti informed its decision making by:

* Using a holistic set of guiding principles and premises.
* Applying constant assessments/forecasts of likely future developments that could challenge the short-term cost focus (e.g. by developing a set of likely hypotheses).
* Using games and simulations and what-if scenario planning. Here the design team considered numerous different supply chain design configurations over several months.
* Including both monetary and qualitative criteria in the decision-making process around the different supply chain design options.

Case 5.1
The 'mi adidas' mass customization initiative

Ralf W. Seifert

Rolf Reinschmidt, head of the Forever Sport Division of adidas-Salomon AG, was reviewing adidas' mass customization (MC) initiative 'mi adidas':

> We all talk a lot about experiences these days – experiences that consumers and retailers expect to have with brands like ours [adidas]. Well, here is an experience our brand is uniquely able to offer, differentiating us significantly from the competition and building an incredible image for the Forever Sport Division.

It was October 2001. Reinschmidt sat down in his office and reflected on his experience to date. He had been sponsoring mi adidas to create a customization experience. The journey had started many years earlier, with the company providing tailor-made shoes for top athletes. Now, customized shoes had been made available on a much broader scale. Competitors also tested the market, and a trend toward MC was visible in other industries from PCs to made-to-measure jeans. The time had come to make specific recommendations on the best course of action for mi adidas.

Reinschmidt had three alternative routes to choose from:

Withdraw: Celebrate the success and PR effect accomplished to date but quietly withdraw from MC in order to focus on adidas' core business.

Maintain: Maintain the developed capabilities and selectively run mi adidas fairs and planned retail tours following top events such as the Soccer World Cup and world marathon series.

Expand: Expand mi adidas to multiple product categories and permanent retail installations; elevate it to brand concept status while further building volume and process expertise.

Mi adidas had gained substantial momentum – it needed direction.

Global footwear market[1]

In 2000 the global footwear market was US$16.4 billion.[2] North America accounted for 48%, Europe 32% and Asia/Pacific 12% of the market. The degree of concentration in the footwear segment was relatively high, with the three largest companies controlling roughly 60% of the market: Nike commanded 35%, adidas 15% and Reebok 10% market share. Nike was particularly strong in the US market, with a 42% market share in footwear, but also led in Europe with 31%. adidas was significantly stronger in the European footwear market, holding a 24% market share compared with its 11% market share in US footwear. (*Refer to **Exhibit 1** for regional market share information and trends for adidas, Nike and Reebok.*)

Adidas-Salomon AG

For over 80 years adidas had been part of the world of sports on every level, delivering state-of-the-art sports footwear, apparel and accessories. (*Refer to **Exhibit 2** for a history of adidas.*) In 2001 adidas-Salomon AG's total net sales reached €6.1 billion and net income amounted to €208 million. Its main brands were adidas with a 79% share of sales, Salomon with 12%, and TaylorMade-adidas Golf with 9%. The company employed 14,000 people and commanded an estimated 15% share of the world market for sporting goods. Headquartered in Herzogenaurach, Germany, it was a global leader in the sporting goods industry, offering its products in almost every country of the world: Europe accounted for 50%, North America for 30%, Asia for 17% and Latin America for 3% of total sales.

Forever Sport division

In 2000 adidas was reorganized into three consumer-oriented product divisions: Forever Sport, Originals and Equipment.[3] Forever Sport was the largest division with products 'engineered to perform'. Technological innovation and a commitment to product leadership were the cornerstones of this division. Sales fell into a few major categories: Running 32%, Soccer 16%, Basketball 11%, Tennis 9% and Others 32%.[4] Reinschmidt was the head of the division. He reported directly to Erich Stammringer, head of global marketing for adidas-Salomon AG.

Mi adidas

'Mi adidas' was envisaged as an image tool and a center of competence for the Forever Sport Division. Christoph Berger, director MC, was responsible for mi adidas and led a small but dedicated team. Berger came from an old shoemaking family and followed a traditional apprenticeship as a shoemaker himself. Having earned an Executive Master of Business Administration (EMBA), he started working for adidas in 1995. The pilot was sponsored directly by Reinschmidt and Stamminger. Without formal line authority, however, Berger had to draw implementation support from the various functions and use external contractors to complement his team. (*Refer to **Exhibit 3** for a project breakdown.*)

Mi adidas was launched in April 2000 to provide consumers with the chance to create unique athletic footwear produced to their personal specifications. The idea was not entirely new, as adidas had provided tailor-made shoes to top athletes for many years. Now mi adidas could be experienced by many consumers at top sporting events and select retailers. The project initially offered only soccer boots but was to be expanded in 2001 to offer running shoes. For 2002 the plan was to further build volume and expand the offering into the customization of basketball and tennis footwear. (*Refer to **Exhibit 4** for the initial mi adidas rollout plan.*)

Phase I: The mi adidas pilot

The first phase of the mi adidas project was a small pilot to evaluate the feasibility and prospects of mass customizing athletic shoes. The objectives were clear-cut: offer a customized product, test consumers' demands for customized products and fulfil their expectations as far as possible. The pilot allowed both project team and functions to gain hands-on experience in marketing, information management, production, distribution and after-service of customized shoes. It also provided a basis for a rough cost–benefit analysis and future budgeting.

Product selection

The pilot mandate was soccer boots. A Predator® Precision boot already in production was offered for customization with regard to fit (size and width), performance (outsole types, materials and support) and design (color combinations and embroidery).

The pilot was 100% event based. Over a two-month period in 2000, six events were held in different European cities: Newcastle, Hamburg, Madrid, Marseille, Milan and Amsterdam. Consumer recruitment was very selective, using local market research agencies, phone calls, written invitations and pre- and post-event questionnaires. (*Refer to **Exhibit 5** for details of the customer recruitment process for the pilot.*) The target group was 50 participants per event and country.

The MC unit was designed in a rather neutral technology-oriented style stressing the brand's tradition as the athlete's support. A white cocoon (evoking a mysterious atmosphere with its shape and color) housed the 3-D foot scanner,

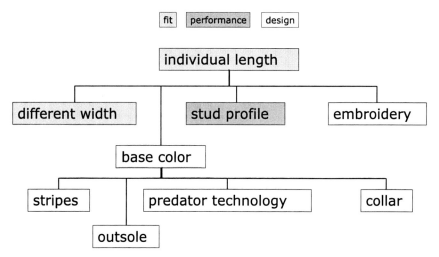

Figure 1   Combination logic of Predator® Precision soccer boot marketing: Event concept and communication

the heart of the unit (*refer to image of MC Unit: 3-D foot scanner station*). A newly developed matching matrix software supported scanning and fitting. At a separate fitting terminal, a selection of sample boots was available for testing fit preferences (*refer to image of fitting terminal*).

MC Unit: 3-D foot scanner station

Fitting terminal

In addition, a design terminal (*not shown*) had a laptop on which the participants, assisted by adidas experts, could customize their soccer boot in terms of materials and design. The stations also displayed material and color samples to facilitate the decision-making process. (*Refer to **Exhibit 6** for details of the customization steps.*)

Today, it is a brand new, revolutionary, and futuristic experience. Soon it will be as normal as buying individualized glasses at an optician.

Consumer feedback

adidas consumers greeted mi adidas with tremendous excitement, 'Consumers loved the product. 100% want a customization service available in the future.'

Shortly after the introduction of mi adidas, even adidas headquarters started to receive direct inquiries from interested consumers who wanted to purchase a customized shoe. Franck Denglos, marketing coordinator, reflected on his experience with the mi adidas pilot:

> The concept and its execution gave consumers a strong positive impression of the brand. They left with the perception that adidas was acting as a leader. However, we have to keep in mind that their perception was highly influenced by the impressive tool, run by highly qualified adidas experts. Plus, during the pilot, the shoe was free.

Competitors' footwear customization initiatives

Several competitors offered a similar service:

Nike Inc.

Nike Inc. decided to bring MC to the web in November 1999. Nike's NIKEiD program enabled online customers to choose the color of their shoe and add a personal name of up to eight characters.[5] For this service, Nike asked the regular retail price for the shoe plus a $10 custom design fee and shipping charges. Delivery of the footwear was advertised as being within three weeks for the US market. To keep fulfilment and distribution under control, however, Nike imposed an artificial ceiling and only accepted up to 400 US-based orders per day.[6]

Reebok International, Ltd

As of 2001, Reebok had not launched (or announced) its own mass customization initiative. Instead, it marketed its full foot cushion for its top of the range running shoe, the Fusion C DMX 10. Utilizing DMX®10 technology and 3-D ultralite sole material, Reebok provided 10 air pods to help distribute air for custom cushioning and to achieve the ultimate in shock absorption.[7]

New Balance Athletic Shoe, Inc.

New Balance opened its first 'width center concept unit' at Harrods in London in April 2001. Coming from a long tradition of making arch supports and prescription footwear to improve shoe fit, the US-based company first manufactured a performance running shoe in 1961. By 2001 New Balance featured a range of athletic shoes and outdoor footwear. Although New Balance did not offer a customization of shoes, it typically offered its products in three (at times up to five) different width sizes to optimize shoe fit.[8]

Custom Foot Corp.

Custom Foot Corp. was one of the leading pioneers of mass customizing shoes in terms of fit and design. Featured in cover stories of the *New York Times*, *Forbes* and *Fortune*, the company seemed to show a whole industry new ways of doing business: Custom-made Italian shoes, delivered in about three weeks, at off-the-shelf prices. But after a glorious start in 1995, Custom Foot went out of business and closed operations in summer 1998. Its concept for blending customization and mass production had failed, as the whole system could not handle the enormous complexity of the process.[9]

Creo Interactive GmbH

In 1998 Creo Interactive designed a totally new shoe based on a modular concept for the sole, the main body and the tongue. This shoe could be produced in just 83 working steps compared with Custom Foot's 150 to 300 steps.[10] Leveraging the internet as an interface for configuration, Creo offered pure design customization in terms of colors and patterns. By locating production in Germany, it was possible to swiftly fulfil European market needs. However, three years into the venture, Creo Interactive closed operations in 2001.

Customatix.com of Solemates, Inc.

Based in Santa Cruz, CA, Customatix.com allowed consumers to log onto its internet site and choose from a vast array of colors, materials, graphics and logos to create their own personalized portfolio of designs online. '150 choices you can put on the bottom of your sneakers.'[11] The blueprints were then transmitted to the company's factory in China, where the shoes were manufactured and shipped to the consumer's doorstep within two weeks. The shoes retailed for $70 to $100 per pair, including import duty and delivery charges. 'The biggest problem we have is, people don't believe we can do what we do' (Dave Ward, CEO of Customatix.com).[12]

Phase II: The mi adidas retail tours

The decision to proceed with the 'Customization Experience' project was made after the successful completion and stringent evaluation of a pilot project conducted in the second half of 2000 in six European countries. During the test project some 400 pairs of the revolutionary adidas Predator® Precision soccer boots were custom built and delivered to a select group of consumers in Germany, France, England, Spain, Italy, and the Netherlands. Delivery time took two weeks on average. Consumer satisfaction was overwhelmingly positive.[13]

The pilot project was mainly seen as a first attempt to evaluate the requirements of 'normal' consumers, as opposed to those of top athletes, with whom adidas had an ongoing relationship. Taking the successful concept of the pilot to the retail channel, however, meant facing different and new challenges. For the pilot, certain issues to do with back-end processes were adapted to current processes or not covered at all. Now, these would require more attention. In addition, a new retail unit (*refer to image of new retail unit running*) had to be created that was smaller (10 to 20m²), easier to transport, more durable, and user friendly.

New retail unit running

Retailers

Retailer interest in mi adidas was overwhelming. In Germany alone, almost 1,000 athletics specialty shops wanted to participate. However, only 50 German retail stores could be part of this second phase: the first retail tours in 2001. Soon retailer selection became a sensitive issue within adidas: Marketing preferred small athletics specialty shops for a maximal image effect and utmost retailer commitment.[14] Sales, however, favored big key accounts for reasons of relationship management. In addition, country selection was controversial: In some countries retailers were accustomed to paying a fee to a manufacturer for being able to host a promotion such as mi adidas. In other countries, retailers had never paid a fee for in-store promotions and might even demand a fee from the manufacturer instead. Depending on the final selection verdict, retailer feedback ranged from enormous enthusiasm to vast disappointment (even sporadic threats to withdraw business from adidas altogether).

Once selected, the retailers took care of consumer recruitment. To support them in marketing mi adidas, they were given a package of communication tools: CDs, posters, invitation cards, registration cards and folders. Some retailers felt that the material was not engaging enough and demanded more support. Subsequently, the countries modified and translated the tools to fit the needs of their consumers more directly. Yet consumer turnout (and order placement) varied greatly from one retail store to another, depending on the commitment to mi adidas.

Whereas the pilot was 100% event based, retailers played the central role in the second phase and accounted for roughly 90% of the order volume. Using multiple mi adidas retail units, well over 100 retailers participated across Europe in 2001.

Customization process

The customization process was still run by adidas experts and emphasized the 'brand experience' theme. The 3-D foot scanner, however, had been replaced by a simpler Footscan™ unit, which was used in combination with a static measurement device for length and width measures. At the same time, the proprietary matching matrix software continued to evolve and directly conformed to consumer preferences in three out of four cases. The overall process had become very stable. 50 to 80 'customization experiences' could be handled per day during an event while about 15 to 20 were possible at a retail outlet.

Recent survey results seemed to confirm European consumers' interest in customized shoes. Although a focus on design customization was much simpler from a configuration perspective, consumers rated a customized design as much less important than a customized fit. In addition, individual preferences varied significantly across different European countries (and to a lesser extent also between men and women), necessitating further research for a targeted offering.[15]

Product and pricing

The athletics footwear market was characterized by rapid product turnover. In 2001 mi adidas already featured its second product generation in soccer boots. The customized version of this soccer boot sold for a 30% to 50% price premium over the catalog price of €150.[16] In addition, the product offering was expanded into running shoes. After successful internal presentations of mi adidas for Running at the adidas global marketing meeting in March 2001 and the Investor Day in July 2001, preparations were made to launch the project in the Running market. In September 2001 mi adidas for Running was introduced to the market during the Berlin Marathon. Consumers were either recruited or invited by PR, or they were impulse buyers who passed by and became interested. Within three weeks, they received the shoes. For 2002 the plan was for mi adidas for Running to be present at all adidas-sponsored marathons (i.e., Paris, Boston, London, Madrid, Rotterdam, Prague and Berlin) and to go on a retail tour in the relevant country after each event.

Consumers

Consumer feedback was excellent. In particular, the short delivery time and the opportunity to design their own shoes impressed the consumers. Mi adidas also attracted strong interest from the press: Two television stations (Bayerischer Rundfunk and Fox TV) and many articles featured adidas' MC initiative and hailed it as a major milestone.

> Although we received this good feedback, there were several technical problems that had to be tackled. These problems caused delays and in some cases wrong production…

Information management

Information management throughout the entire process was critical: Basic consumer data, product options, biometric knowledge and product specifications had to be merged for order taking. In addition, sourcing, production, distribution, payment and reordering required appropriate IT backing.[17] 'Information is the most important conversion factor of successful mass customization.'

Many challenges in terms of the scope and integration of the required IT infrastructure remained:

a   The mi adidas kiosk system for order creation led to technical problems with synchronizing information generated offline (e.g., order numbers and customer records) with adidas backbone systems such as the sales system and customer master database.
b   The traditional sales system was not designed to process orders of individually customized shoes with detailed information on each article.
c   The IT systems for distribution needed to be extended for an organized distribution and return process.
d   Consumer data captured via mi adidas could not be transferred to the adidas CRM system.

There were ways around these problems, but they resulted in limited centralization and poor accessibility of data.

> The initial rollout was clearly under-budgeted. For example, eRoom (*refer to **Exhibit 10***) was chosen as the web accessible repository for the technical documents. This decision was not entirely supported by Global IT and is seen as a short-term solution until an alternative can be found.

All development, configuration and support for mi adidas had thus far been absorbed by the business and no costs had been charged to the project budget for IT solutions, beyond the mi adidas kiosk application and scanning software. The kiosk application was developed by a contractor. However, no helpdesk was available for support and future system integration. The IT department was worried:

> The speed of implementations, the time needed to support both SAP and non-SAP countries and the limited resources Global IT presently has to support this, leads to the conclusion that we may fail to maximally deliver mi adidas globally.

Mi adidas had progressed fast – calling for a completely new set of requirements.

> Mi adidas, even such a small project, has forced the IT department to think about how close we are getting to our consumers and what is needed to support this development.

Production

By 1992 most sporting goods companies had outsourced the main part of their footwear production to the Far East to reduce production costs. adidas followed suit and outsourced all textile production and 96% of footwear production during its turnaround in the mid-1990s. The outsourced footwear production was divided between Asia (China, Indonesia, South Korea, Taiwan, Thailand and Vietnam), Eastern Europe and North Africa. Depending on the quality of the shoe, between 20% and 40% of production costs were related to personnel costs, which were the main driver for cost differences between regions.[18] Contract manufacturers focused on footwear assembly and sourced input materials from local suppliers as needed. (*Refer to* **Exhibit 8** *for a supply chain overview.*)

Adidas maintained a small footwear factory in Germany, in Scheinfeld, near its headquarters. Here, models, prototypes and made-to-measure performance products could be manufactured and tested. In addition, special shoes for Olympic sports such as fencing, wrestling, weightlifting and bobsled were made. However, Scheinfeld was not excited at the prospect of taking mi adidas production in-house. Furthermore, material provisioning for a vast set of customization options could be more costly in Scheinfeld because it was too far away from volume production sites and suppliers.

The production processes used for the mass customization shoes were the same basic processes used in mass production. For the MC events, however, a combination of development sample room and mass production facilities was used (*refer to* **Exhibit 9** *for a comparison*). This combination was chosen to allow for the highest level of control and quality while providing a minimal 'disruption' to the factory's daily mass production schedule. 'A program like mi adidas, without dedicated facilities, manpower and materials resources, will always be perceived as an interruption to the overall process of creating shoes.'

Yet the capacity of the sample rooms was limited[19] and its operational format was not designed for volume scale effects. The mass production facilities, by contrast, were not meant to handle a lot size of one[20] nor were they set up to allow for close linkage of individual product flow with corresponding customization information. Such a process was not in place and the workers lacked training and language capabilities to handle production according to detailed written product specifications. 'Variability is simply not in our business model!'

Although the assembly of a customized shoe was theoretically straightforward, provisioning the required material proved to be time consuming. Delays were exacerbated when material was needed that was not currently available for in-line production. In this case, special material provisioning resulted in significant inventory costs as materials for the top of the range models in question were expensive. From a production perspective, a better understanding was needed of the value–cost trade-off between the marketing perception of customer value-added versus inventory and production costs for specific customization options. For example, design customization in terms of multiple colors was not ideal from a material provisioning perspective because different shoe sizes already meant different component sizes (e.g., strip length varied with the shoe size), which would now have to be available in a range of colors. These trade-offs and the options available for new shoes should ideally play a much more prominent role right from the start – in designing products for MC. Karl-Josef Seldmeyer, vice president, head of global supply chain management, summarized his experiences: 'For today's volumes, the combined complexity of fit, performance and design is too much.'

Distribution

Timely mass customization also depended on proper execution of communications and logistics to meet the seven-day lead time from order receipt to ex-factory shipping. Starting from July 2001, the mi adidas process was changed from a pilot with deliveries direct to the final consumer to a process that involved the retailers in customization and distribution. After customization at the retailer shops, orders were no longer transferred directly to the sourcing systems. Instead, they were routed from the retailer to the respective subsidiary's sales system and from there to Logistics Ordering Systems, using the subsidiary's regular buying process. The addressee was no longer the final consumer but the individual retailer in whose shop the customization had taken place. The individual retailer was now responsible for distribution to the end consumer. (*Refer to* **Exhibit 10** *for an overview of the mi adidas order and product flow.*)

Communication and competing initiatives

With the push into multiple product categories, communication became more difficult. In particular, the extremely technical and highly advanced customization process could not be adequately promoted as the mi adidas budget did not support targeted messaging by category. However, increasing the marketing spend was not then an option, since marketing saw MC as just one of many initiatives. After all, they already supported top athletes via a special care team and tailor-made shoes made in Scheinfeld. Since it was naturally in competition for resources and management attention with other recent initiatives, mi adidas was often seen as secondary to designated brand concepts such as a³,[21] and ClimaCool™,[22] Hence a³, 'Football never felt better' and Clima acted as overriding messages for the upcoming marathons, soccer World Cup and Roland Garros, respectively. 'Communication activity and spend needs to be regulated, ensuring that brand concepts are not undermined by ongoing mi adidas activity.'

Adidas' own retail activities

To further strengthen its brand, adidas had also just stepped up its own retail activities, increasing the number of its own retail outlets from 37 in 2000 to 65 in 2001. Most notable here was the opening of two concept stores in Paris and Stockholm as well as an adidas Originals store in Berlin.[23]

Negotiating continued internal support

By October 2001 mi adidas was an established initiative and the generally positive brand image effect was widely accepted within the organization. Although mi adidas had become bigger, the organizational set-up had not substantially evolved. To date, much of the support for the project from different functions of adidas was granted on a goodwill basis. As time progressed and volumes increased, it naturally became more and more difficult to persuade core business units to fully support this initiative, especially out of their own cost centers. 'The annual budget for mi adidas had basically stayed identical during its first years.'

The situation was not ideal. Although the functions continued to support mi adidas and took pride in its success to date, the ultimate responsibility for mishaps, of course, rested with the project team. Should mi adidas be elevated and play a more independent role or should it be better integrated into the existing matrix to be in sync with adidas' core business, with the functions in turn assuming more accountability? A clear evaluation was made difficult by the current practice of attributing mi adidas sales to the respective countries, hindering separate accounting.

The future of mi adidas

Reinschmidt wondered if the time was right to scale mi adidas to the next level (Phases III and IV; *refer to Exhibit 3*). The pilot (Phase I) had been very successful and adidas had developed and refined important new capabilities. Consumer feedback was enthusiastic and retailers fared much better during repeat offerings of mi adidas. Yet the initial retail rollout (Phase II) had been somewhat slower than projected, falling 40% to 50% short of the targets established in the original rollout plan.

Future alternatives

Reinschmidt had come to the conclusion that mi adidas needed clearer direction. Once again he reviewed the three generic alternatives that the company could embark on: 'mi adidas could be turned into a commercial tool over the course of the next years and now was the time to decide upon this.'

Alternative 1: *Withdraw* – Celebrate the success and PR effect accomplished to date but quietly withdraw from MC in order to focus on adidas' core business.

> Mi adidas had been launched two years earlier and now featured a soccer and running shoe. As the product life for these model cycles ended, so would mi adidas. Current commitments would be honored but any further investments in the MC initiative were to be avoided. New PR tools would soon take the place of mi adidas.

Alternative 2: *Maintain* – Maintain the developed capabilities and selectively run mi adidas fairs and planned retail tours following top events such as the soccer World Cup and world marathon series.

> Mi adidas would continue in its current form and scope and be allowed limited organic growth. Investment would be minimal and MC responsibilities would be more fully integrated into the existing functions. Mi adidas would be part of (and governed by) adidas' annual planning cycle. As new boots were introduced to the market, a customizable derivative of those models would be created for mi adidas; the kiosk application, promotional material and back-end processes, etc. would be adapted accordingly.

Alternative 3: *Expand* – Expand mi adidas to multiple product categories and permanent retail installations; elevate it to brand concept status while further building volume and process expertise.

> Mi adidas would be scaled up in terms of both volume and product categories. Increased marketing spend and revised back-end processes would support its rollout. Permanent installations at select retail stores would complement the event and retail tour concepts to foster more continuous order flow and steady volumes. Further investments would ensure a degree of independence for mi adidas and help develop MC into a potential business model in its own right for adidas.

Decision looming

Reinschmidt had the alternatives lined up and it was up to him to come to a sensible recommendation based on the various inputs received. He had just started to summarize a set of key issues that should determine which alternative to choose, as well as his assessment of the alternatives, when he was interrupted ...

adidas footwear sales[24]

Region	2001 Net Sales	Net Change vs. 2000
North America	€818 million	− 10%
Europe	€1,200 million	+ 15%
Asia	€371 million	+ 39%
Latin America	€122 million	+ 3%

Note: adidas' total net sales in 2001 were €4.8 billion.

Nike footwear sales[25]

Region	2001 Net Sales	Net Change vs. 2000
USA	$3,209 million	− 4%
Europe	$1,423 million	+ 9%
Asia Pacific	$632 million	+ 14%
Americas	$360 million	+ 5%

Note: Nike's total net sales in 2001 were $9.5 billion.

Reebok footwear sales

Region	2001 Net Sales	Net Change vs. 2000
USA[1]	$931 million	+ 1%
UK*	$484 million	+ 1%
Europe*	$410 million	− 4%
Row*	$256 million	− 4%

[1] Reebok International, Ltd., 2001 Annual Report, Year Ended 12/ 31

* Footwear share of net sales estimated based on Reebok International, Ltd., 2001 Annual Report.

Note: Reebok's total net sales in 2001 were $3.0 billion.

Exhibit 1 Global footwear market: Regional overview

It all began in 1920, when Adolf 'Adi' Dassler and his brother Rudolf made their first shoes in Herzogenaurach, a small village in the south of Germany. Using the few basic materials available after World War I, Rudolf began making slippers with soles made from old tires. Adi converted the slippers into gymnastics shoes and soccer shoes with nail-on studs or cleats. The idea was as simple as it was brilliant: Provide every athlete with the best possible equipment.

At the 1928 Amsterdam Olympics, German athletes showcased Dassler shoes to the world. In 1936, the brothers achieved a major breakthrough when Jesse Owens agreed to wear their shoes in the Berlin Olympics, where he won four gold medals. By 1937 the Dassler brothers were manufacturing shoes for more than 11 different sports. In 1948 the two brothers quarreled and Rudolf left to establish the Puma sports company, while Adi registered the name adidas and, the following year, adopted its now famous three diagonal stripe trademark. The first samples of adidas footwear were used at the 1952 Helsinki Olympics.

In 1954 Germany won the World Cup, wearing new screw-in studs on adidas soccer shoes. In 1963 the first adidas soccer ball was produced, and clothing was added to the product range in 1967. By the Montreal Olympics in 1976, over 80% of medal winners were adidas-equipped athletes. Business was booming. adidas had become a household name in the sporting arena, synonymous with sporting achievement.

In 1972 Nike entered the American market with low-quality, fashionable leisurewear targeting teenagers. Reebok followed suit in 1979. Following the death of its founder in 1978, adidas struggled through turbulent organizational and management changes and was quickly outrun by changes in the industry. Its street popularity faded as newer, more aggressive companies like Nike and Reebok stepped up the pace of competition.

In 1989 the Dassler family withdrew from the company, and the enterprise was transformed into a corporation. Bernard Tapie, a French business tycoon, took over but was soon jailed following his involvement in a soccer-fixing scandal. Subsequently, adidas was declared bankrupt and left to a number of French banks. In 1993 French-born Robert Louis-Dreyfus was appointed chairman of the executive board of adidas. Having purchased 15% of the company, Louis-Dreyfus was a majority shareholder and led a stunning turnaround for the company and initiated adidas' flotation on the stock market in November 1995.

In 1997 adidas acquired Salomon Group, and the company's name changed to adidas-Salomon AG. With the brands adidas (athletic footwear, apparel and accessories), Salomon (skis, bindings, inline skates, adventure shoes and accessories), TaylorMade (golf clubs, balls and accessories), Mavic (cycling components) and Bonfire (snowboard apparel), adidas-Salomon AG substantially broadened its portfolio of sports brands, offering products for both summer and winter sports.

In 2001 Herbert Hainer took over as chairman and CEO. adidas-Salomon AG's total net sales grew to €6.1 billion with net income of €208 million. It employed 14,000 people and commanded an estimated 15% world market share.

Source: http://www.adidas.com and IMD adidas case IMD-3-0743 (GM 743), January 26, 1999.

Exhibit 2 A short history of adidas: 1920–2001

Project Management	Product Development	Product Configurator / Design tool	Marketing → Event → Communication	Information Management	Production	Logistics / Shipment	Service/ Fulfillment	Payment Tracking
• project organization tracking • budgeting / payment • project kick-off • project evaluation • meetings & presentations • handle critical situations	• product development • pattern engineering • foot bed • fit test • sample production • budget	• layout • image to transport • configuration principle • handling • general architecture • potential for future other categories • eCommerce • intelligence • data flow • interfaces • budget	**Product Configuration** • color variations • positioning / layout of all decorations • clarify: stitching or printing of deco's • cosmetics **Event** • concept • message we want to bring across • PR-image we want to create • communication strategy (name of program / product!) • pre-event • event organization • post-event • cooperation with regions • conceptualization of product Configurator • budget	• general IT structure • data tracking handling • storage • research • speed • intelligence • future plans • budget	• data reception • creation of bills of material • planning operation • production on demand • QC on demand • preparation for shipment • packaging • interfaces to systems and projects (e.g. scanner, payment, eCommerce, content management) • production site selection • budget	• customized packaging and shipment • define partner for shipment • speed • costs • quality • budget	• hotline • satisfaction panel • returns / replacement • next steps • new offers • ensure enduring customer-brand-relationship	• clarify types of payment: → online (credit card) → credit card at event location → invoice → currencies → accounting and billing

Exhibit 3 Working breakdown structure plan

Source: Company information

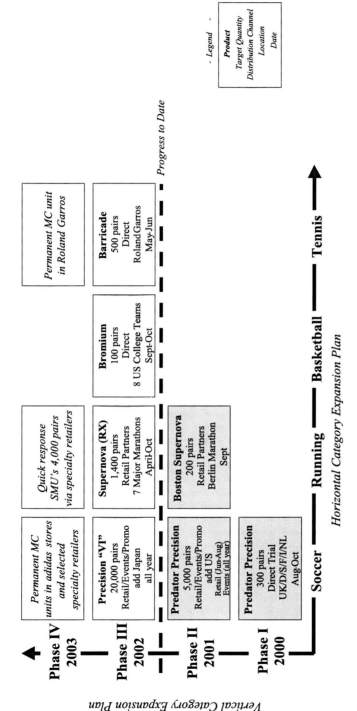

Exhibit 4 Mass customization rollout plan

Source: Berger, C. 'The Customized Revolution at adidas.' *Kundenindividuelle Massenproduktion: Von Businessmodellen zu erfolgreichen Anwendungen*. Eds. M. Schenk, R. Seelmann-Eggebert, F.T. Piller. Die dritte deutsche Tagung zur Mass Customization, Frankfurt, November 8, 2001.

– 15 days		Local market research agency contacts potential participants. Questionnaire-guided telephone interview.
– 10 days		Selection of recruits based on questionnaire answers. Telephone availability-check of the recruits. Set-up of substitute list.
– 7 days		Official written invitation accompanied by pre-event questionnaire.
– 2 days		Ultimate check if recruits will take part in the event. Telephone invitation of substitutes as required.
Event		adidas customization experience and on-site interview
+ 2 weeks		Delivery of customized soccer shoes.
+ 6 weeks		Telephone follow-up interview.

Not only should the product and services be individualized and unique, but also the personal relationship and interaction with the consumer as being part of the customization experience. Are we prepared?

Christoph Berger, Director MC

Exhibit 5   One-to-one communication with the event participants/recruits

Source: Company information

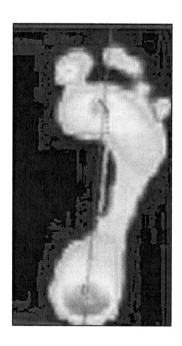

Step 1 check in >	Step 2 scanning >	Step 3 fitting >	Step 4 testing >	Step 5 design >
Get ready for 'mi adidas'! Get registered now for the chance to create your unique pair of customized shoes.	First your feet will be scanned by means of the adidas Footscan system to determine the exact length, width and pressure distribution of each foot. This will enable you to determine which technologies your shoe will need for optimal performance.	Here you consult with an adidas fitting expert to review the results of your footscan. Then this information, combined with your personal fit preferences, is entered into a computer to determine the best-fitting shoe.	Once you have determined your personalized function and fit, you will have the opportunity to test your shoes before heading into the final design phase.	Now you can put the finishing touches on your one-of-a-kind shoes. You will be able to choose different colors, materials and even personalized embroidery – all of which can be viewed on the computer screen as you make your selections.

All that is left now is to confirm and order your customized shoe.[26] Within two weeks your personalized footwear will be with you ready for a new level of performance.

Exhibit 6 The customization process

Source: http://www.miadidas.com

Custom-built footwear for consumers – Retail launch mid 2001 – Pilot project unit on display at ISPO

Herzogenaurach, 02/04/2001 – adidas, as the first brand in the sporting goods industry, is set to launch a pioneering 'Customization Experience' project in footwear. The project starts in the Soccer category, but will be expanded into other major sports categories. With the 'Customization Experience' project, adidas will give consumers the opportunity to create their own unique footwear to their exact personal specifications in terms of function, fit and looks, thus providing services that were so far only available to soccer stars like David Beckham and Zinedine Zidane.

The decision to proceed with the 'Customization Experience' project was made after the successful completion and stringent evaluation of a pilot project conducted in the second half of 2000 in six European countries. During the test project some 400 pairs of the revolutionary adidas Predator® Precision soccer boots were custom built and delivered to a select group of consumers in Germany, France, England, Spain, Italy and the Netherlands. Delivery time took two weeks on average. Consumer satisfaction was overwhelmingly positive.

With the start of the 'Customization Experience' project, adidas is entering the new age of the 'experience economy'. adidas introduces a new business model in the industry, influencing and changing the whole value chain and potentially the sporting goods marketplace, creating a new level of relationship between the consumer and the brand.

The adidas 'Customization Experience' unit used during the pilot project will be on display at ISPO in Munich, February 4–6, 2001. Launch in the retail marketplace is scheduled for mid 2001.

Exhibit 7   Press release: 'adidas to Launch Customization Experience'

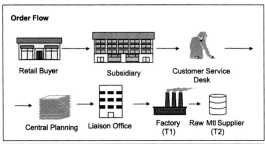

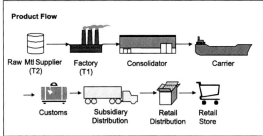

Exhibit 8   Traditional order and product process flow Three mi adidas production sites
Source: adidas-Salomon AG   Source: Company information
Source: www.maps.com, company information

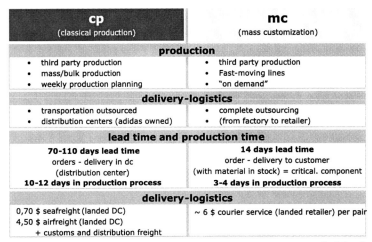

cp (classical production)		mc (mass customization)	
production			
• third party production • mass/bulk production • weekly production planning		• third party production • Fast-moving lines • "on demand"	
delivery-logistics			
• transportation outsourced • distribution centers (adidas owned)		• complete outsourcing • (from factory to retailer)	
lead time and production time			
70-110 days lead time orders - delivery in dc (distribution center) **10-12 days in production process**		**14 days lead time** order - delivery to customer (with material in stock) = critical. component **3-4 days in production process**	
delivery-logistics			
0,70 $ seafreight (landed DC) 4,50 $ airfreight (landed DC) + customs and distribution freight		~ 6 $ courier service (landed retailer) per pair	

Exhibit 9   Comparison: Classical production versus mass customization of adidas footwear

Source: Berger, C. 'The Customized Revolution at adidas.' *Kundenindividuelle Massenproduktion: Von Businessmodellen zu erfolgreichen Anwendungen.* Eds. M. Schenk, R. Seelmann-Eggebert, F.T. Piller. Die dritte deutsche Tagung zur Mass Customization, Frankfurt, November 8, 2001.

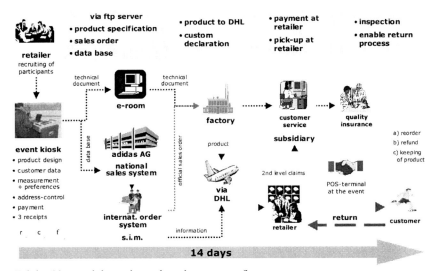

Exhibit 10   mi adidas order and product process flow

Source: Berger, C. 'The Customized Revolution at adidas.' *Kundenindividuelle Massenproduktion: Von Businessmodellen zu erfolgreichen Anwendungen.* Eds. M. Schenk, R. Seelmann-Eggebert, F.T. Piller. Die dritte deutsche Tagung zur Mass Customization, Frankfurt, November 8, 2001.

This case won the 2006 European Case Award, in the category Production and Operations Management, granted by ecch in association with Business Week.

This case also won the 2004 POMS International Case Writing Award sponsored by the Center for International Business Education and Research (CIBER) at Indiana University.

Case 5.2
Hilti: Gearing the supply chain for the future (A)

Kerstin Langenberg and Ralf Seifert

September 2005, Schaan, Liechtenstein. Stefan Nöken, head of supply chain at Hilti, was reflecting on Hilti's current initiative to make its supply chain fit for the future – Plant Structure Project II (PSP II): 'During our meetings, the executive board pushed for substantial cost savings. But, at the same time they made it clear that by no means was quality to be put at risk.'

PSP II had been launched to help realize the ambitious cost targets set by Hilti's Vision 2008 initiative. Cost-cutting trends were also evident among its competitors. Nöken knew that to sustain the firm's competitiveness, he had no choice but to restructure Hilti's supply chain. But he could not risk damaging the firm's high quality standards, engrained values or culture.

Since the project started in January 2005, Nöken and his project team leader, Frank Brandenburg, had developed three alternatives for restructuring Hilti's supply chain:

1 **Low pain low gain**. Buy parts of the product portfolio, instead of making them in-house, and move all small tools to Hilti's prototype plant in Shanghai, which would affect 8% of Hilti's cost of goods sold (COGS).
2 **Consolidate around existing structures**. In addition to alternative 1, consolidate Western European production, which would affect 30% of COGS, but require plant closures.
3 **Greenfield**. In addition to alternative 1, move tool production from Western Europe to a new, cost-competitive plant in Eastern Europe. This alternative would affect 45% of COGS, but would require all tool production facilities in Western Europe to be closed.

The three alternatives were lined up. In the upcoming executive board meeting the team would have to make its recommendation to the members of the board.

Global construction tools industry

The main players in the global construction tools industry were Bosch, Black & Decker (with Dewalt), Hitachi, Makita and Hilti. Hilti was positioned as an innovation leader in the industry's premium price segment with outstanding quality and high service standards, including guaranteed delivery within 48 hours for all of its products. As a result, Hilti was able to command price premiums as high as 30%.

After experiencing some difficult years from 2001 to 2003, the construction industry saw an upturn in 2004. Further growth was forecast and new customer markets were gaining importance (e.g. Asia). In line with these trends, the industry had seen increased moves towards globalization and consolidation. US giant Black & Decker, for example, had just finalized a comprehensive restructuring program and had transferred production from the US and England to low-cost areas such as Mexico and Eastern Europe.[27] Bosch had announced plans to double its already strong engagement in China by 2007.[28] And TTI, a leading Chinese producer of electronic tools, had just bought German and US electronic tool makers AEG and Milwaukee to strengthen its global presence.

Hilti Corporation

In 1941 Martin and Eugene Hilti founded the 'Maschinenbau Hilti OHG',[29] a mechanical workshop with five employees in Liechtenstein. Its main activities included the production of various kinds of mechanical and machine parts. By 1960, Hilti had established itself in European markets and had set up a major production facility in Liechtenstein. To ensure premium customer service, the company established a direct sales force, rather than selling via distributors or dealers. Subsequently, between 1960 and 1980, Hilti was transformed from an OHG to Hilti AG.[30] During the same period, the firm entered the South American and Asian markets. Throughout the 1980s and 1990s, Hilti continued to expand into new markets, including Algeria, Korea, Hungary and East Asia. In 1993 Pius Baschera was the first non-family member to be appointed CEO. In the late 1990s Hilti established a new corporate strategy called the Champion 3C strategy. The three Cs stood for *customer* focus, building on strong *competences* (innovation, total quality, direct customer relationships and effective marketing) and *concentrating* on core markets and products, where leadership positions could be achieved and sustained.

By 2004, Hilti employed approximately 15,000 people. The firm was present in more than 120 countries and had annual sales of approximately CHF 3.3 billion and a net income of CHF 231 million (*refer to Exhibits 1 and 2*). All market regions showed considerable growth compared with 2003: Europe/Africa had increased by 11%, North America by 6%, Latin America by 9%, and Asia/Pacific by 10%. Europe/Africa contributed 67% of total sales, North America 21% and Latin America and Asia/Pacific 2% and 10%, respectively.

Products

Hilti's product range included systems for drilling and demolition, direct fastening, diamond coring and cutting, anchoring, fire prevention, insulation, installation, measuring and screw fastening, as well as cutting and sanding systems. The products were categorized into consumables and tools, accounting for approximately 40% and 60% of Hilti's sales, respectively. Tools (e.g. electric hammer drills), typically showed a high value density,[31] whereas consumables (e.g. anchors) showed a considerably lower value density.

Supply chain

Hilti's supply chain was also classified according to tools and consumables. Most processes were set up jointly (e.g. distribution centers, transportation), but production plants for each product category were separate in most cases. In

September 2005 Hilti operated a total of eight plants, five of which were located in Western Europe. The firm manufactured consumables in plants in Liechtenstein (Schaan), Germany (Kaufering and Strass), Hungary (Kecskemet) and China (Zhanjiang-Guangdong). Tools were manufactured in Liechtenstein (Mauren), Austria (Thüringen), China (Shanghai) and Germany (Kaufering and Strass). The German plants produced both consumables and tools (*refer to **Exhibit 3***).

In the past, Hilti had undertaken two major supply chain restructuring initiatives: Struktur und Ausrichtung der Werke (SAW) in the early 1990s and Plant Structure Project I (PSP I) from 2002 to 2005 (*refer to **Exhibit 4***). Hans-Karl Moser, responsible for Hilti's tools supply chain, reflected: 'Success stems from continuity. The people concerned experience [supply chain] projects as a revolution, but at Hilti it is more a continuous evolutionary process.'

During SAW, Hilti restructured its in-house production. As a result, the firm increased its outsourcing activities and closed a plant in the United Kingdom.

As part of PSP I, which focused on consumables, Nöken – then the project leader – not only revised Hilti's in-house production, but also assessed its sourcing strategy. By then, the notion of 'supply chain' had evolved to include sourcing and distribution, rather than merely focusing on production. As a result of PSP I, Hilti closed its consumables plants in Mexico and the US to better leverage economies of scale. At the same time it opened a prototype plant for tools in Shanghai to produce one family of tools. Management wanted to explore the benefits of producing in China for its tool products, since Hilti's Chinese consumables facility in Zhanjiang-Guangdong had already been operating successfully for several years. The plant in Shanghai was initially seen as an experiment to investigate whether tool production was feasible in China, but it also served as a platform to facilitate access to the Asian market. During this time, Hilti also built up sourcing markets for parts and components in China and Eastern Europe.

In addition, make and buy decisions were increasingly integrated at Hilti, as the firm constantly challenged which assembly parts of its products to make in-house and which parts to source externally. Hilti responded to this trend and merged sourcing and manufacturing into an integrated supply chain function.

Premises

Hilti had established a set of premises to protect the firm's business model, the Champion 3C strategy, its brand and its social and environmental policies. Decisions made within the firm had to be in line with these premises. Examples of premises are:

BUSINESS MODEL

- The value add in Liechtenstein should be high enough to support high prices in this high-cost production location.

CHAMPION 3C STRATEGY

- Economic and technological independence should be protected (competence).
- Hilti was to produce only Hilti products and not products for third parties (concentration).
- Sustainable technology leadership should be a focus (competence).

BRAND PROTECTION

- The company's present position as a high-quality and high-value supplier must be maintained.

SOCIAL AND ENVIRONMENTAL POLICIES

- Hilti was not to cooperate with suppliers of fake products.
- Change had to be socially acceptable.

Step 1: Launching PSP II

In January 2005 PSP II was launched to help the firm attain the targets established in its Vision 2008. The plan forecast revenues of CHF 4 billion with profits of CHF 450 million by 2008. The focus of PSP II was to revise Hilti's manufacturing footprint for tools. Minor project goals were reconfirming strategic make or buy positions and product regions, and analysing the cost structures of plants.

Within the project, a work stream targeting Hilti's allied products[32] was initiated. (*Refer to **Exhibit 5** for a project plan of PSP II.*)

Alongside its main focus, results from PSP I had indicated that there were supply market opportunities for tools in the following markets:

- Asia, which would result in a 30% cost reduction on average at product level.
- Eastern Europe, which would result in only a 10% cost reduction, but transport costs would be less and supply lead times would be shorter.

There was also untapped potential for outsourcing more plastic and machined parts and the firm had investigated what technologies were available in the supply market and at what prices.

Team

The project team consisted of two full-time employees, a project manager, Frank Brandenburg, and a co-project manager. In addition, key employees concerned with the project outcomes (e.g. plant managers) and key supply chain managers were involved. Focal sub-teams were created to investigate specific topics, for example, machining technologies or plastics. Business units were involved whenever necessary to constantly keep the project aligned with the business and product strategies and to be fully transparent from the outset (*refer to **Exhibit 6** for an illustration of the project team structure*).

Make vs. buy

Only 20% of total product value at Hilti stemmed from in-house production, while 80% of product value was purchased, including parts for assembly and allied products. In line with its Champion 3C strategy, Hilti had established rigorous standards on what to make in-house. Only those products that differentiated the firm from its competitors (through cost or quality advantages) or those that needed protection of know-how and intellectual property were produced in-house. All other products/components had to be sourced externally (*refer to **Exhibit 7***).

The project's main focus on the make was not indisputable and was debated within the firm:

> The executive board constantly challenged our project by saying the battle is not won in the make, but in the buy. And that we shouldn't focus on what we are good at already! … [But] You can't push spaghetti across the table; you need somebody at the other side of the table to pull it! No manager of a European plant would assemble parts sourced from China. They would rather rely on quality suppliers that they have known for 20 years.

The project team was convinced that to benefit from new sourcing regions, the firm first had to assemble within a particular region. Regional plant managers would create the necessary 'pull' for a local sourcing network and help overcome internal organizational barriers. Indeed, the project team drew on Hilti's experience from a few years before, when building up sourcing in Hungary and China had proved to be extremely difficult.

Remaining true to the premises

Any decision made within the framework of PSP II had to be in line with Hilti's premises. Some of the premises had the potential to impact the project's recommendations in a significant way. Brandenburg reflected on the Shanghai plant that had been set up a few years earlier:

> We don't cut back. [The Shanghai plant] fulfils Hilti standards, e.g. with a fire sprinkler system and emergency generators to hedge against electric power outages. We invested much more money than other firms would have. Others go to Asia and set up to Asian standards. But this is where quality problems arise.

Developing hypotheses

Hilti's decision drivers were based on several hypotheses that the team compiled together with the respective business units. For example, in terms of costs, they hypothesized that local costs in China and Eastern Europe would increase relatively quickly – nevertheless Hilti could still benefit from producing in China or Eastern Europe. In terms of quality, one assumption was that the Chinese and

Eastern European supply markets would increasingly fulfil Hilti's requirements on product quality. Other hypotheses targeted the development of Hilti's product range, price levels of standard raw materials and future advantages due to certain production technologies.

Such hypotheses served to evaluate whether or not a restructuring alternative was feasible before the alternative was assessed in detailed.

Step 2: Developing restructuring alternatives

After the project had been launched and the scope defined, the project team developed multiple restructuring options for cost savings taking into account Hilti's premises and the newly established hypotheses. In what they called 'sandbox games', the team considered numerous options over two months. As in a sandbox game, product families were moved virtually back and forth between plants and segmented into manufacturing techniques. Finally, the team constructed 11 options ranging from 'keep plant structure as is' as the most conservative to 'move to Asia and Eastern Europe and buy' as the most aggressive. From these 11 options, the team essentially compiled three main reorganization alternatives that were to be evaluated in detail:

1   **Low pain low gain**. Shift semi-complex plastic and machined parts of the production portfolio from make to buy, and move all small tools to Hilti's tool plant in Shanghai. This alternative would affect 8% of Hilti's COGS.
2   **Consolidate around existing structures**. In addition to alternative 1, consolidate Western European production, for example by producing all plastic parts where they would be assembled. This alternative would affect 30% of COGS, but would require plant closures. The plant in Strass, for example, could not survive without producing plastic parts for tools.
3   **Greenfield**. In addition to alternative 1, move production from Western Europe to a new, cost competitive plant in Eastern Europe. This alternative would affect 45% of COGS, but would mean that all tool production facilities in Western Europe would have to be closed.

Each of the three alternatives was feasible and had supporters in the firm.

> We chose what to shift in a way that it would work. [...] At Hilti, [such projects] are run in a rather conservative way. Once a decision is made, we are extremely sure that we will make it happen. The question then becomes whether it will take three months more or not.

Step 3: Assessing restructuring alternatives

Hilti evaluated the three alternatives with monetary as well as qualitative evaluation criteria (*refer to* **Figure 1**). Sustainability was a key factor in the decision making:

If you only go [to China] because of the cost factor, then it is wrong ... [We are looking for a] long-lasting strategy. We can't afford to set up in China today and go to Vietnam tomorrow – then we would be constantly occupied with managing only ourselves.

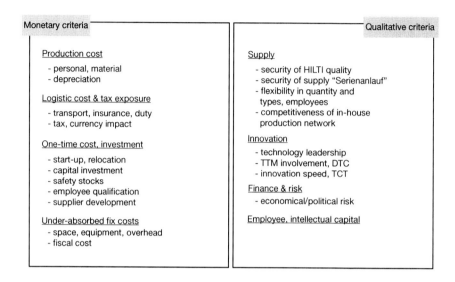

Figure 1 Evaluation method[33]

To enable efficient evaluation of the alternatives, the firm established a stepwise approach with decision filters. The process started with a comparison of production costs and concluded with a qualitative assessment. Only if the previous step had shown potential, did the firm transfer to the next step (*refer to* **Exhibit 8**).

Monetary assessment

For the monetary assessment the team looked at different future scenarios. To do this they had to collect cost data for various stages and make certain assumptions.

Collecting accurate cost data was crucial for the project's success. Project policy demanded that the people concerned should always be involved. As a consequence, plant managers were asked to quantify the potential costs of closing the plant they supervised. As expected, this biased the data:

Of course, every plant manager initially estimated sums as high as CHF 5 million to close his plant. But then we asked: Do we really need to overhaul every tool for the shifted production? No! Again CHF 2 million less. ... But such discussions helped us acquire consolidated knowledge.

In parallel, scenarios were constructed that helped estimate how uncertain future trends might impact the business case of each alternative (e.g. changes in wages).

Naturally, scenario building was controversial, e.g. whether even to consider moving production entirely to China, say, or Eastern Europe. To minimize risk, the project team compiled detailed sensitivity analyses for worst-case scenarios. Nonetheless, risk could not be avoided: 'If we set assumptions too conservatively, then we don't change anything in the end, because the business case looks bad.'

Due to their large impact on the business cases, the assumptions and resulting scenarios had to be approved by top management.

Qualitative assessment

Quality considerations encompassed quality of supply and innovation, finance and risk, and employees and intellectual capital.

Quality had always come first at Hilti, so quality of supply and innovation were essential decision drivers. Safeguarding Hilti's quality, the reliability of supply lead times and continuing technology leadership, among others, were all important quality considerations. The project team evaluated, for example, the Chinese suppliers (using the firm's experiences from the prototype plant in Shanghai) and benchmarked them against the firm's European suppliers.

Finance and risk was another decision driver. Among other things, this category included currency fluctuations and local risks. In China, for example, the first iconic red Hilti boxes containing pirate copies of Hilti's tools had appeared a long time earlier. Hilti was a premium player in the market, and suppliers would quickly learn how to copy its technologies. Therefore, the project team developed strategies to hedge against these risks (e.g. never source many parts for the same tool from one supplier).

Employees, firm culture and social responsibility had a long tradition and high standing at Hilti. In 2003, the firm had been awarded the Carl Bertelsmann Prize for excellence in corporate culture, i.e. an employee- and customer-driven culture and outstanding management. Naturally, the project posed a threat to jobs in Hilti's plants. According to Jochen Neuberger, a project leader in Hilti's supply chain division:

> These were one or two difficult years. Most of the project team was situated in Hilti's headquarters in Schaan; they didn't have direct contact with assembly workers every day. But I was in the middle of them. Not a day passed when I wasn't approached by a worker who asked, 'Wait a moment, I don't understand!' The discussions were fair and open, but hard. It's very draining, emotionally speaking, but you have to take the time to talk to people to accommodate their concerns.

In view of Hilti's deep-rooted tradition and culture, ethical considerations were important drivers for decision making.

Decision looming

Nöken had the alternatives displayed, and it was up to him to come to a sensible recommendation for the upcoming board meeting:

1   **Low pain low gain**. Looking at 2004's numbers, this alternative seemed sufficient. Hilti was under no pressure to take a more radical approach, with the associated hassles and risks. However, the executive board was looking for cost savings, and competitors were working on pushing down their costs too. Would alternative 1 be sufficient to make Hilti's supply chain competitive for the future?

2   **Consolidate around existing structures**. The business case for alternative 2 showed that the forecast net savings were slightly positive. The planned consolidation would certainly help foster the competitiveness of Hilti's highly valued historic structures in Western Europe. But would the relatively small net savings justify the unavoidable plant closures and the possibility of having to lay off workers? And were the planned activities enough to ensure Hilti's ongoing success in the future?

3   **Greenfield**. The business case for alternative 3 showed considerable net savings. However, the risks involved were also considerable, as it was a complete shift and would have a significant impact on Hilti's workforce. Was such a big cut necessary and was Hilti ready to pursue it? And would such a move damage Hilti's quality and reputation?

The board meeting was coming up. It was time to make a decision.

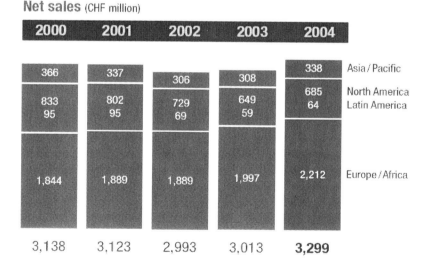

Exhibit 1   Development of sales (2000–2004)

Source: Hilti AG, Annual Report 2004.

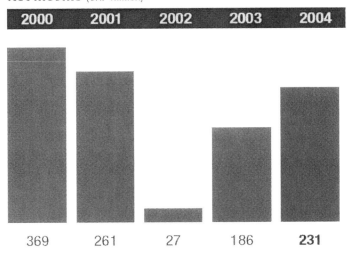

Net income (CHF million)

| 2000 | 2001 | 2002 | 2003 | 2004 |

369   261   27   186   **231**

Exhibit 2 Development of net income (2000–2004)

Source: Hilti AG, Annual Report 2004.

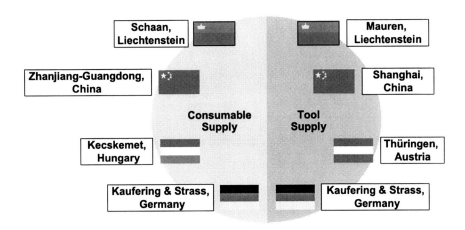

Exhibit 3 Plant structure tools

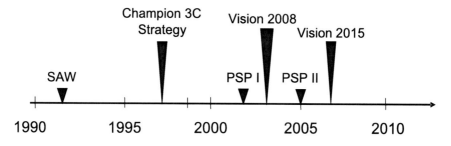

Exhibit 4 Timeline of events and projects related to the supply chain

SAW = Struktur und Ausrichtung der Werke
PSP I = Plant Structure Project I
PSP II = Plant Structure Project II

Source: Company information

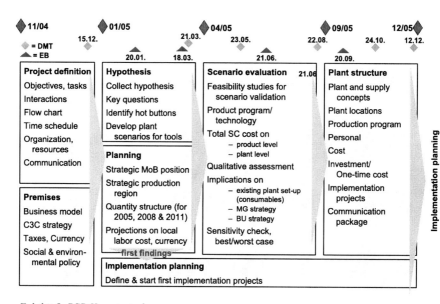

Exhibit 5 PSP II project plan

Source: Company information

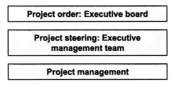

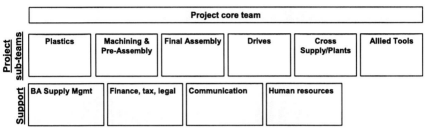

Exhibit 6 PSP II project team

Source: Company information

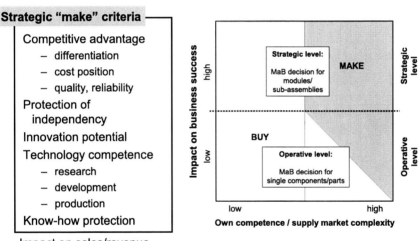

Exhibit 7 Criteria for deciding whether to make production segments

Source: Company information

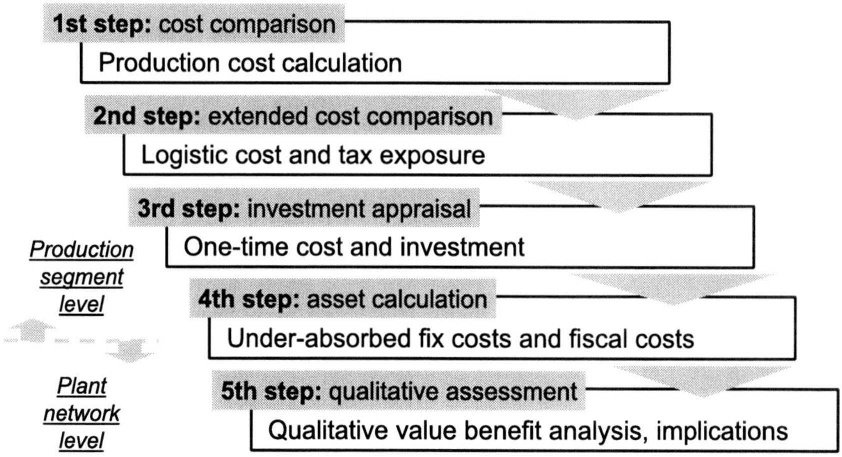

1st step: cost comparison
Production cost calculation

2nd step: extended cost comparison
Logistic cost and tax exposure

3rd step: investment appraisal

Production segment level

One-time cost and investment

4th step: asset calculation
Under-absorbed fix costs and fiscal costs

Plant network level

5th step: qualitative assessment
Qualitative value benefit analysis, implications

Exhibit 8 Stepwise evaluation approach

Source: Company information

Case 5.3
Hilti: Reflections and outlook (B)

Kerstin Langenberg, Ralf Seifert

January 2006, Schaan, Liechtenstein. Hilti had completed the implementation of PSP II in just three months. Events had unfolded quickly since the board decided which alternative to pursue.

After carefully weighing the pros and cons of the three alternatives for restructuring Hilti's supply chain, the project team recommended alternative 2 in September 2005, which included closing the plant in Mauren, Liechtenstein. The team felt this alternative offered the right balance between necessary structural change and social responsibility.

Decision

Although the executive board approved the team's recommendation for alternative 2 – to extend the prototype plant in Shanghai, pursue a consolidation initiative and shift selected parts from make to buy – they did not approve any plant closures. Instead, they asked for an action plan to be developed to take up the excess capacity caused by the shifts to Asia and consolidation in various plants. Setting up a repair center in Mauren and establishing new working conditions (e.g. shift model) were possibilities.

This amendment to alternative 2 would mean that the workforce in Mauren and Strass would decrease only slightly, from 1,600 to 1,500 over the next five or six years. The workforce in China would increase from 400 to 600 employees. From a mid-term perspective, Hilti felt that growth options would help prevent social hardship – as new employment opportunities would be created. CEO Pius Baschera commented:

> Social responsibility towards our employees was a key decision driver, next to know-how and quality assurance. The competency of our employees makes the difference. We want to continue to strengthen this competitive advantage. In addition, with these optimization activities, we can make our plant structures fit for future requirements and use the potential for growth as best as possible to sustain our global competitiveness.

Once the decision was made, implementation was completed in three months, and the project goals were overachieved. Net present value exceeded its target by more than 10%. However, there were some misjudgments and some surprises along the way. Frank Brandenburg, project leader, and Hans-Karl Moser, head of Hilti's tools supply chain, summarized their key learnings.

Key learnings

Establish a broad corridor for scenarios

The company's rapid growth – materializing at 9% instead of the forecast 3% – took the project team by surprise. Brandenburg noted: 'Nobody had dared to come up with ambitious numbers.'

As a result, Hilti's capacity was inadequate for the next few years, until the firm was able to ramp up production. While the team had carefully evaluated worst-case scenarios during the project, they had not analysed aggressive best-case scenarios for growth within PSP II.

Don't underestimate political influence

Shortly after Hilti's relocation decision, China announced a rise in value added tax. Moser remembered: 'People got nervous very fast then.'

Luckily, this development had only a minor impact, and Hilti was successful in far exceeding its project targets. This affirmed that cost factors should not be the only driver of major restructuring shifts; sustainability should also be key.

Implement decisions quickly

Moser reflected on the importance of fast implementation once decisions had been made. 'Towards the end [of the implementation], we entered a critical phase. Vision 2015 – with new growth targets – came up and newly appointed heads of business units started to question the decisions of PSP II.'

Don't underestimate supplier relations

The project also reconfirmed the importance of first-rate supplier quality for Hilti:

> Building up a supply base was backbreaking work for the team. We only succeeded because we pursued technology transfers and taught the new suppliers how to do it. … It's different from Europe, where you show drawings to your suppliers and then ask for suggestions on how to advance the idea.

Hilti hedged supply risks in China by always appointing two suppliers for the same task and by affording a two-month safety stock of inventory in Shanghai. Such security measures were necessary. If a small tool, for example, had to be sent by plane for an emergency delivery, the 25% to 30% of savings attained by producing in China were easily eaten up. But Hilti was optimistic about the future, as Moser noted: 'As the partnership grows, we will reduce such safety activities.'

Don't underestimate the cost of capital

Long lead times from Asia to the European market – where most of Hilti's sales were still generated – challenged the firm's 48-hour delivery standard. As quality came first at Hilti, this meant that it had to keep high inventory levels throughout the chain, which tied up large amounts of capital. To reduce inventory levels, Hilti was investigating techniques to reduce the number of product variants within the chain.

Further developments

After the implementation of PSP II was completed in early 2006, Hilti's business continued to boom. In 2006 Hilti outlined Vision 2015 with the goal of doubling its revenues from CHF 4 billion to CHF 8 billion. To support these targets, the firm launched a new supply chain project called Global Supply Footprint in 2006. This initiative further indicated the increasing importance of a holistic approach to supply chain management. As part of the Global Supply Footprint Initiative, Hilti made the following moves.

South America

Hilti decided to reopen a consumables plant in Mexico to serve America's markets. While the firm continued to consolidate the production of its tool products, larger production volumes and lower value density led to a localization strategy for its consumable products. In addition to reducing currency risks due to its more dispersed production footprint, Hilti expected the Mexican plant would generate additional savings of CHF 7 to CHF 10 million.

Europe

Existing structures in Western Europe also benefited from Hilti's record numbers. Plants could be extended, despite the shift to Shanghai, and supplier volumes in Europe remained at a constant level, which resulted in continuing good supplier relationships.

In March 2008, despite its massive growth, Hilti announced that it would close its plant in Mauren, Liechtenstein in 2011. Thanks to the firm's strong sales numbers, the closure did not require laying off workers. Instead, employees were offered new jobs in either Liechtenstein or Austria. Brandenburg explained: 'To some extent and to my surprise this [the closure of the plant in Mauren] was accepted quite positively. But understandably, the workers are now demanding: Show us where our new jobs are.'

China

Now that small tool production had successfully been shifted to China, the next step was to move the development of small tools to Shanghai. Experience showed that European developers were having difficulty designing tools to cost made up of only parts that were obtainable also in China. Moser explained: 'In Europe, you always find a supplier that makes a certain part … But in the non-premium segment, Hilti is under more pressure and this provoked us to develop these parts in China.'

With this series of supply chain restructuring activities behind it, Hilti had come a long way. But there was no time to rest. Hilti had to continue advancing its supply chain activities – constantly initiating renovation – if it wanted to continue being successful. The project team firmly believed they had to address potential problems when times were good rather than waiting until competitive pressures took away the freedom to act.

Chapter notes

1 Pine, B., B. Victor, and A. Boynton. 'Making Mass Customization Work.' *Harvard Business Review*, September–October 1993: 103–114.
2 Lee, H. L. 'The Triple-A Supply Chain.' *Harvard Business Review*, October 2004.
3 Lee, H. L. 'The Triple-A Supply Chain.' *Harvard Business Review*, October 2004.

Case study notes

1 Sporting Goods Intelligence (SGI).
2 Total market value based on wholesale prices.
3 The reorganization officially took effect January 1, 2001. In 2002 the organization was revised again and the Forever Sport Division became the Sport Performance Division.
4 adidas-Salomon AG, 2001 Annual Report.
5 http://nikeid.nike.com
6 'Nike offers mass customization online.' *Computerworld*, November 23, 1999.
7 http://www.reebok.com
8 http://www.newbalance.com and New Balance Athletic Shoe, Inc., Press Releases, April 20, 2001.
9 Piller, F.T. *Mass Customization*. Wiesbaden: Gabler Verlag, 8/2001: 397.
10 Piller, F.T. 'The Present and Future of Mass Customization: Do It – Now!', adidas internal management report, 2001.
11 http://www.customatix.com
12 K. Smith, 'Fancy Feet.' *Entrepreneur's Business Start-Ups*, 7/2001.
13 adidas-Salomon AG, Press Release, April 2, 2001 (*refer to* **Exhibit 7** *for the full press release*).
14 Some specialist stores got very excited about mi adidas and lined up local sponsors to equip entire sports teams with customized shoes while hosting the mi adidas retail unit at their outlet.
15 Jäger, S. 'Market Trends: From Mass Production to Mass Customization.' EURO ShoE project, March 3, 2002, Innovation in the European footwear sector conference, Milan.
16 'Individuelle Maßanfertigung von Sportschuhen.' *Schuhplus/infocomma*, October 15, 2001.
17 Dulio, S. 'Technology Trends: From Rigid Mechanical Manufacturing to Mass Customization.' EURO ShoE project, March 3, 2002, Innovation in the European footwear sector conference, Milan.
18 IMD adidas case IMD-3-0743 (GM 743), January 26, 1999.
19 For the mi adidas pilot, volume was limited and production was not a problem. In general, a development sample room, however, could not handle more than 500 to 1,000 pairs per month.
20 Production set-ups were often made only once per day producing large batches of footwear.

21 a^3 was a functional technology combining cushioning, stability and light weight. It managed the foot's natural movement by dissipating harmful impact forces, stabilizing and guiding the foot through the entire footstrike, and retaining and redirecting energy from the rear foot to the front foot. adidas planned to introduce the concept for running shoes in 2002 as the most technical, functional design available.

22 ClimaCool™ was a footwear technology concept offering 360 degrees of ventilation and moisture management. In scientific tests, it produced 20% dryer and 20% cooler feet. Targeting regular or serious athletes, adidas planned for a staggered market introduction across products in 2002.

23 adidas-Salomon AG, 2001 Annual Report.

24 adidas-Salomon AG, 2001 Annual Report, Year Ended 12/31.

25 Nike Inc., 2001 Annual Report, Year Ended 5/31.

26 Customers were not pushed to accept a customized shoe – returns upon delivery were minimal.

27 Black&Decker Annual Report 2004.

28 na presseportal (www.presseportal.de/pm/60282/740644/robert_bosch_gmbh).

29 Offene Handelsgesellschaft (general partnership).

30 Aktiengesellschaft (public company).

31 Product value with respect to the product's weight.

32 Allied products are finished products bought from suppliers or competitors to complement the firm's product offering.

33 Hilti corporation.

Index